# A BOOK OF THE PYRENEES

# LECTOR HOUSE PUBLIC DOMAIN WORKS

This book is a result of an effort made by Lector House towards making a contribution to the preservation and repair of original classic literature. The original text is in the public domain in the United States of America, and possibly other countries depending upon their specific copyright laws.

In an attempt to preserve, improve and recreate the original content, certain conventional norms with regard to typographical mistakes, hyphenations, punctuations and/or other related subject matters, have been corrected upon our consideration. However, few such imperfections might not have been rectified as they were inherited and preserved from the original content to maintain the authenticity and construct, relevant to the work. The work might contain a few prior copyright references as well as page references which have been retained, wherever considered relevant to the part of the construct. We believe that this work holds historical, cultural and/or intellectual importance in the literary works community, therefore despite the oddities, we accounted the work for print as a part of our continuing effort towards preservation of literary work and our contribution towards the development of the society as a whole, driven by our beliefs.

We are grateful to our readers for putting their faith in us and accepting our imperfections with regard to preservation of the historical content. We shall strive hard to meet up to the expectations to improve further to provide an enriching reading experience.

Though, we conduct extensive research in ascertaining the status of copyright before redeveloping a version of the content, in rare cases, a classic work might be incorrectly marked as not-in-copyright. In such cases, if you are the copyright holder, then kindly contact us or write to us, and we shall get back to you with an immediate course of action.

**HAPPY READING!**

# A BOOK OF THE PYRENEES

## SABINE BARING-GOULD

ISBN: 978-93-93794-85-7

Published:                1907

© 2021
LECTOR HOUSE LLP

LECTOR HOUSE LLP
E-MAIL: lectorpublishing@gmail.com

La Vallée du Lys

# A BOOK OF THE PYRENEES

BY

## S. BARING-GOULD

AUTHOR OF "A BOOK OF BRITTANY,"
"A BOOK OF THE RIVIERA," ETC.

IT IS THE SOUL THAT SEES; THE OUTWARD EYES
PRESENT THE OBJECT, BUT THE MIND DESCRIES.

*LONGFELLOW*

**WITH TWENTY-FIVE ILLUSTRATIONS**

*First Published in 1907*

# PREFACE

This *Book of the Pyrenees* follows the same lines as my *Book of the Rhine* and *Book of the Riviera*. It is not a guide, but an introduction to the chain, giving to the reader a sketch of the History of the Country he visits.

# CONTENTS

## CHAPTER IV

### S. JEAN-PIED-DE-PORT



## CHAPTER V

### ORTHEZ



## CHAPTER VI

### PAU

## CHAPTER VII

## OLORON



## CHAPTER VIII

## THE VAL D'OSSAU



## CHAPTER IX

## LOURDES

## CHAPTER XIV

## THE VAL D'AURE



## CHAPTER XV

## LUCHON



## CHAPTER XVI

## COUSERANS

## CHAPTER XVII

## FOIX



## CHAPTER XVIII

## LA CERDAGNE



## CHAPTER XIX

## THE CANIGOU

## CHAPTER XX

## PERPIGNAN

# LIST OF ILLUSTRATIONS

From a photograph by Messrs. Levy and Sons, Paris

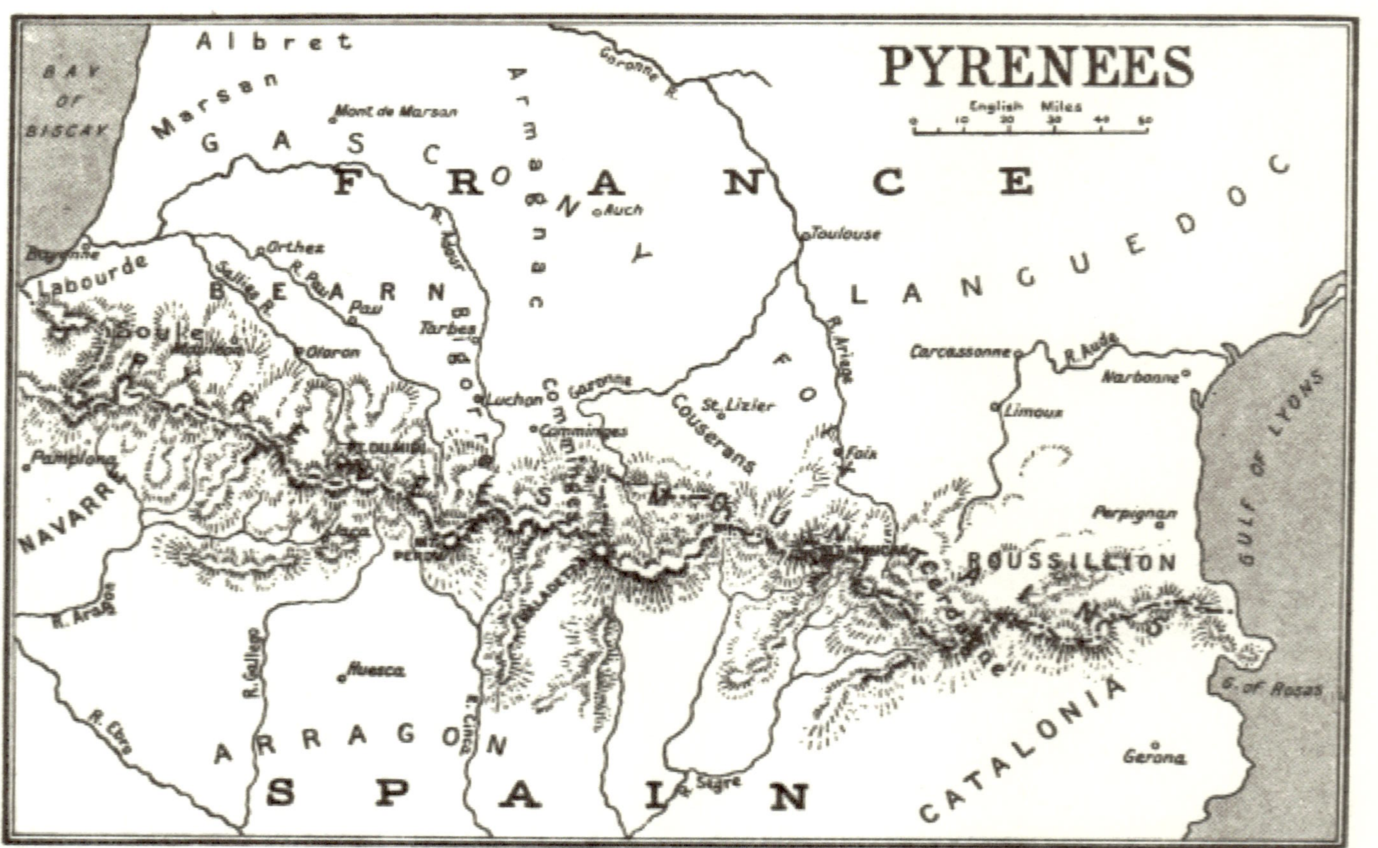


Map of the Pyrenees

# THE PYRENEES

## CHAPTER I

### THE PYRENEAN CHAIN

The wall of division—A triple chain—Contrasts—Deforesting—The
Catalan of Roussillon—The Basque of Navarre—Roman roads—
The three ports—Central ridge—Trough to the north—Watershed—Glacial moraines—Lakes—Cirques—Abrupt termination
of the lower valleys—Cave dwellers—Dolmens—That of Buzy—
Landes of Pontacq—The Iberian stock—Development of language—Auxiliary verbs—The Basque villages and people.

THE Pyrenees stand up as a natural wall of demarcation between two nations,
the French and the Spaniards, just as the mountains of Dauphiné sever the
French from the Italians. It has been remarked that these natural barriers are
thrown up to part Romance-speaking peoples, whereas the mountain ranges sink
to comparative insignificance between the French and the Germans. Over the Jura
the French tongue has flowed up the Rhone to Sierre, above the Lake of Geneva, so
the Spanish or Catalan has overleaped the Pyrenees in Roussillon, and the Basque
tongue has those who speak it in both cis-Pyrenean and trans-Pyrenean Navarre.
The Pyrenees are the upcurled lips of the huge limestone sea-bed, that at some
vastly remote period was snapped from east to west, and through the fissure thus
formed the granite was thrust, lifting along with it the sedimentary rocks.

Consequently the Pyrenees consist of from two to three parallel chains. The
central and loftiest is that of granite, but where loftiest is hidden on the north side
by the upturned reef of limestone. On the south the calcareous bed is lifted in great
slabs, but split, and does not form so ragged and so lofty a range.

The Pyrenees start steeply out of the Mediterranean, which at a distance of
five-and-twenty miles from Cape Creuse, has a depth of over 500 fathoms, and
there the limestone flares white and bald in the line of the Albères. But to the west
the chain does not drop abruptly into the Atlantic, but trails away for 300 miles,
forming the Asturian mountains, and then, curving south, serves to part Galicia
from Leon. The range of the Pyrenees dividing France from Spain is 350 miles in
length.

The chain to the west wears a different aspect from that in the east. The Basque
mountains are clothed with trees, pines and birch, walnut and chestnut, and above

them are turf and heather. But the eastern extremity is white and barren. This is due to the fact that the Western Pyrenees catch and condense the vapours from the Atlantic, whereas the Oriental Pyrenees do not draw to them heavy and continuous rains. The boundary between the regions and climates is Mont Carlitte. In the Western Pyrenees the snow line lies far lower than in the east. On the former of these glaciers hang in wreaths, whereas there are none in the east.

The contrast between the northern and southern slopes is even more marked than that between the extremities of the chain. On the French side are snow, ice, running streams, fertile vales, luxuriant meadows and forests, and valleys and hillsides that sparkle with villages smiling in prosperity. But on the southern slope the eye ranges over barren rocks, sun-baked, scanty pastures, and here and there at long intervals occur squalid clusters of stone hovels, scarce fit to shelter goats, yet serving as human habitations.

To the mountaineers the French side is *bach*, that in shadow; the Spanish is *soulane*, the sunny. At one time this latter slope was not as arid and desert as at present, but the thriftlessness of man has shorn down the forests and the teeth of the goats have nipped off or barked every seedling or sapling thrown up by nature to cover its nakedness and redress the evil. Thereby the rainfall has been diminished, and the soil is exposed to be carried away into the plain by every storm that breaks over the heights.[1] Trees are the patient workers that reconstitute the flesh over the bones of the mountains. They derive their elements from the air and the rock, and they perform transformations far more wonderful than those attributed to the philosopher's stone. As Victor Hugo sang:—

> "Les arbres sont autant de mâchoires qui rongent
> Les aliments épars dans l'air souple et vivant;
> Ils dévorent la pluie, ils dévorent le vent.
> Tout leur est bon: la nuit, la mort. La pourriture
> Voit la rose, et lui va porter sa nourriture."

When the trees disappear from a country it shows the thriftlessness of the inhabitants—"sufficient unto the day is the evil thereof"; with the axe and the firebrand they destroy in a day what it will take centuries to replace.

Two non-French races occupy the extremities of the chain and the lowlands at its feet. In the Basses Pyrénées are the Basques, in Pyrénées Orientales are the Catalonians, speaking a dialect of the Spanish of Barcelona.

The whole of Aquitaine, from the Loire to the Pyrenees, the whole of Western Spain and Portugal, was once occupied by the Iberians, of whom the Basques are the shrunken residue. All Eastern France and Eastern Spain were overflowed by the Celts. The Romans recognized that Spain was in the possession of two races totally distinct, ethnographically and linguistically, and they termed the population of the peninsula Celtiberians.

When the Romans arrived on the scene they carried one main causeway from Arles to Narbonne, and thence to Toulouse, and from Toulouse to Dax. From this, roads branched to the south and crossed the Pyrenees into Spain by three gaps,

[1] É. Reclus: *Géographie universelle*, II. "La France."

natural doorways—one to the east, the easiest of all, by Le Perthus, where Pompey set up a trophy; one by Somport leading from Iluro (Oloron) to Saragossa; a third by Roncevaux to Pampeluna.

By the first of these ports Hannibal crossed from Spain on his way to Italy; by it also poured the Saracens to devastate the fields of Gaul. By Roncevaux Charles the Great passed to menace the Saracen power, and on his return met there with disaster at the hands of the Basques, which has been immortalized in song.

East and west were debatable lands. Navarre sat astride on the ridge, with a foot in Spain and the other in Gascony. To the east was Roussillon, that pertained to the kings of Aragon, till ceded definitely to France in 1659.

**Natives of Roussillon**

But to revert to the geological structure of the Pyrenees. The central chain is, as already said, composed of crystalline rocks, granite, and micaceous schist, whereas the northern chain exhibits the upturned beds of superincumbent deposits, and on the Spanish side the limestone lies on the granite. In the department of Haute Garonne the chains are soldered together by a transverse bar of mountain.

J. H. Michon, author of *Le Maudit*, says well:—

"These mountains reveal to me almost the entire history of the successive periods in the terrestrial crust. I have but to follow the torrent of the Arbouste, and mount to the Lac de Seculéjo, and push farther to the Pic d'Espingo, to find myself on the crest of the ridge dividing France from Spain. Often at these altitudes, reaching to 3000 metres above the sea, the prodigious force which has rent the terrestrial crust in a fault of eighty leagues in breadth, which has upheaved, as in the Marboré, enormous masses of limestone that once formed the basin of seas succeeding each other at different epochs—often has this phenomenon filled me with amazement. There in the Marboré lie the beds, retaining their horizontality, as though the aqueous deposits had been formed at this great elevation.

"But more commonly the central chain presents to our view masses of granite of astounding thickness. What a terrible cataclysm must that have been which thus reft and upset the globe, changing an extensive plain long submerged into a gigantic wall of granite shielded right and left with encasing masses of sedimentary formations which the upheaved granite has split and displaced in all directions."

To the north of the Pyrenees lies a deep trough extending from the Bay of Biscay to the Corbières that links the Pyrenees to the Cevennes, and which at the present day forms the watershed between the Mediterranean and the Atlantic. This gulf was gradually silted up by the torrents from the Pyrenees. Masses of rubble may be seen backing and capping isolated hills of sandstone, and forming long ridges, as that of the Park at Pau. The drift was from east to west. All the low hills are crowned with rolled stones. The boulders vary in size in proportion to the distance they have travelled. At Pamiers, Tarbes, and Pau they are of the size of a child's head, but farther north dwindle to pebbles and gravel, and finally we enter on a region of clay and sand, which heavy rains convert into quagmires. Indeed, those of Armagnac, between the Garonne and the Upper Adour, have hardly their equal in France. These are not glacier deposits, for the stones and pebbles have been rolled, and the clay or mud is the chewed or mumbled remains of boulders. At a later period the entire basin thus choked was lifted high above its original level.

That there was a glacial period in the south of France is certain, and the glaciers have left their moraines behind them. The glacier of Argelez extended in one stream to Lourdes, and then fanned out towards Tarbes. At Argelez it filled the valley to the height of 4430 feet. To morraine is due the desolate plain of detritus of Lannemezan. Separated from the mountain spurs by the profound depression in which flows the Neste, it is attached to the main chain solely by the isthmus that runs out from the Pic d'Arneille towards the plains.

**The Cascade, Gavarnie**

*From a photograph by Messrs. Levy and Sons, Paris*

The true watershed, between the Atlantic and the Mediterranean, lies far to the east, on the frontier between Ariège and the Pyrénées Orientales. All the streams and rivers to the west of the insignificant chain there flow into the Bay of Biscay. The rivers to the east are comparatively unimportant, the Aude alone being of a respectable size; and this does not derive its waters from the main chain of the Pyrenees, its sources are in the spur that acts as the watershed.

The lakes of the Pyrenees are nothing more than mountain tarns; the largest is the Lac Lanoux, in Pyrénées Orientales, lying below an irregular cirque, commanded by the Pic Pédroux. It stands 6500 feet above the sea-level, and is about two and a half miles long. It is usually frozen over from September to the end of June.

But if the lakes be insignificant, the cirques are of the most imposing character. There are none in Europe comparable to that of Gavarnie. This consists of an immense cul-de-sac, a vast amphitheatre, the stages of limestone capped with snow and ice, and above it tower five huge snow-clad mountain crests. The arena is heaped up with rubble brought down by the cascades. The mighty walls are wept over by water from the thawing glaciers. The highest fall of all is that in the lap of the cirque; it is a stream that precipitates itself from a height of 1270 feet, and, speedily resolving itself into spray, waves in the air like an ostrich plume. Superb as is the Cirque de Gavarnie in summer its appearance in winter is even more sublime. Especially is it so when the mountain-tops are enveloped in vapour. Then the aspect is as of a series of walls with snow bars intervening, mounting as a giant staircase into heaven; and the cascades are transformed into crystal columns.

There are other cirques deserving of notice, as that of Estaubé, commanded by the Pic de Pinède, behind which rises the Mont Perdu, on Spanish ground.

Troumousse, to the east of Estaubé, is a basin of pasture, girded about by a rampart 3000 feet in height, above which soars the Munia, a mass of snow and ice.

From the French side long lush valleys run to the roots of the first chain between the buttresses, but above this the character of the scenery changes abruptly. The melted snows descending from peak and terrace have sawn their way through the barrier imposed by the northern belt of limestone, feeling for and finding faults, through which they have torn their way, and debouch abruptly on to the lower broad valleys out of restricted ravines. Above these gorges we light on basins, such as that of Luz, green, in spring a sheet of gold from the crocuses. These were lake-beds, dried up when the torrents had contrived their escape. The rich vale of Ossau, between monotonous spurs, ends abruptly above Laruns, and there, through a cleft in the precipice, rages forth the Gave. It is much the same with the other Gave. Above Lourdes it glides through a broad, well-cultivated valley, but at Pierrefite, the mountain barrier is cleft in two places, through one of which roars forth the river from Luz, through the other the Gave from Cauterets. The Val de Campan, the Val d'Arreau, and that of Luchon, have much the same character.

Of the mountains, undoubtedly the Pic de Midi d'Ossau is the most conspicuous, not on account of its height, for it attains only to 8700 feet, but from its form, resembling a dog's tooth, cleft near the summit, glittering with snow, and rising in singular majesty above the Val d'Ossau, where the mountains fall back respectfully to allow a full view of its majesty. There are many noble mountains,—the Pic de Midi de Bigorre, 9436 feet; the Vignemale, 10,820 feet; Mont Perdu, 11,168 feet; Maladetta of the same height almost to a foot; but these last hold themselves screened behind the inferior but snow-clad northern range. The Canigou, however, belongs to this latter range, and is afflicted with none of the retiring qualities of the crystalline range. It steps boldly, ostentatiously forth above the plain of Roussillon, and for long was supposed to be the highest peak of the Pyrenees, though actually reaching only to 8360 feet. M. Élisée Reclus says of it:—

> "Like Etna, the Canigou is one of those mountains which rise vigorous as masters over a wide stretch of country. From below this grey pyramid, cleft with ravines, streaked with detritus between salient ribs of rock, of every tint, is not a whit less striking in aspect than the Sicilian volcano."

To the lover of flowers the Pyrenees present greater attractions than even the Alps. They lie farther to the south, enjoy more sun, and exhibit a greater luxuriance of vegetation and more variety in species. We meet in the Pyrenees with all old Alpine friends and make fresh acquaintances. Nowhere does the *Saxifraga longifolia* or *pyramidalis* throw up such a *jet-d'eau* of blossom. I have grown it at home, but it does not equal the beauty and abundance of flower as here wild. Nowhere are the geraniums in greater abundance and variety, springing up among the tufts of sharp-scented box. The crimson *Erodium manescavi*, the yellow *Hypericum mummularium*, the imbricated *Dianthus monspessulanus*, and the still more tattered *Dianthus superbus*, the purple toothwort, the blue stately aconite or monkshood, the lemon-coloured *Adonis vernalis*, the violet *Ramondia pyrenaica*, the *Primula viscosa* and *P. auricula*, the *Lilium bulbiferum*, the *Lilium pyrenaicum*, and a thousand more. Strange is it that the Alpen rose, the *Rhododendron ferrugineum*, should be as capricious a plant as it is. It luxuriates on the Alps, in the Pyrenees, and in the Dauphiné Alps; but does not appear in the Cevennes, the mountains of Auvergne, or Corsica. The great central plateau of France, though the heights rise to considerable altitudes and the constituent rocks are the same as those of the Pyrenees and the Alps, yet are totally devoid of this beautiful shrub.

The earliest inhabitants of the chain of the Pyrenees have left their traces in the limestone caverns. They were contemporary with the reindeer, the cave-bear, and hyena. Hardly a grotto that has been explored does not reveal that these men had lived there.

There are not many megalithic monuments to the north of the chain, but sufficient remain to show us that the dolmen-builder occupied the land from sea to sea. At Buzy, near the entrance to the Val d'Ossau, is a fine dolmen. I saw it first in 1850; it had been recently dug out by a treasure-seeker. A peasant told me that the man who had rifled it had found a bar of gold so soft that he could bend it. In fact, it consisted of pure gold without alloy. Near the dolmen lay a slab of red sandstone, with circles carved on it, some concentric, much like the carvings on the stones of Gavr'innis, in Brittany, and in the great covered way at Drogheda, in Ireland. Not having a drawing book with me nor a scale, all I could do at the time was to sketch the sculpture on my cuff. Three weeks later I revisited Buzy to make a careful drawing to scale of the slab, and found that in the meantime it had been broken up by the road-menders.

The road from Pau to Tarbes traverses a vast plateau, rising 300 feet above the plain of the Adour. It is composed of marshy moorland covered with fern and gorse. This is actually the old moraine deposited by the glacier of Argelez. It is made up of angular blocks brought down from the mountains, excellent material from which to construct mortuary cells. And on this plateau we find tumuli in remarkable abundance. This, as well as Lannemezan, must have served as huge cemeteries. Of late these cairns have been excavated, and prove to cover dolmens and covered avenues; one, the Grande Butte of the lande of Pontacq, contains a megalithic chamber, recalling the finest monuments of the kind in Brittany.

The tumulus of La Hallade had been violated in the Iron Age, and used then as a place of interment; but underneath the cinerary urns of the Early Gaulish period was discovered the prehistoric monument intact—a long low gallery of stones set on edge and covered with flat slabs. It was subdivided into eight cells, and contained twenty-three vases, some of which contained burnt bones, flakes of schist and quartz, a handful of turquoise beads, and a little blade of gold.

That the people of the rude stone monuments have their modern representatives in the Basques is probable. All this region was held by the Vascones, who gave to it their name—Gascony. They were driven over the Pyrenees by the Gauls, but in the sixth century they forced their way back to their old dwelling places and the tombs of their fathers, and falling on Novempopulania, as the territory was then called, defeated the Duke Bladastus, in 581, and settled down on the plains. But they were beaten in their turn, and, abandoning the plains, settled in those districts known as Labourde, Soule, and Lower Navarre.

The Basques are a people of great interest to the ethnologist, as the last shrunken remains of that Iberian race that once occupied all Western Europe from Scotland to Portugal and Spain, and, indeed, overleaped the Straits and spread as Kabyles and Berbers in Northern Africa. Although overlapped by other races this Basque element forms the main constituent of the French race in the south-west.

Every cook knows what "stock" is. It is the basis on which almost every known kind of soup is built up, whether Julienne, soupe claire, à la marquise, à la vermicelle, and Mrs. Beeton only knows how many more. The Iberian has been the stock out of which the English, Irish, Welsh, French, Italians, and Spaniards have been concocted. In France there was a dash of Gaulish, a smack of the Roman, a soupçon of Frank, *et voilà*; the Frenchman of to-day is at bottom an Iberian.

This same Iberian was an accommodating personage. He was ready to abandon his own rudimentary tongue and adopt the language of his conquerors. He cast his agglutinative tongue behind his back, took in as much Latin as he could swallow, and produced the French language. In Wales he adopted the British tongue, in Ireland the Gaelic.

He was wise in so doing, for his own language, as represented by the Basque of the present day, is crude, unformed, and wanting in flexibility. The first stage in the formation of speech is in the utterance of nouns substantive. A child embraced by a stranger says, "Man kiss baby." Kiss is a noun substantive. The child has not as yet arrived at the formation of a verb; and baby is a substantive, he has not yet attained to the use of a personal pronoun. The Chinese language remains in this primitive condition. In it the position of the words in a sentence governs the signification.

The second stage is that reached by the agglutinative tongues, where a differentiation of the parts of speech has taken place, and pronouns and particles acting as prepositions are tacked on to the nouns and verbs, but in such an elementary manner as never to become fused into them so as to affect and alter them. Always their separate existence is manifest. The third stage is where they are united and interpenetrate each other. The soldering has been so close that only a skilled eye can discover that an inflexion in a verb, a case in a noun, are composite words.

*Amo, amas, amat*, are actually formed of the root *ama*, love, with primitive pronouns welded on to them so as to distinguish the person who loves.

In Basque the auxiliary verbs alone undergo conjugation, and they exhibit a peculiarity that deserves notice. Take an instance: the auxiliary verb *izan*, to be. "I am" may be rendered in four different ways, according to the person addressed. In speaking to a male familiarly "I am" is *nuk*; but a woman addressed in like manner is *nun*; "I am," when used in address to a person highly respected of either sex, is *nuzu*; "I am" spoken without any particular reference to any one is *niz*. So "he or she is" may be rendered *duk, dun, duzu, da*; and "we are" by *gaituk, gaitun, gaituzu, gare*.

The Basque language is capable of an incredible amount of agglomeration in the formation of words, and of indefinite modification of times, conditions, forms of words.

*Etche* is a house; *argizagi* is the moon; *elhur* is snow; *chori* is a bird; *sagar* an apple; *oski* a shoe; *aurhide* a child; *arrolze*, an egg.

We feel at once that we meet here with a language which has no relations that we can detect with any of the European tongues with which we are familiar.

The Basque has not distinguished himself in literature. It is true that a set of poems pretending to be ancient has been produced and published as relics of Early Basque poetry, but they were forgeries, like Macpherson's *Ossian*.

The nucleus of the Basque country may be said to be S. Jean-de-Luz. Formerly it was Ustaritz (i.e. the Oak of Judgment), where the Elders assembled in Council; but at the French Revolution this oak was cut down.

The Basque villages have a character of their own. Erected by a people who do not feel eagerness to look in at one another's windows, a people pushing independence to fanaticism, the villages consist rather of isolated buildings loosely united than of close agglomeration of houses. Like the Welsh, the Basques love whitewash, but paint their shutters brilliant red. The churches stand in the midst of a clump of trees, their towers surmounted by three points, symbolical of the Trinity. They are a healthy people, clean in mind and clean in body, religious and honest. The whole population has been described as "la plus belle, la plus saine, la plus alerte, la plus joyeuse qui se puisse se trouver en Europe."

# CHAPTER II

## GASCONY

The province of Gascony—Protest against inclusion in Aquitaine—
Union of Béarn, Foix, and Bigorre—Navarre—Interest of Gascony
to English people—Gascony annexed to the Crown of England—
Viscounty of Béarn—The Fors—Independence of the people—A
babe with open hands—An elderly wife—John of Béarn's treatment of a Pope—Charles of Viana—Schemes of Juana—Murder of
Blanche—The coveted crown—Death of Francis Phœbus—Choice
of a husband—Gascon braggarts.

THE province of Gascony included Labourde, of which Bayonne was the capital;
the viscounty of Soule, with Mauleon as its chief town; Basse Navarre; Béarn,
a viscounty, with its residential châteaux at Orthez and at Pau, and its cathedrals
at Lescar and Oloron; Bigorre, a county with its capital at Tarbes; Cominges, and
to the south of that Couserans; and finally the county of Foix, on the frontier of
Languedoc.

The whole of this stretch of land was included by Augustus in Aquitaine. This
the peoples of Vasconia did not like, and they sent to him an embassy to request
that they might be organized into a separate province. To this the emperor agreed.
Concerning this transaction history is silent; but we know about it from a Roman
inscription at Hasparren, set up by the ambassador, to commemorate his journey
and the favourable reply he received.

In the thirteenth century the viscounty of Béarn was annexed to the county
of Foix, and the intervening county of Bigorre fell to Foix in 1425, through the
marriage of an heiress. Finally, Navarre also was united to Foix-Béarn-Bigorre in
1479. It furnished the holder with a royal title, nothing more save the scrap of land
on this side the Pyrenees called Basse Navarre, of which the principal town was S.
Jean-pied-du-port.

Gascony should be of special interest to us English, as it was for so long a possession of the English Crown.

Louis VII, before the death of his father, had contracted marriage with Eleanor
of Guyenne, heiress of Poitou and of the duchy of Aquitaine. He obtained the most
splendid dower that ever fell to the lot of a French king. It consisted of nothing less
than half of the south of France. Eleanor was a passionate, frivolous girl; Louis, a
pale, feeble prince, a prey to petty religious scruples. He took the cross and started

on the disastrous and disgraceful crusade of 1147. He took Eleanor with him. She made no secret of her contempt for her husband. "He is a monk, and not a man." She became over-intimate with her uncle, Raymond of Antioch, the handsomest man of his time. She was accused also of carrying on an intrigue with a Saracen. On her return to Europe she insisted on being divorced from Louis, and she cast herself into the arms of Henry Plantagenet, Count of Anjou, Duke of Normandy, and heir to the crown of England. Thus she detached all these provinces from France and annexed them to the realm of England. Indeed, Henry, by the marriage of one of his sons to the heiress of Brittany, found himself master of nearly the whole of Western France. The House of Anjou had sprung into domination on Gaulish soil equal to that of the French king and his other vassals put together, and controlling the mouths of the three great rivers. Add to all this the possession of the English kingdom. The long protracted and desolating wars that ensued on French soil was a struggle between the kings as to whether France should be annexed to England, or Aquitaine to France.

"By the peace between Henry III and Louis IX," says Mr. Freeman, "Aquitaine became a land held by the King of England as a vassal of the French crown. From that time it became one main object of the French kings to change this feudal superiority over this great duchy into an actual possession. The Hundred Years' War began through the attempt of Philip of Valois (1337) on the Aquitanian dominions of Edward III. Then the King of England found it politic to assume the title of King of France. But the real nature of the controversy was shown by the first great settlement. At the Peace of Bretigny (1360) Edward gave up all claim to the crown of France, in exchange for the independent sovereignty of his old fiefs and of some of his recent conquests. Aquitaine and Gascony, including Poitou ... were made over to the King of England without the reservation of any homage or superiority of any kind. These lands became a territory as foreign to the French kingdom as the territory of her German and Spanish neighbours. But in a few years the treaty was broken on the French side, and the actual possessions of England beyond the sea were cut down to Calais and Guines, with some small part of Aquitaine adjoining the cities of Bordeaux and Bayonne. Then the tide turned at the invasion of Henry V. Aquitaine and Normandy were won back; Paris saw the crowning of an English king, and only the central part of the country obeyed the heir of the Parisian kingdom. But the final result of the war was the driving out of the English from all Aquitaine and France except the single district of Calais.

"The French conquest of Aquitaine (1451–3), the result of the Hundred Years' War, was in form the conquest of a land which had ceased to stand in any relation to the French crown."

Thus Aquitaine, including Gascony, had belonged to the crown of England from 1152 to 1453, just three hundred and one years.

But, although nominally pertaining to England, it contained stubborn and recalcitrant elements, notably the counts of Foix, who were viscounts of Béarn.

Towards the close of the eleventh century the viscounty of Béarn had enjoyed sovereign rights, admitting allegiance to none. Later, when Louis XI went in pilgrimage to Notre Dame de Sarrance, he lowered the sword of France on entering Béarn, as being no longer in his own kingdom. This little territory during the Middle Ages was perhaps the best governed corner of the earth, the freest and happiest in France, and perhaps in all Europe. The *fors* of Béarn were the liberties to which the viscount was required to swear adhesion before he was recognized as sovereign. The earliest of these *fors* is that of Oloron (1080), renewed in 1290, and it is one of the earliest monuments extant of the Romance tongue. By these constitutions the inhabitants of the viscounty governed themselves.

An instance or two of the independent spirit of the Béarnais may be given.

Marie, daughter of Peter, Viscount of Béarn, upon the death of her brother, in 1134, became heiress. She had been reared at the Court of Aragon, and had married William de Moncada, a Catalonian noble. She had the weakness to do homage to the king for Béarn. The people rose in revolt, deposed her, and elected as their viscount a knight of Bigorre, well spoken of for his virtues. He, however, disregarded the *fors*, and attempted to rule as a feudal lord, whereupon within a year he was assassinated. Then a knight of Auvergne was chosen, and held the viscounty for two years. But he also disregarded the constitution and was put to death. Then his estates of Béarn sent a deputation to Marie de Moncada, to inform her that it had come to their ears that she had given birth to twin boys, and the people authorized their commissioners to select one of the twins to be their viscount. The deputation were shown the cradle in which the infants lay; one slept with his hands open, the other held his fists clenched. "We will have the open-handed lad," said the Béarnais, and he became Viscount Gaston VI. On his death in 1170 his brother, the close-fisted William Raymond, claimed the inheritance, but the Béarnais refused to acknowledge his claim as one of right, protesting that the viscountship was elective. They compelled him to submit to their will, and accepted him only when he had granted still greater liberties than they had hitherto enjoyed, and this not till five years after the death of his brother.

William Raymond died in 1223, leaving a son, William, to succeed him, but he was killed in battle against the Moors in 1229, and William's son Gaston succeeded under the regency of his mother Garsende. She is described as having been so stout that only a large wagon could contain her, and then she overlapped the sides. Gaston VII, son of this plump lady, left an only child, a daughter Margaret, the heiress of Béarn, which she carried with her when married to Roger Bernard, Count of Foix. Thus it came about that Foix and Béarn were united in one hand.

Roger Bernard and Margaret had a grandson, Gaston IX of Béarn. At the age of eighteen he was married to Eleanor of Cominges, a lady considerably older than himself. Some one without tact remarked to the Countess on the disparity of their ages. "Disparity of ages!" exclaimed she, "Why, I would have waited for him till he was born."

## I. PEDIGREE OF THE VISCOUNTS OF BÉARN, COUNTS OF FOIX

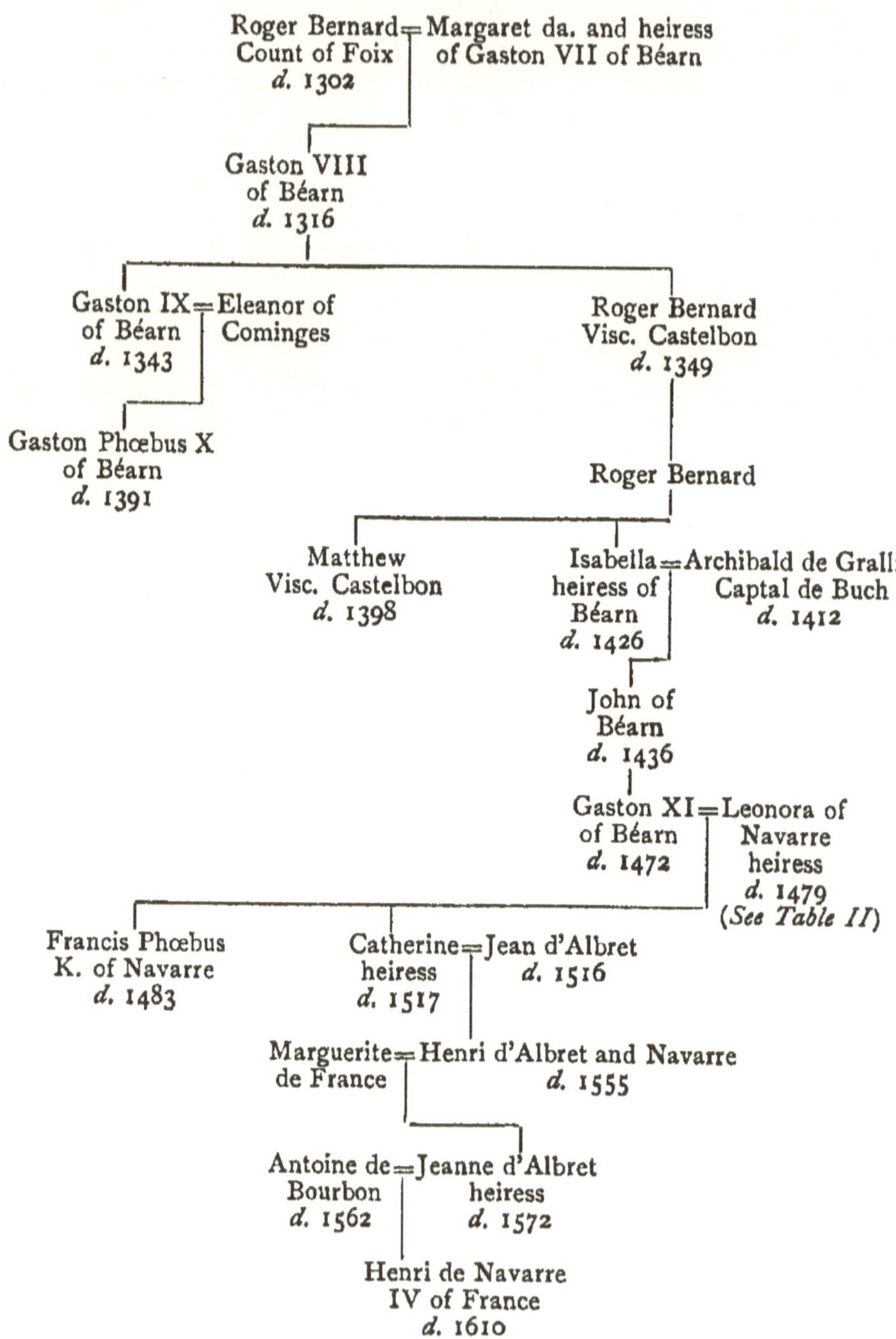



The young husband fell fighting against the Moors in 1343. By his elderly wife he left a son, Gaston Phœbus, of whom more when we come to Orthez.

## II. PEDIGREE OF LEONORA, HEIRESS OF NAVARRE

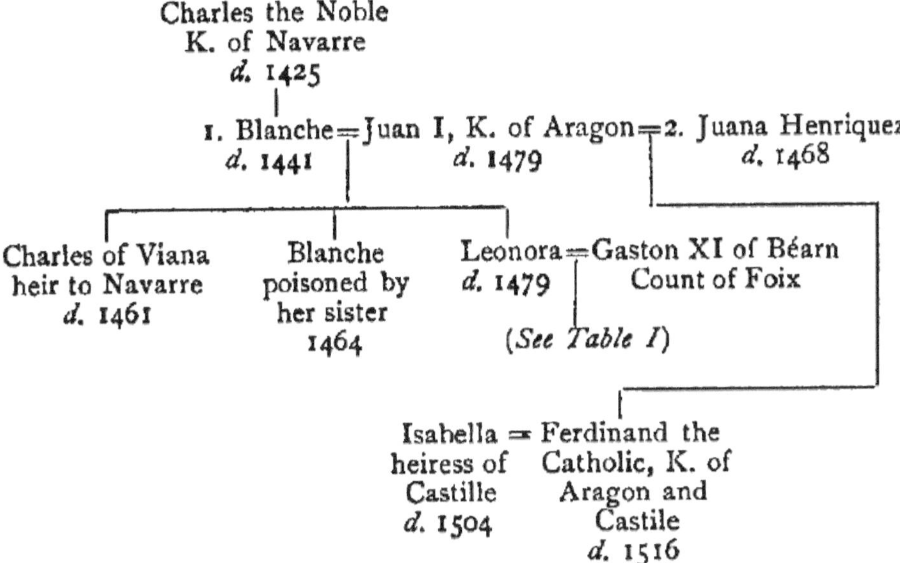

Gaston Phœbus was succeeded by a cousin, Matthew de Castelbon, who died in 1398, without issue, and he was followed by his sister Isabella, married to Archibald, Captal de Buch, a just and worthy ruler. They had a son, John of Béarn, who succeeded his mother in 1426. He captured the antipope, Benedict XIII, and threw him into a dungeon in one of his castles, where he died of ill-treatment, and then John denied Christian burial to his body. This so delighted Pope Martin, the rival of Benedict, that he conferred on John the title of "Avenger of the Faith." Jean was succeeded by his son Gaston, who placed his sword at the disposal of Charles VI. At Bordeaux with his aid the English underwent a signal defeat. He was married to Eleanor of Navarre, through whom the claim to the title of King of Navarre came to her descendants. How that was, and the crimes that brought it about, must now be told.

Charles the Noble, King of Navarre, died in 1425. Having lost his only son, he bequeathed crown and kingdom to his daughter Blanche, married to Juan of Aragon, brother of Alphonso, King of Aragon and the Two Sicilies, and by reversion after her death to their son Charles, Prince of Viana. Juan of Aragon acted as viceroy to his brother whilst Alphonso was in Italy. On the death of Charles the Noble Juan and Blanche assumed the titles of King and Queen of Navarre. Blanche died in 1441, and by her will bequeathed the kingdom, in accordance with her father's desire, to her son Charles of Viana. But Juan had no thought of surrendering the crown to his son. He married a young, handsome, and ambitious woman, Juana Henriquez, daughter of the Admiral of Castille, and she became the mother of Ferdinand, afterwards known as "the Catholic." Thenceforth she schemed to obtain all that could be grasped for her own son Ferdinand.

Charles was an amiable, accomplished youth, fond of literature and of the arts. Queen Blanche, in her will, had urged him not to assume the government without the consent of his father; but when, in 1452, the estates of Aragon recognized him as heir to the crown, and Juan declined to resign, Charles openly raised the standard of revolt. Juan marched against his son, and Charles was defeated, taken prisoner, and consigned to a fortress. There he remained for a year, and would have remained on indefinitely had not the Navarrese armed for his deliverance. Juan was forced to yield, and as a compromise confirmed Charles in the principality of Viana, and promised to abandon to him half the royal revenues.

The reconciliation thus forcibly effected was not likely to last; in fact, the compromise suited neither party. The father burned to chastise sharply his rebellious son, and Charles chafed at being defrauded of the crown which was his undoubted heritage. Hence in 1455 both prepared to renew the contest. The following year, 1456, the prince was again defeated by his father, and was compelled to fly to his uncle Alphonso, who was then at Naples. During his absence Juan summoned the estates and declared that both Charles and his eldest daughter Blanche were excluded from succession to the throne—Charles on account of his rebellion, Blanche for having espoused his cause—and Juan proclaimed his youngest daughter Leonora to be his heir. Blanche had been married to, and then separated from, Henry the Impotent, King of Castille. Leonora was married to the Count of Foix.

The inhabitants of Pampeluna, and the people generally throughout Navarre, were indignant at the injustice committed by Juan; they elected Charles to be their king, and invited him to ascend the throne. Unfortunately for him, Alphonso, King of Aragon and the Two Sicilies, died in 1458, whereupon Juan ascended the throne that had been occupied by his brother. Charles now hoped for a reconciliation, which he had reason to expect, as his father now wore three crowns which had come to him by right; and he hoped that Juan would readily surrender to him that of Navarre, which he had usurped, and to which he had no legitimate claim. The Prince of Viana landed in Spain in 1459, and dispatched a messenger to Juan entreating him to forget the past and to recognize his claim to Navarre at present and his right to succession to Aragon. But Juan would allow nothing further than restoration to the principality of Viana, and expressly forbade his son setting foot in Navarre. Had the misunderstanding ended here, it had been well for Charles; but a new occasion of dispute arose.

Henry IV of Castille offered his sister Isabella, heiress to the crown after his death, to Charles of Viana. This alarmed and enraged Juana, the stepmother of Charles, who calculated on effecting this alliance for her own son Ferdinand, and uniting under his sceptre the kingdoms of Aragon and Castille. To obtain this end Charles must be got rid of. Accordingly she induced his father Juan to invite him to a conference at Lerida. The prince went thither unsuspiciously, and was at once arrested and thrown into prison. The Estates of Aragon and Catalonia were incensed at the harsh and unjust treatment of one whom they hoped eventually to proclaim as their sovereign. They demanded his liberation. The King refused. Insurrection broke out, became general, and so menacing that Queen Juana was alarmed and herself solicited the release of the Prince. She did more; she went in person to Morella, whither the captive had been transferred, to open the prison gates. He was conducted by her to Barcelona, which admitted him, but shut its gates in her face. All Catalonia now recognized the Prince, and proclaimed him heir to the thrones of Aragon, Navarre, and Sicily. But the rejoicing of the people was of brief duration, as shortly after his release from durance Charles fell ill, lingered a few days, and died. By his testament he bequeathed the crown of Navarre to his sister Blanche as next in order of succession to himself.

The death of Charles was too opportune for it not to have been attributed to poison, administered by an agent of his stepmother. Soon after a ray of sunlight focussed by a mirror set fire to Juana's hair. This was at once set down as a Judgment of Heaven falling on her, an indication by the finger of God that she was the murderess of her stepson.

Charles was now out of the way; Blanche, however, obstructed the path, and the will of her brother in her favour proved fatal to her. Juan was resolved to retain the sovereignty of Navarre during his own life, and none the less to transmit it at death to his favourite daughter Leonora, Countess of Foix, or her issue. He determined to compel Blanche to renounce her rights. To effect this she was sent across the Pyrenees, closely guarded, under the pretext that she was about to be given in marriage to the Duke of Berri, brother of the French king. But she perceived clearly enough what was her father's purpose, and at Roncevaux, on her way, she caused a protest to be prepared in all secrecy, in which she declared that she was being carried out of Spain by violence, against her will, and that force would be used to compel her to renounce her rights over Navarre; and now she declared beforehand against the validity of such a renunciation. Upon reaching S. Jean-Pied-du-port, she was, as she had anticipated, constrained to make a formal surrender of all her rights, in favour of her sister and brother-in-law, Gaston, Count of Foix. In a letter addressed to Henry, couched in pathetic terms, she reminded him of the dawn of happiness that she had enjoyed when united to him years before, of his promises made to her, and of her subsequent sorrows. As she was well aware that her father was consigning her to imprisonment, and perhaps death at the hands of her ambitious and unscrupulous sister, she conferred on him all her rights to the crown of Navarre, to the exclusion of those who meditated her assassination, the Count and Countess of Foix. On the same day that this letter was dispatched she was handed over to an emissary of the Countess Leonora, 30 April, 1462, and was conveyed to the Castle of Orthez. The gates closed on her, and she was seen no more, but not long after they opened to allow a coffin to issue to be conveyed to Lescar, there to be interred.

The secret of Blanche's death was closely kept, till the Navarrese Cortes took the matter up, and demanded her release as their rightful queen. Then only was it announced that she was dead, but on what day and in what manner she died was never revealed.

The Count and Countess of Foix now congratulated themselves on having secured the crown of Navarre to themselves and to their descendants, and their son Gaston was at once invested with the title of Prince of Viana. But the crime committed brought but a barren gain. A few years later Gaston of Viana, their hope, was killed by a lance in a tournament at Lillebourne. Count Gaston never obtained the kingdom, and died at Roncevaux in 1472. His widow, Leonora, was balked to the very last. Her father retained the title of King and the rule over Navarre up to his death in 1479, and when the coveted diadem fell to her, she retained it but for fifteen days, and then died also. Her grandson, Francis, called Phœbus on account of his beauty, was indeed crowned at Pampeluna. He was a gallant and amiable boy, but the doom of the ill-gotten crown was on him. Ferdinand the Catholic, son of the wicked Joanna, would not allow a pretty boy to stand in his way. One day, 29 January, 1483, after dinner, the prince, *adonné à toutes gentillesses*, took a flute on which he was wont to play. Scarcely had he raised it to his lips ere he turned deadly white and sank into a chair. In two hours he was dead, at the age of sixteen. As he lay dying he turned to his mother with a smile and said, "My kingdom is not of this world."

It was the conviction of all contemporaries that Ferdinand the Catholic had contrived to have the lad poisoned.

The claim to the crown of Navarre now passed to Catherine, the sister of Francis Phœbus, married to Jean d'Albret. This marriage is interesting. It was determined by the Estates of Béarn. No sooner was Francis Phœbus dead than Ferdinand of Castille, his supposed murderer, sent to demand the hand of Catherine for his son, a child in the cradle. But the mother, Magdalen of France, coldly replied that the choice of a husband for her daughter was a matter for decision by the Assembly of the delegates of Béarn. The Estates were convoked to Pau, and the majority voted for Jean d'Albret, whose lands adjoined Béarn, and who was himself then but a child. During the infancy of Catherine and Jean d'Albret Magdalen acted as regent. The Count of Grammont and others formed a plot to poison her in favour of Jean de Foix, Catherine's uncle. It was discovered, and the minor conspirators were executed at Pau; the instigators, being grandees, escaped scot-free.

Catherine, on growing to woman's estate, left no stone unturned in her attempt to obtain the kingdom of Navarre, but feebly supported by her amiable husband. "Would that I had been born John and you Catherine!" exclaimed the impetuous princess; "and then we would have secured Navarre." In the end Catherine died of disappointment at the failure of all her schemes, and in dying turned her eyes in the direction of Navarre.

The rest of the story of the viscounts of Béarn, counts of Foix, and titular kings of Navarre, shall be told when we come to Pau.

By some fatality, surely unjustly, the Gascons are credited throughout France with being braggarts, cowards, the makers of bad bulls and as bad jokes. This is what a writer says of them in *Le Passe-temps Agréable*, Rotterdam, 1737:—

> "If in France you would speak of a braggart and swash-buckler, whose magnanimity and courage are discoverable in his speech, and in his speech alone; who speaks of war, without having been in it; say but, He is a Gascon, and this explains everything. Those friends at the table who are faithful so long as it is spread with good cheer, but who vanish when the platter and the

beaker are empty—say that they are Gascons, and that explains all. Should you encounter a fellow who boasts of his gallantries and the favours he has received from fair ladies, intimate that he is a Gascon, and all will know the worth of his statements. The word Gascon suffices to comprehend various characters never estimable. But it must not be supposed that all Gascons are such sorry creatures as those spoken of above. There are to be found among them men of rare merit, and men with plenty of courage, men as honest as are any others. But, actually, all Gascons do not come from Gascony. Every nation under the sun breeds its braggarts and false braves. 'The true Gascons,' says a writer who knew them well in their own land washed by the Garonne, 'the true Gascons possess a good deal of heart, and are desirous of making all the world aware of the fact.' But I am not satisfied that they do not make display of more heart than they actually possess."

A collection of bons-mots and blunders made by Gascons is found in *Vasconia*, Lyons, 1730. The description of a Gascon, as given by a fellow-countryman, is more flattering than that above. He says: "To be a Gascon is to be a happy mixture of dazzling virtues and of agreeable and convenient faults. Everything in us is charming, even our imperfections. What if there be blemishes perceptible in us? There are spots in the sun itself."

# CHAPTER III

## BAYONNE

Approach to the Pyrenees—Colour of the mountains—Bayonne—Cathedral—Attachment of Bayonne to the English—Quarrels with Norman towns—Taken by the French—Bayonets—Meeting of queens—Wild Scotchmen—Napoleon lures the Infante and King of Spain to Bayonne—Dethrones the King—The crossing of the Pyrenees by Wellington—Battles—About Bayonne—Cemetery—Lakes in the Landes—Biarritz—The Refuge—S. Jean de Luz—Riding *en cacolet*—Heaving at Eastertide—The Bidassoa—Peace of the Pyrenees—Fontarabia—Passages—San Sebastian—Siege—Charges brought against the English.

MICHELET, with florid eloquence, describes the approach to the Pyrenees from Bordeaux in the first chapter of the second volume of his *History of France*.

"However beautiful and fertile may be the valley of the Garonne, one cannot lag there. The distant summits of the Pyrenees exercise on us a too powerful attraction. But it is a serious matter to reach them. Whether you take the way by Nérac, a doleful *seigneurie* of the Albrets, or whether you follow the coast, it is all the same, you must either traverse or skirt an ocean of *landes*, covered with cork trees and vast pine forests, where nothing is met save black sheep under the conduct of a shepherd of the department, that have left the mountains for the plains in quest of warmth. The roving life of these shepherds is one of the most picturesque elements in the South. These nomads, companions of the stars in their eternal solitude, half astronomers, half sorcerers, carry their goods with them. Here in the West they continue to lead the Asiatic life of Lot and Abraham.

"The formidable barrier of Spain now rises before us in all its majesty. The Pyrenees are not, like the Alps, a complicated system of peaks and valleys, they are simply a mighty wall that drops to lower elevations at its extremities. Two peoples, distinct from one another—the Basques at the west, the Catalans at the east—hold the doors of two worlds. These irritable and capricious porters open and shut at will, wearied and impatient at the incessant passage of the nations through these ports. They opened to Abderaman, they shut to Roland. Many graves lie between Roncevaux and the Seu d'Urgel."

Certain it is that the approach to the Pyrenees across the long level of the Landes lends to them an advantage only possessed by the Alps when seen from the plains of Lombardy. I know nothing so impressive as the scene from a swell on the surface of the Landes, when the eye sees the great range in silver and cobalt stretching to the south from a dim east, in which snowy peaks and silver clouds are indistinguishable, to die away beyond the reach of the eye in the west, and all beheld over a vast sheet of dark green forest, like a sea stretching to their roots. Nowadays we whirl from Bordeaux to Dax and Bayonne by rail. I recall the journey by carriage, when before our eyes for two days we saw that blue ridge tipped with silver half-way up the sky, hour after hour becoming more distinct. I have spoken of the colours of the mountains as cobalt and silver. So they are in the remote distance, but when near at hand the tints are richer. I had a drawing-master at Bayonne, to whom I showed some water-colour sketches of English scenery. He shook his head. "Cobalt!" said he; "that will not do for the shadows of our Pyrenees. For them you must employ ultramarine and carmine." He spoke the truth. Such are the royal purples of Pyrenean shadows worn in summer and autumn.

Bayonne is a trefoil. There are three towns, but the third is on the north side of the Adour, and in the department of Landes. It has grown up about the railway station and the citadel. Old Bayonne is a city planted on both banks of the Nive, where it joins the Adour. Bayonne is the capital of the Basque country, and the population of the town is composed of Basques, Spaniards, Jews, with a sprinkling only of French. The cathedral, the old castle, the Mairie, and the theatre are in Grand Bayonne on the left bank of the Nive. In Petit Bayonne, on the right bank, are the arsenal, the Châteaux Neuf, and the military hospital.

The old town, cramped within its fortifications, capable of expansion upwards only, has narrow and gloomy streets.

The cathedral was left incomplete by the English when driven out of Bayonne. It lacked a west front and towers; but these have been supplied of late years. Externally the cathedral is not striking, but within it is well-proportioned. Choir and apse pertain to the thirteenth century, the nave to the fourteenth, all constructed when the English were masters of the town. The arms of England, of Talbot, and other noble families that are English, are emblazoned on the keys of the vaulting ribs. On the south side of the church are the beautiful cloisters, almost the largest in France. Their date is 1240.

A good many houses in the town have cellars vaulted with ribs to a key, and on some of these latter are English arms. But few old buildings in the town are of interest. The château dates from the twelfth and thirteenth centuries, and the new château is of the fifteenth and sixteenth, but neither is architecturally remarkable.

**The Cathedral, Bayonne**

Bayonne and Bordeaux were warmly attached to England during the three hundred years that they pertained to the English crown. Their love was not altogether sentimental; it sprang out of self-interest, as these two ports furnished the wine that was supplied to Britain and Ireland. Our kings did what they could to attach the citizens to their crown by the grant of extensive privileges, and undoubtedly Bayonne reached its greatest prosperity when under the sceptre of England. This prosperity roused the jealousy of the commercial ports of Normandy, especially was this the case when that duchy was detached from the English crown. To avenge the death of a Rouen merchant killed in an affray in Bayonne the Normands attacked and butchered a whole ship's crew that had entered one of their ports. On another occasion they surprised sixty-two Bayonnais merchant vessels in the port of S. Malo, and hung from the yardarm one of the crew of each side by side with dogs. This latter insult was more keenly felt by the Bayonnais than the execution itself. They appealed to Edward I "against these bad persons who have put your subjects to death, hanging mastiffs alongside of Christians, in defiance of Christianity and of your Majesty, and of your subjects."

The outrage had to be chastised. Large armaments were equipped on both sides, and in one engagement the Normands lost five thousand men. The grim joke with the dogs proved costly to them in the end.

But at the close of the thirteenth century these petty quarrels between rival cities were merged in the general war that raged between England and France. Philip the Fair got possession of Bayonne in 1294. Edward I hastened into Gascony, besieged the town, retook it, and thenceforth the leopards of England waved from their battlements till July, 1451, when the English were expelled from Bayonne by Charles VII. The Bayonnais watched the entry of the French with sullen dissatisfaction, and were only consoled for the change of master by a miracle. A luminous white cross appeared in the sky, and this led them to suppose that Heaven had decreed that the white cross of France should take the place of the red cross of England. Bayonne has given its name to the bayonet, which was invented there about the year 1647. Originally it was a dagger with a round handle that fitted into the bore of a gun, and was fixed only after the soldier had discharged his piece. The use of the bayonet fastened on to the barrel was an improvement introduced by the French. In the battle of Marsaglia in 1693 the success of the French was mainly due to the employment of this weapon. The enemy were unable to stand against so formidable a novelty.

In 1565 the queen-mother, Catherine de Medici, here met her daughter, Isabella of Spain, who had just recovered from a severe illness.

"Political motives were not forgotten, and among other matters to be considered between the sovereigns of France and Spain—for Catherine hoped that Philip would accompany his wife—was undoubtedly the repression of heresy. There exists among the state papers at Simancas what is called by diplomatists an 'identical note' of the subjects to be discussed at Bayonne. In it we read that the two powers engaged not to tolerate the Reformed worship in their respective states, that the canons of the Council of Trent should be enforced, that all nonconformists should be incapacitated for any public office, civil or military, and that heretics should quit the realm within a month, permission being accorded them to sell their property. Although Catherine gave her assent to these declarations, so far as the discussion of them was concerned, we have indisputable evidence that she did not intend to adopt them in the same sense as Philip of Spain."[2]

It has been supposed that on this occasion the massacre of S. Bartholomew was planned. Such, however, was not the case. Catherine at the time was indisposed to adopt violent measures. She sought to hold the balance between the contending parties. Moreover, the massacre did not take place till seven years later. The meeting at Bayonne in 1565 was rather one of rejoicing, with a series of magnificent fêtes, and political business was transacted only at odd moments. Some years later, when Walsingham referred to this Bayonne meeting as the occasion of an inauguration of a general league against the Protestants, Catherine replied that it had no such result at all, and that it "tended to no other end but to make good cheer."

One of the masques performed on this occasion was a representation of "Wild Scotchmen." The Duke of Guise and six others were equipped in what was fondly believed to be the Highland costume. Over a white satin shirt embroidered with gold lace and crimson silk they wore a jacket of yellow velvet, with short skirts closely plaited "according to the custom of these savages," trimmed with a border of crimson satin, ornamented with gold, silver, pearls, and other jewels of various colours. Their yellow satin hose were similarly adorned, and their silk boots were trimmed with silver fringe and rosettes.

> "On their heads they wore a cap *à l'antique* of cloth of gold, and for crest a thunderbolt pouring out a fragrant jet of perfumed fire—the said thunderbolt being twined round by a serpent reposing on a pillow of green satin. Each cavalier wore on his arm a Scotch shield or targe covered with cloth of gold and bearing a device. The horses' trappings were of crimson satin with plumes of yellow, white, and carnation. So much for the Frenchman's ideal of a Scotchman!"—White.

We must pass on to the time of the First Empire, before Bayonne became the scene of any political event of importance.

Napoleon had resolved on dethroning the King of Spain, and on converting the peninsula into a kingdom for his brother Joseph. The condition of affairs in Spain was favourable. The King, Charles IV, was the feeblest of the fainéant race of the Bourbons. He retained a tame confessor about his person, for whom he would whistle when he was conscious of a twinge of conscience. The Queen, Louisa Maria of Parma, had made a paramour of Manuel Godoy, a lusty private in the Guards. Him she created Prince of the Peace and Prime Minister. His power over her and over the mind of the poor King was complete.

The Infante, the Prince Ferdinand, was also feeble-minded. He was the rallying point of the faction opposed to Godoy. Ferdinand appealed by letter to Napoleon (11 October, 1807), and the Emperor at once, through his agent Savary at Madrid, pressed him to throw himself on his protection by coming to Bayonne, "where," said Savary, "you will hear him salute you as Ferdinand VII, King of Spain and

---

[2] White (H.), *The Massacre of S. Bartholomew.* London, 1868.

the Indies." The stupid Bourbon prince walked into the trap. On 16 April, 1808, he crossed the frontier. "Ha! is the fool actually come!" exclaimed Napoleon, who was at Bayonne. "I could hardly have thought it possible."

Napoleon received him graciously, but instead of hailing him as king, endeavoured to induce him voluntarily to resign his pretensions to the throne. But Ferdinand, though stupid, was stubborn, and he refused. It was accordingly necessary for the Emperor to ensnare the old king as well. He wrote to him and to the Queen, inviting them to Bayonne so that he might settle the dispute between him and the Infante, in order to place the throne of Charles beyond danger of usurpation by Ferdinand. The King was also dull enough to walk into the snare.

On 30 April a huge, lumbering coach drawn by eight Biscayan mules rolled over the drawbridge of Bayonne. It contained the monarch, his queen, his youngest son, and some attendants. Two other antiquated chariots discharged their cargoes of chamberlains and ladies-in-waiting. Godoy, who had preceded the royal party, welcomed it, and assured his sovereign that the intentions of the Emperor towards him were most generous. This assurance was speedily corroborated by Napoleon, who appeared in person. The childish king threw himself, weeping, into the arms of Napoleon, and called him his best friend and truest support.

As the infirm old man was unable to walk unassisted, Napoleon took him under the arm to help him up the steps. Charles turned to the Queen and said, "See, Louisa, he is sustaining me!"

The resentment of the old couple against their son had increased. Ferdinand was summoned to their presence before Napoleon, and then ensued a scene to which the Emperor afterwards looked back with disgust. The King loaded his son with bitter reproaches, the Queen broke out into invectives. Losing all command over herself, this royal virago foamed at the mouth, called on her good friend the Emperor to send him to the guillotine, and had the indecency to protest that this son, though borne by her, had not the King for his father. Then the old king, crippled with rheumatism, raised his shaking hand over the prince and threatened him with his cane.

The main quarrel between the King and Ferdinand was due to Charles having abdicated when a riot broke out in Madrid and Ferdinand having been proclaimed. But Charles afterwards revoked his abdication, which had been wrung from him by his terrors, and Ferdinand refused to withdraw his claim to having succeeded his father on the surrender of the crown by the old man. After the deplorable scene described, Ferdinand gave way so far as to consent to resign the crown, on condition that this renunciation was in favour of his father only, and that it was ratified in Madrid. This did not satisfy Napoleon; it was not what he wanted.

At this juncture Marbot, the aide-de-camp of Murat, who had been sent to Madrid, arrived at full gallop to announce to the Emperor that an insurrection had broken out in the capital, in consequence of an attempt made to remove the remaining members of the royal family.

This furnished Napoleon with the excuse he wanted. "Unless," said he to Ferdinand, whom he accused of having provoked the riot, "unless between this and midnight you have recognized your father as king, and have sent information to this effect to Madrid, I will have you dealt with as a rebel."

The terrified prince yielded. On 6 May Ferdinand signed a formal renunciation of the crown. But on the previous day Charles had been induced also to surrender his claims. Ferdinand in return was to have the palace of Navarre and an income of six hundred thousand francs; Charles was accorded the châteaux of Chambord and Compiègne. The despised and disinherited princes were to receive in all ten millions; "but," as Napoleon wrote, "we will reimburse ourselves out of Spain!" Yet even this undertaking was not observed. Ferdinand was interned in France.

The stretch of country from Bayonne to the frontier is full of interest to the Englishman as the scene of the contest between Wellington and Soult, after the former had driven the French over the frontier and out of Spain.

The autumn of 1813 had been passed by the greater part of the allied army of English, Portuguese, and Spaniards under canvas on the cold and cloudy summits of the Western Pyrenees. They endured great privations. Their picket and night duties were incessant and harassing; the weather, moreover, was stormy. The tedium of these camps, and the sufferings from frost and sleet, exhausted the patience and shook the constancy of the soldiers of weakest fibre.

But the fall of Pampeluna released the army on the Pyrenees from its inactivity. It was known that Marshal Soult had prepared a defensive position on the Nivelle stretching from ten to twelve miles from the sea at S. Jean de Luz to the Petite Rhune before the village of Sare.

Soon after midnight, on the morning of 10 November, the columns of the allies under Wellington wound down the passes of the mountains in silence, lighted by the moon. At earliest dawn the attack was made on the lines of the enemy, and by sunset, in a succession of brilliant charges, the allies had broken the line. Soult had been out-manœuvred and out-fought on his own long-prepared ground, and beaten at every point. The French, numbering seventy thousand men, had been placed in carefully selected positions. Strongly entrenched, they knew the roads, and were fighting to protect their native land from invasion; yet they suffered themselves to be dislodged from every point assailed with a lack of spirit that surprised the allies.

Under cover of night Soult withdrew and concentrated his forces in front of Bayonne. Wellington took up a position within two miles of the enemy, his left resting on the sea and his right on Cambo. As the weather was stormy and wet, all operations ceased. The roads were execrable, the crossroads a quagmire. It was not possible at that time of the year to move artillery over the sodden ground, and even communication between the wings was difficult.

Sir Rowland Hill on the right crossed the Nive at Cambo, and the French in front of him fell back on Bayonne; he then occupied the heights of Villefranche. The forces of the allies were disposed in a semicircle, their communications intersected by a river, and made difficult by the muddy roads. The position of the French was central, with short and easy communications, and was supported by the guns of the fortress. Soult could fling himself with all his weight on any point where the allies were weakest in his estimation, and that before they could bring up reinforcements. This, in fact, is what he did. On 10, 11, and 12 December, the Marshal directed repeated attacks on Sir John Hope on the left; but met with no success. Then hastily passing through the town with his main force, on the night of the 12th, he hurled thirty thousand men against the position held by Sir Rowland Hill on the British right. Sir Rowland mustered but thirteen thousand men, British and Portuguese. The French columns advanced steadily, disregarding the crushing bullets of a well-served artillery, the grape and the musketry of the light troops. They were gaining ground by sheer weight of numbers, when the reserve advanced, arriving from the centre, and the French were beaten back with terrible slaughter, all Bayonne looking on from the ramparts.

The battle was fought by Sir Rowland Hill with his own corps, unassisted. Wellington did not arrive on the field until the victory was won.

Soult now strongly garrisoned Bayonne, and withdrew along the road to Orthez and Pau, in order to defend the latter. Wellington followed him, but not until the close of January, and he left Sir John Hope to watch Bayonne. It was necessary for this gallant officer to cross the Adour, as the citadel was on the right bank. The river was three hundred yards wide at the point selected, one where a bend in its course concealed it from the view of the garrison of Bayonne.

"At one in the morning of 23 January Sir John Hope marched from his cantonments to direct and support this movement. The pontoons were unavoidably delayed by the depth and softness of the sandy road, therefore the design of sending a detachment across the river before daylight was defeated. However, the attention of the garrison was entirely occupied by the lively demonstrations upon their entrenched camp. Sir John Hope determined to commence passing the river as soon as ever a few boats and pontoons could be launched. Owing to light and baffling winds the bridge flotilla had not arrived off the bar. The pontoons from Bidart did not accomplish their march in the time expected, and at noon four jolly-boats and five pontoons, which the men took on their shoulders and carried over the sand-hills, were the only means of passage at the disposal of the general. To protect the launch of these boats some field guns were moved forward. At sight of the troops the enemy's picket retired without firing a shot, and walked leisurely to the citadel. Fifty men were instantly rowed over to the right bank. A hawser was stretched across the river, the five pontoons were formed into rafts, and a detachment of the Guards was ferried over. When about 600 men had been put across, the tide flowed so strong that the rafts could no longer work; and, save a few sent over in the jolly-boats, the passage of troops ceased. At this time only six companies of the Guards, two of the 60th Rifles, and a small party of the rocket corps, had been passed to the right bank. All seemed quiet in their front; when, suddenly, about five o'clock in the evening, two columns issued from the citadel to attack this detachment. Colonel Stopford, in command, drew up his troops in a position that secured his flanks, and enabled him to avail himself of the support of the guns on the opposite bank. His right rested on the Adour, his left on a morass. The artillery could sweep his front with a defensive fire, and he judiciously placed his rocket men on each flank. The French had nearly 1500 men, and advanced to the attack with some show of resolution; when the rockets opened on them, and being well directed, swept through their ranks with so rushing a sound, and so destructive an effect, that the novelty startled and appalled them. They seemed paralyzed with astonishment, and a few quickly following discharges of the ground-rockets drove them back in haste and fear. More men were crossed over in the night at slack water; and on the following evening the first division, two guns, and a squadron of dragoons, were established on the right bank."[3]

The flotilla appeared off the Adour on the morning of the 25th, the bar was successfully passed, thirty-four *chasse-marées* were brought into position, and anchored head and stern upon the line selected; the sappers worked all night, and by noon next day a solid bridge was laid down. Troops and artillery now filed over it, and the citadel of Bayonne was invested.

Upon the morning of 14 April the governor of the citadel made a furious sortie upon the investing corps, which was wholly unprepared for the attack, as peace had been declared, and Bonaparte had abdicated on 5 April. The news had reached Bayonne; the commandant of the citadel was well aware of it, but could not resist the treacherous attempt to retrieve his laurels by catching the British unprepared.

His assault was repulsed, with the loss of 830 men to the British, and with the capture of Sir John Hope, who was wounded. The French attack was supported by the fire of the gunboats on the river, which opened indiscriminately on friend and foe. The French lost 910 men.

The cemetery where our gallant fellow-countrymen lie who thus fell is on the edge of the Landes, on the north side of the Adour. When Queen Victoria visited Biarritz, as also recently when King Edward VII was there, this cemetery was duly visited by both monarchs. No one who remains any length of time in Bayonne should omit a visit to the beautiful lakes that lie embosomed in cork woods and pine forests in the Landes, in the abandoned course of the Adour. The river, instead of entering the sea where it does now, formerly turned north, and had its mouth at Cape Breton, something like ten miles distant. But at the close of the fourteenth century a violent tempest blowing from the west threw up a barrier of sand and blocked the mouth of the Adour, which then pursued its course northward, and finally discharged its waters into the Atlantic at Vieux-Boucau, and that remained its mouth for two centuries. But in 1579 the inhabitants of Bayonne, aided by a flood, managed to pierce the isthmus of sand-hills which separated their town from the sea, and thus created a new mouth for the river. The Adour, however, pours into the bay in a contrary direction to the prevailing winds, consequently

[3] Sherer, *Military Memoirs of the Duke of Wellington.* London, 1832.

there is an incessant struggle going on there between the current and the waves, resulting in a deposit of mud, sand, and pebble, and the building up of a bar which the sea is incessantly driving towards the shore, whereas the river is as incessantly engaged in repelling it. The existence of this bar makes the entrance to the Adour difficult and even dangerous, and has necessitated expensive works.

The lakes in the Landes are a haunt of wild fowl, and afford good fishing.

Biarritz needs little more than a mention, though a place of some antiquity. It is spoken of in the eleventh century, when some Basques harpooned a whale in the Bay of Biscay. It throve on the whale fishery, and so wealthy did it become that the tithe of its revenue constituted the principal source of the income of the bishops of Bayonne. In course of time the whales abandoned the coast and migrated to the north, and then the prosperity of Biarritz declined, and it sank to being an insignificant fishing village, till the Empress Eugénie took a fancy to it, and a new era of prosperity began. It is now a fashionable resort, especially for Spanish nobles. The heaths around in early summer are lovely with the intensely blue *Lithospermum*, and the crimson *Daphne cneorum*.

Visitors to Biarritz make an expedition to the "Refuge," distant about three miles, over a heath. The Abbé Céstac had founded an orphanage at Bayonne for girls, and had placed it under the charge of the Servantes de Marie. Not content with this good work he gathered about him a number of penitents and lodged them in the attics of the orphanage. Then in 1839 he bought a little property near Biarritz, and moved his penitents to it and placed them under the control of his sister Madelaine.

> "Complete isolation, absolute silence, total abstinence from flesh meat, manual labour in the garden and graveyard, constant prayer in the church, or meditation in their cells, constitute their rule of life. Like the Trappists, their bed is a hard board, to which they retire at eight in the evening to rise at four in the morning. On Friday they take a meal which serves for dinner—unseasoned vegetables—on their knees. They never read a book, except one of devotion, and are entirely ignorant of the politics and changes of society. This holy Thebaid is shut out from all view of the external world; neither ocean nor river, nor plain nor hill, can be discerned from it, although Nature, immediately outside its limits, presents herself in her loveliest aspects of sea and mountain. Unbroken silence and solitude prevail, and the stranger who enters its sacred seclusion becomes involuntarily overpowered by the sentiment that pervades the atmosphere and fills the mind with awe and wonder."[4]

I should add, with indignation that human beings, even penitents, should be reduced by this method to stultification.

---

[4] Lawlor, *Pilgrimages in the Pyrenees*. London, 1870.

The Coast, Biarritz

S. Jean de Luz is a favourite bathing place for such as desire more quiet and less heavy hotel charges than Biarritz affords. In 1660 the church saw the marriage of Louis XIV and Maria Theresa, Infanta of Spain. In commemoration of this event, the magistrates walled up the door by which the bridal pair passed out, and it has remained thus shut to this day. At S. Jean de Luz may be seen what is usual in Basque and Béarnais churches, as also in Tyrol, the men occupying the galleries, not infrequently in double tiers, whilst the women fill the body of the church. In the Maison Lobobiagne, with turrets, lodged Louis XIV; the Infanta and her mother, Anne of Austria, occupied the Maison Joanoëna.

I can recall rides *en cacolet* as customary among the Basques some sixty years ago, now quite obsolete. A horse was furnished with two baskets, one on each side, and two persons were accommodated, one in each basket. Inglis says in 1835:—

> "Morning, noon, and evening, the road between Bayonne and Biarritz is crowded with travellers *en cacolet*. The horses belong generally to the women who drive them; these women are generally young, many of them handsome. They generally speak French, Basque, and a little Spanish, and are rather intelligent than otherwise, always carrying on an unintermitting conversation during the whole ride. The horses are usually indifferent; they go at a small trot, and perform the *trajet* in about forty minutes."

One of the most puzzling facts in the study of mankind is the manner in which the most unmeaning customs are found extended far and wide. I shall have something to say of the *couvade* in another chapter. There is another which is met with in the Basque country, and which is also, or was, usual in Yorkshire. On Easter Monday the girls seize on lads and heave them up in the air, and hold them aloft till they redeem themselves with a coin or a kiss. On Tuesday the boys enjoy the same privilege with the girls. I have been so lifted up near Bayonne. I recall an instance in Yorkshire, where H.M. Inspector of Schools, a grave and reverend signor, came to a manufacturing town on Easter Monday. As he was sedately walking from the station he encountered a bevy of mill lasses, when at once he was uplifted by them and carried in triumph, in vain expostulating, and a kiss from him was demanded by each before he was released.

So with April Fools' Day—*le poisson d'avril*—it is honoured in the same fashion in Hindustan as in Europe.

Few visitors to Biarritz fail to take a run over the frontier into Spain. The Bidassoa for about twelve miles forms the line of demarcation between France and Spain. Near the bridge of Behobia are the remains—they are nothing more—of the Ile des Faisans, on which conferences were held between Cardinal Mazarin, plenipotentiary for France, and Don Luis da Haro, acting for Spain, which led to the conclusion of the famous Treaty of the Pyrenees, in 1659, cemented by the marriage of Louis XIV with the daughter of Philip IV. At the meeting on the Ile des Faisans each party advanced from its own territory by a temporary bridge to this patch of neutral ground in mid-stream. The death of Velasquez, the painter, was due to exposure whilst superintending the decoration of the tent for the minister of Spain—a duty more befitting an upholsterer than a great artist. By the treaty France received la Cerdagne and Roussillon, but surrendered Lorraine to Duke Charles IV, on condition that he should dismantle all its fortresses. As he delayed doing this Louis retained his hold on the duchy.

Fontarabie (Fuenterrabia) does not signify the Fountain of Arabia, and retains in its name no reminiscence of Moorish domination; the derivation is from the Latin *fons rapidus*. It is a picturesque, dirty town, malodorous; bearing as its arms in quarterings an angel holding a key, to signify that the town holds the key of Spain—a squalid beggar would be more appropriate than an angel; a whale and two syrens, the whale to indicate the fishing of the leviathan, now long departed; and lastly a castle between two stars. These arms were accorded to Fuenterrabia by Philip IV in 1638, when the admiral of Castile repulsed the Prince of Condé, who was besieging it. The church, Gothic in style, has been modernized externally; within it is overloaded with barbaric ornament. The castle, known as the palace of Charles V, dates originally from the tenth century, but has undergone much re-building and adaptation. The courtyard is picturesque, and the terrace commands a beautiful view.

Fuenterrabia brings no pleasing remembrances to an Englishman. The citizens begrudged a lodging to our sick and wounded during the passage of the Pyrenees by the allied troops under Wellington when in pursuit of Soult in the depth of winter. The town authorities even wanted to take away the boards on which were stretched the disabled soldiers. "These," wrote the Duke, "are the people to whom we have given medicines, etc., whose wounded and sick we have taken into our hospitals, and to whom we have rendered every service in our power, after having recovered their country from the enemy."

Irun signifies in Basque "the good town," but it contains little that is good, nothing that is interesting. Passages, however, will arrest the traveller, owing to its picturesque harbour, land-locked, and the entrance commanded by the castles—reminding a Devonshire man of Dartmouth. The port has been neglected and suffered to be silted up, although the rock-bound coast possesses no better harbour of refuge for storm-tossed boats.

San Sebastian has suffered so severely from sieges that it has lost its medieval character; but nothing can destroy its natural beauty of situation. The Monte Urgull, on which is the castle, was originally a rocky island, but it has been united to the land by the deposits of the River Urumea, and the town now occupies this neck. Beyond is the concha, a semi-lunar bay, with excellent sands, and with the Isle of Sta. Clara breaking the force of the waves that roll in from the Atlantic. San Sebastian is the most fashionable seaside resort in Spain, and is much frequented by the nobility and by well-to-do citizens of Madrid. The church of S. Vincent is a Gothic edifice of 1507. San Sebastian is memorable for its siege by Wellington. Mr. Ford says:—

> "It was obtained in March, 1808, by Therenot, when the French got in under false pretences. They held it during the war, and being in the rear of the Duke when advancing in 1815 on

the Pyrenees, it retarded his progress, and its possession became absolutely necessary. This was a work of great difficulty, for the naturally strong position was garrisoned by 3000 brave French veterans under General Rey, and the Duke, from the usual neglect of our Government, in spite of repeated applications to Lord Bathurst, was forced to wait from 25 July to 26 August for want of means even to commence operations, during which time the active enemy strengthened their defences, being supplied from France by sea.

"In vain the Duke had warned Lord Melville, under whose fatal rule the navy of England was first exposed to defeat, and who now did his best to ensure a similar misfortune to the army. And to make matters worse, Graham, to whom the siege was entrusted, neglected the advice of Sir C. Felix Smith and of Sir R. Fletcher. Graham having failed in a night attack on 24 August, the Duke was forced to come in person to set matters right. His arrival was, as usual, the omen of victory. Now the town was assaulted as it ought to have been at first, from the *chafres* or sand banks, and was taken on 31 August. The French, after a most gallant defence, retired to the upper citadel, on which, by the almost superhuman efforts of the engineers, backed by the bluejackets, guns were brought to bear, and it surrendered on 9 September, two-thirds of the valorous garrison having perished, while nearly 5000 English troops were killed and wounded."

Wellington—then only the Marquess Wellesley—had not bombarded the town, so as to spare the inhabitants, but General Rey himself had set fire to the town on 22 July, as is admitted by him in his own dispatch, and it was done for the express purpose of hampering the progress of the English, when he saw that the place must inevitably fall; and this, when Wellington would not suffer his batteries to play upon the town.

When finally San Sebastian was taken, all control over the soldiers, who were exasperated by the stubborn resistance, was for a while lost. A thunderstorm burst at the same time that the soldiers broke in, and a scene of riot and rapine ensued. In the midst of explosions of thunder and lightning the city was sacked. Fires broke out in various places, and flames waved over such houses as had been spared by Rey. At the same time the garrison of the castle ploughed the streets with their artillery, killing alike inhabitants flying from the English, Spanish and Portuguese soldiery, as well as the soldiers themselves. It was found impossible to extinguish the flames or to control the soldiers. The most was made of this. Napoleon wrote: "Les Anglais commettent des horreurs dont les annales de la guerre offrent peu d'examples, et dont cette nation barbare était seule capable dans un siècle de civilisation." But Napoleon never minced words. The sack of San Sebastian, though regrettable, was mild in comparison with the atrocities committed by the French elsewhere in Spain. In justice it must be said that it was not English alone who were guilty of these excesses, but the far more lawless Spaniards and Portuguese who formed our allies, and that the sack was stopped as soon as ever Wellington was able to gain control over the maddened soldiery.

San Sebastian

# CHAPTER IV

## S. JEAN-PIED-DE-PORT

Four valleys—The Basque land—Quarrels with Bayonne—The Sieur de Puyane—Cambo—Itxasson—Pas de Roland—Stalagmitic saint—S. Jean-Pied-de-Port—The first book in Basque—Patronal feasts—Roncevaux—The Song of Roland—The history of Turpin—Death of Roland—His horn—Convent—Canons—Virgin with diamonds in her eyes—Spanish kitchen—Smugglers—Escape of the Princess of Beira—The Couvade.

Fʀᴏᴍ the ridge of the Western Pyrenees descend four large valleys towards the north, each with a river running at the bottom. The westernmost and least important is that of the Nivelet, that flows into the Bay of Biscay at S. Jean de Luz. The second thence is the Nive, that discharges its waters into the Adour at Bayonne. The third is the Bidouze, which reaches the Adour just below where that river receives the mingled waters of the two Gaves. The last of these, and the easternmost of these rivers, is the Cenon, that loses itself in the Gave of Oloron, near Sauveterre.

In the ancient geography of France these four valleys were somewhat irregularly divided into districts, of which the westernmost was called Labourde, and the easternmost Soule, and the central portion was Lower Navarre. Taken collectively these districts constitute the Basque land, the population of which was closely related in language, habits, and blood to the inhabitants of Biscay, Guipuzcoa, and Upper Navarre in Spain. The narrow strip of land comprising the two cantons of S. Palais and S. Jean-pied-de-Port was for many centuries regarded as forming a parcel of the province of Gascony, but Alphonso the Noble took it, together with Labourde, from the English King John, so that it became a portion of the kingdom of Navarre, though Bayonne was recovered by the English. Sancho, King of Navarre, strengthened his hold on it more firmly, but eventually, when the claim to the crown of Navarre passed to the Counts of Foix and Viscounts of Béarn, it was the sole portion of that kingdom that these latter were able to retain, the Spanish Navarre having been annexed by Ferdinand the Catholic.

The Basques never obtained political independence. They were always subjected to Frank or English domination; they passed under the rule of the kings of Navarre and counts of Foix, and finally under the crown of France. Nevertheless they succeeded in maintaining a communal right of self-government, and enjoyed great privileges, notably that of conveying their wares and those of Spain free of duty to the markets of Toulouse and Bordeaux; rights these that awoke the jealousy of the citizens of Bayonne, who were incessantly at feud with them. The Bayonnais claimed Villefranche as belonging to Labourde, because the tide flowed through the arches of the bridge there. In an affray over this the mountaineers killed several citizens of Bayonne. In reprisal, in the reign of Edward III of England, Duke of Gascony and Aquitaine, the mayor of Bayonne, a Sieur de Puyane, descended on Villefranche on S. Bartholomew's Day, when a fair was being held there, caught five burgesses of note and fastened them to the arches of the bridge, and let them drown to show by occular demonstration that the tide did rise to Villefranche, and that therefore it was within the jurisdiction of Bayonne. The Basques rose *en masse* and massacred the Labourdins wherever they caught them. Finally, both parties appealed to the arbitration of the Sieur d'Albret, and the town of Bayonne was condemned to pay a heavy sum as indemnity to the families of the drowned men. The Bayonnais appealed to the King of England. He mitigated the fine, but the Basques would only consent to his adjudication on condition of reserving the right to pursue the sons of the Sieur de Puyane till they had exterminated the family. This was the last act by which the Basque nation manifested its political existence. But they retained their special privileges till the French Revolution, when the common law of France superseded all local independence of jurisdiction.

Cambo is a pretty, pleasant place, that has of late years risen to notice as a health resort. It takes its name from what has been supposed to be an Euscaldunic, i.e. Basque camp. I planned this and sent plan and description to the Archæologia, in 1852. But with greater experience of ancient camps than I had then, I have come to doubt whether it is what has been supposed. It consists of a platform on a hillock with a network of trenches about it, and ridges between them sharp as the back of a knife. It may have been used as a camp of refuge, but it could not contain a large force, and the dykes around appear to have been formed by currents of water.

Itxasson is an eminently Basque village. The church contains rich ornaments of silver gilt for the altar, given in the eighteenth century by an emigrant, Pedro d'Echegaray, on his return from America, where he had realized a fortune. The Basques, it may be noticed, do not give their names to houses and farms, but assume as surnames those place names from which they came.

From Itxasson the Pas de Roland is reached in half an hour on foot. It is an archway bored in the crag beside the river. Road and railway have so maltreated the rock that the Pas is now hardly worth a special visit. It was through this arch that the Roman road passed, and through it Roland the Paladin went to his death at Roncevaux. According to local legend Roland set his foot against the rock and burst a way through it by pressure. Road and rail now enter the mountains following the river.

At Bidarray, on the mountain-side, is a grotto, about thirty feet deep. In one corner a ladder conducts to a cavity, at the back of which is a stalagmitic incrustation three feet high, of a livid hue, rudely representing a human torso. This is held in high veneration by the peasantry, and is called "the Saint of Bidarry," though who the saint was whom it is supposed to represent nobody can say. A very similar incrustation occupies a niche in the Gorge of the Ardèche, and is there held to be a lively presentation of Charlemagne. Sick people seek this cave and soak rags in the water that dribbles from the figure, and which has in fact built it up. They apply the rags to the suffering parts of their bodies, and depart believing themselves to be healed, but the rags are left behind as *ex votos*.

**Pas de Roland**

S. Jean-Pied-de-Port was the key to the port or pass into Spain, and especially to the communication between Upper and Lower Navarre. It occupies a point where three streams fall into the Nive. There had been a Gallo-Roman town three miles distant at S. Jean-le-Vieux, but it had been destroyed by the Saracens. The present town was founded by the Garcias, kings of Navarre, in the eleventh and twelfth centuries. S. Jean, from the Treaty of the Pyrenees to the Revolution, during three reigns, was the capital of French Navarre. There are several old houses in the town, some of the Renaissance Period, and owing to their being built of red sandstone have a warm and pleasant aspect. The citadel was constructed by Deville in 1668, but was remodelled by Vauban, as were also the ramparts of the town.

The first book in Basque that was printed and published was by Bernard d'Echepare, curé of S. Jean-Pied-de-Port, in 1545. It consists of two parts. The first contains Christian doctrine, moral sentences, and passages from Scripture, good for edification. But strangely united with this, under the same cover and with continuous numeration of pages, is a collection of the priest's erotic poems.

> Si ... turpiter atrum
> Desinat in piscem mulier fermosa superne,
> Spectatum admissi risum teneatis, amici?

He frankly admits that he had had his love adventures. "I would not go to heaven, not I," he tells us, "unless I were sure of meeting women there."

He gives us a picture of female charms too highly coloured to bear reproduction. He throws in episodes from his own experience. In one of his escapades he got into such a scrape that he was incarcerated by order of the king of Navarre. "Il est à regretter," says Michel, "qu'il se soit borné à nous parler de sa détention, sans en indiquer ni la cause, ni le lieu, ni l'époque."

S. Jean-Pied-de-Port should be visited at the time of its patronal fête, 15 to 18 August, where day and night are given up to concerts, games, masquerades, and allegorical dances performed by the peasants of la Haute Soule.

But should a visitor be there at midsummer he should make an effort to push on to Pampeluna for the fête of 7 July, when for over a week the city keeps holiday—*les gigantes* parade the streets, monstrous figures, representing Moors; and the Alcalde and Corporation dance in front of the cathedral in honour of S. Firmin, the patron saint. He will, moreover, have an opportunity of seeing the pretty Navarrese girls, who have come out of the country for the great annual merry-making.

But the place of highest historic and romantic interest to be visited from S. Jean-Pied-de-Port is Roncevaux. Here, on 15 August, 778, the army of Charlemagne met with a crushing defeat, in which Roland and the twelve peers of the emperor were overwhelmed by rocks hurled down on them by the Basques.

The contemporary Eginhard tells us that the king invaded Spain at the head of a huge army, pushed on as far as Saragossa, and there received hostages from the Saracen chiefs. On his return, whilst entangled in the Pyrenean pass, the Basques attacked his rearguard, which perished to a man. Most of the officers of the palace, to whom Charlemagne had confided the command of the troops, were among the slain, and with them "Roland, prefect of the Marches of Brittany."

No revenge could be taken for this disaster, as the light-footed mountaineers dispersed, and could not be reached. This is all we know for certain, but even in this account the existence of Roland among the captains slain is doubtful, as the passage referring to him is an interpolation, and is not found in the best MSS. copies.

In 810 Louis "le Debonaire," at that time King of Aquitaine, on his return from an expedition into Spain, took the precaution of securing the wives and children of the Basques and retaining them as hostages till he was safely through the pass. But in 824 the Frank army descended to Pampeluna, under two counts, and on its way back was surprised at Roncevaux by the Basques; the troops were slaughtered and the counts taken. These two disasters in popular tradition were run into one, and gave occasion to the composition of the "Song of Roland," one of the finest pieces of medieval poetry that we possess.

> "'The Song of Roland,'" says Mr. Ludlow, "apart from any question of literary merit, has a peculiar interest for our country, not only as forming one of the treasures of the Bodleian, but from its connexion with one of the half dozen greatest events in our history—the Battle of Hastings. For there, as we are told by Wace, William of Normandy's minstrel 'Taillefer who full well sang, on a horse that was swift, went before them singing *Of Charlemagne and of Roland, and of Oliver and of the vassals who died at Roncevaux.*'"[5]

The very earliest text extant of this poem is in the Bodleian Library at Oxford. All other songs of Roland are amplifications of later date.

Thus it appears that to the chanting of this ballad by a minstrel William went forward to the conquest of England.

One of the most popular books of the Middle Ages was the *History of the Life of Charlemagne and of his Nephew Roland*, which passed as the composition of Turpin, Archbishop of Rheims, a man who died about 800. It was a historical romance based on old ballads, composed in the twelfth century, and of no historic value whatsoever. Pope Callixtus II formally decided, however, in 1122, that it was veracious history.

In this book we have the fully-developed story of the defeat at Roncevaux. In it, declared by an infallible Pope to be authentic and trustworthy, we are informed that Charlemagne was eight feet high, measured by his own feet, "which were of the largest size," that at a meal he would consume a quarter of a sheep, and if that were not at hand, then he would appease his appetite with two fowls, or a duck, a peacock, a crane, or a hare.

The army had marched into Spain, and Roland and Ganilon the Traitor had been sent forward to Saragossa on an embassage to the Soudan, who, according to the counsel of Ganilon, spake fair and consented to all Charlemagne's demands. Consequently the host of the Franks returned through the Pyrenees, unsuspicious of evil. Charles led the van, and Roland and Oliver the rearguard. Meanwhile the Saracens had gone about by bypaths, and they suddenly appeared to intercept the march of that body of men which was under the command of Roland and

[5] Ludlow, *Popular Epics of the Middle Ages*. London, 1865.

Oliver. A furious fight ensued, Oliver fell, and Roland alone survived. Then he put his ivory horn to his lips and blew such a blast that Charles heard it, though many leagues away, and he knew thereby that his nephew was in danger. With the blast Roland broke a blood-vessel, and, sinking to the ground, he dashed his good sword Durandal against the rocks with intent to break it, lest it should fall into the hands of the paynim.

To this day at Roncevaux a mass is said in May above the tombs of the paladins, in the little chapel supposed to have been founded by Charlemagne, and this mass is for the repose of the souls of those who fell in the massacre of Roncevaux.

Roncevaux itself consists of a few poor huts about a monumental convent, from the midst of which rises the church with a massive square tower. The "royal and illustrious collegiate church" was considered in Spain to be the fourth in order of the holy spots on earth. The other three were Jerusalem, Rome, and Compostella. The chapter was under the special protection of the Holy See, and the King of Spain nominated the prior. This dignitary and six canons are all that remain of the ancient order of Roncevaux. Throughout the convent may be seen its badge, a cross, the middle member curved at the head like a pastoral staff, and with a sword at the feet.

Pilgrims from France, Germany, and Italy were wont to cross the Pyrenees on their way to Compostella, and many lost their lives in the snow. On this account, in 1131, the Bishop of Pampeluna founded a hospital at Roncevaux for their accommodation, and he dispatched one of the canons of his cathedral to attend to the requirements and comforts of the pilgrims. This was the origin of the convent that grew rich with the gifts of kings and princes who were lodged there. The canons of Roncevaux wear a sleeveless surplice and a black amice over their shoulders in summer, but in winter a thick black cloak and a furred hood. When they go out they wear a short linen scapular over their cassocks.

Under the tower is a Gothic hall. This, with the cloister and the church, was erected by Sanchez the Strong, King of Navarre, in the thirteenth century. He and his wife repose in the church under a marble tomb.

In this church is a Mater Dolorosa, the eyes of which are apparently full of tears. This appearance is due to the insertion of diamonds, but the ignorant peasantry are fully convinced that the eyes of the Madonna really brim with tears for their sorrows, and out of profound compassion.

Near the convent formerly stood a pillar commemorative of the defeat of Charlemagne's rearguard, but the monument was destroyed in 1794 by two commissioners of the French Republic, to the performance of a "musique touchante." These men headed a column called l'Infernale; it entered Spanish territory, and carried fire and sword everywhere. They pillaged the church and the convent, and wrecked all they could lay hands on.

Over this pass fled Joseph Bonaparte, without his crown, after the rout of Vittoria. At Roncevaux is a little inn where the traveller has an opportunity of seeing a Spanish kitchen, with a central hearth, about which are ranged as many little saucepans as there are visitors to be entertained, and of hearing the custom-house officers play the guitar, and seeing the muleteers dancing the fandango.

Smuggling thrives in the Pyrenees, indeed it is impossible to suppress it. The most daring and successful of all smugglers are the Basques, and the mountains in their part not being of the loftiest, free trade can be carried on with comparative ease. F. Michel, in *Le Pays Basque*, says:—

> "Contraband is a veritable profession that employs a great many hands. Men thoroughly upright and strictly honest take part in it. The chiefs are well known, and one is certain of meeting with fidelity, integrity, and chivalrous devotion among them. This may be understood, because their profession depends mainly on the confidence which their character inspires, and without which the merchants would not venture to have recourse to them."

Consider what the length of the chain is—350 miles as the crow flies, 500 if you follow the frontier line. Tobacco is a Government monopoly in France, and French tobacco is execrable. There are in that 500 miles a thousand passes: some easy, others difficult. The douane cannot be everywhere; it can be planted at certain fixed points, but the officers are not ubiquitous, cannot guard every port, for the ports are in the region of perpetual snow, where, if stationed, the officers would freeze at their posts. Besides, the douanier gravitates instinctively towards the cabaret, where he can have his wine, his coffee, his absinthe, about a stove. And none of the taverns are planted on the more difficult cols. Consequently a very considerable traffic is done across the frontier by these honourable and intelligent men, the smugglers.

In November, 1835, the Princess of Beira was on her way from Naples to Spain to be married to the Pretender, Don Carlos. She was his sister-in-law, but at Rome dispensations are ever obtainable for money.

Ferdinand VII, by his third wife, Maria Christina, daughter of Francis I, King of the Two Sicilies, had a daughter, Isabella, born in 1830. Now Don Carlos was the brother of Ferdinand. When this latter died, in 1834, Carlos claimed the crown. Queen Christina had become regent, whilst Isabella was a minor. Carlos went to the north of Spain, and war broke out between the Carlists and the Christinos. Spain, Portugal, England, and France united in quadruple alliance to support the claims of Queen Christina. Carlos was in the Spanish Biscay, and he summoned to him his son by his wife Maria Frances, who was dead, and also his intended wife, the Princess of Beira. This lady undertook to leave Naples, traverse France, pick up on her way the Prince of the Asturias, who was at Toulouse, and join her intended husband in the Basque province of Spain.

Her journey had to be carried out with precaution, as France opposed the pretensions of Don Carlos. She managed, attended by the Count Custine and a Portuguese lady, to secure the Prince of the Asturias and to make her way to Bayonne. There she remained awhile in concealment till warned that her retreat was discovered, when she fled and delivered herself up to the protection and guidance of some smugglers. After a day spent in wandering through the forest of Mixe, with which her guides were unfamiliar, she reached in the evening the valley of Mîharin, between Hasparren and S. Palais. It had been arranged that she should sup at the cabaret of Sallubria; but the place was so squalid that Count Custine advised the Princess to throw herself on the hospitality of the Viscount de Belsunce, who had a château hard by. This she did, and was received with the utmost civility, though it was not allowed to transpire who she was. Thence one of the smuggler guides, Baptista Etchegoyen, was dispatched with instructions to the contraband Captain Ganis to aid the Princess in her escape. He arrived in the middle of the night with some of his band, and with horses carrying bundles containing disguises.

In order to reach the frontier it was necessary to pass through Hélitte, a station of douaniers, on the high road from Bayonne to S. Jean-Pied-de-Port. In order to effect this, Ganis took advantage of a funeral that was to take place at half-past ten in the morning. He left Méharin at 9 a.m. attending the two ladies, dressed as mourners. At a little distance from the place the Princess and her attendant had to alight and go direct to the church, where Ganis informed her they were to place themselves behind a tall woman in mourning, and to follow her when she left the church. The ladies assisted at the office for the dead, with hoods concealing their faces. They followed the corpse to the cemetery, and passed the station of the douaniers without attracting attention. On reaching a valley they found horses awaiting them, and by evening they had reached Macaye, near Hasparren, where they lodged in the house of Ganis.

Fatigued by the journey, the Princess hoped to pass a quiet night, but soon after dark an alarm was given. Fifteen to eighteen hundred men—soldiers, gendarmes, and douaniers—were patrolling the country in quest of the Princess. A party of these men, suspecting that she was under the protection of Ganis, approached the house with the purpose of searching it. The smuggler roused the ladies, made them follow him on foot, and under his conduct they reached the banks of a river that was swelled by the rain then descending in torrents. Ganis took the Princess on his back, and stepped into the water. He was followed by his brother with the lady-in-waiting. The flood rose to his armpits, and he had the utmost difficulty in struggling across. Before he had reached the further bank he heard shouts, and looking back, saw a crowd of uniforms on that he had quitted. The smugglers and their charges now made for the road into Spain by Anhoue, and succeeded in passing the frontier without further adventures.

Next morning the south wind bore to Bayonne the joyous clatter of the bells of Urdase, and of all the Spanish villages over the frontier, celebrating the marriage of the Princess of Beira with the Pretender, Don Carlos of Bourbon. In the meantime the Count Custine had remained with the Prince of the Asturias in the château of M. de Belsunce. Baptista now returned for them. They were disguised as Basque peasants, mounted horses, and departed under the conduct of the energetic and indefatigable Etchegoyen, who conducted them by a different route from that taken by the Princess, to where they met her and the Prince, his father.

It would be unpardonable to quit the Basques without a few words on the Couvade, a custom once prevalent among them, but by no means peculiar to them, as it has been found in Asia, Africa, and America.

Immediately after childbirth the woman rises and goes about the business of the house, whereas the husband at once retires to bed with the baby, receives the congratulations of the neighbours, and is fed on broth and pap during ten days. Strabo mentions this usage above eighteen hundred years ago as prevalent among the Iberians, the ancestors of the Basques. "The women," he says, "after the birth of a child, nurse their husbands, putting them to bed instead of going to it themselves." That this custom was widely spread in the south of France appears from the medieval tale of *Aucussin and Nicolette*. In it the hero finds King Theodore *au lit en couche*, whereupon he takes a stick and thrashes him till he vows to abolish the Couvade in his realms. Diodorus Siculus, at the beginning of the Christian era, tells us that this custom also prevailed in Corsica.

Marco Polo, in the thirteenth century, met with it in Eastern Asia, so that the widow's remark to Sir Hudibras was not amiss—

> "Chineses go to bed
> And lie-in in their ladies' stead."

The same custom is found among the American Indians.

What can be its meaning? What topsy-turvydom of the human brain can have originated it? Mr. Tylor, in his *Early History of Mankind*, says that it proceeded from a notion that the woman was a mere machine for the turning out of babies, and that the babes were not in the least supposed to belong to her, but to the father. Also that the child was part and parcel of the father, a feeble and frail parcel, and that the utmost precaution had to be taken to keep the male parent in health lest the child should suffer. If the father were to take a pinch of snuff, the infant would sneeze its brains away; if he were to eat solid food, the babe would suffer indigestion. A missionary found it impossible to persuade his Indian servant to eat anything but slops directly after the birth of a son and heir, as he was persuaded heavy diet would injure the child. Then the missionary belaboured his servant with a stick, and sent him to look at his infant smiling in its sleep, and so convinced the man of his delusion.

This may be the explanation. I cannot say. Mankind does many things out of sheer cussedness.

# CHAPTER V

## ORTHEZ

Court of the counts of Foix—Froissart—Gaston Phœbus—Kills his
son—And a cousin—Death of Phœbus—Evan de Foix—The bastards of Phœbus—Tragic death of Evan—Bridge over the Gave—
Jeanne d'Albret—Her despotic actions—Flight to La Rochelle—
Charles sends La Terride into Béarn—Jeanne invites Montgomery
to her aid—He enters Béarn—Takes Orthez—Massacre—The castle capitulates—Broken faith—Murder of ten barons—Slaughter
of priests and monks—Catholic worship forbidden—Death of
Jeanne—Castle of Belocq—Puyôo—Battlefield of Orthez—Retreat
of Soult.

ORTHEZ has little to occupy it save to brood over its past. It is a dull town, without characteristic features, and it sulks because Pau the parvenue is flourish-
ing, and flaunting, whilst itself, the venerable Orthez, the once capital, sits as a
widow, desolate.

Till the fifteenth century it was the residence of the Court of the counts of Foix
and viscounts of Béarn, whose castle of Moncada occupied the height above the
town. A splendid pile it was, erected by Gaston VII, in 1240, after the pattern of a
Spanish castle of the name that he had taken. This had proved to him a hard nut
to crack, and he hoped to make the new Moncada by additional works wholly
uncrackable. But the tooth of Time has broken it completely, and nothing of it now
remains save the keep.

The town was astir and aglow when Gaston Phœbus resided in the castle.
Froissart so describes it. Minstrels, merchants, knights, adventurers, swarmed in
the streets, and streamed into the castle, which they did not leave empty-handed.
"I have heard him say, when the King of Cyprus was in Béarn proposing a crusade, that if the kings of France and of England had gone to the Holy Land, he
himself would have been the most considerable lord in the host, second only to
them, and would have led the largest contingent."

Gaston Phœbus, Count of Foix and Viscount of Béarn, was the son of Gaston
IX and the elderly Eleanor de Cominges. On account of his beauty he was given
the name of Phœbus, and he adopted the blazing sun as his device. He was arrested by King John of France when at Paris because he refused to do homage for his
lands, but was released and given command of an army in Guyenne to war against
the English.

The Bridge, Orthez

Froissart visited Orthez, and lodged at the tavern "La Lune," now rebuilt and renamed "La belle Hôtesse."

> "I must say," wrote he, "that although I have seen many knights, kings, princes, and other great men, I have never seen any so handsome as he, either in mould of limb and shape, or in countenance, which was fair and ruddy, lit up with grey, amorous eyes, that delighted whenever he chose to express affection. He was so perfectly formed that it is not possible to overpraise him. Gaston Phœbus was a prudent knight, full of enterprise and wisdom. He never allowed men of abandoned character to be about his person; he reigned prudently, and was constant at his devotions. He mightily loved dogs above other animals, and during the summer and winter amused himself with hunting. He employed four secretaries, whom he called neither John, Walter, nor William, but his Good-for-noughts, and to these he gave his letters to copy out."

But this prince was no other than a lusty, handsome animal, incapable of controlling his passions, and whilst profuse in largesses to wandering *jongleurs* and travellers, who would bruit abroad his praises, mean in money matters in other particulars.

Gaston Phœbus succeeded his father in 1343, and in 1348 married Agnes, daughter of Philip III of Navarre. By her he had one son, Gaston, as beautiful as Phœbus himself, and an amiable youth. Before long the Count and his wife fell out. The quarrel was sordid—it concerned money. Phœbus had imprisoned the Sieur d'Albret. The King of Navarre, Charles the Bad, brother of the Countess, interceded for his liberation, and undertook to guarantee payment of fifty thousand francs for his ransom. Accordingly Gaston released him, and d'Albret paid the money into the hands of the King of Navarre, who pocketed it, and declined to send it to the Count of Foix, under the plea that he was trustee for his sister and reserved it as her dower. The Count resented this upon his wife, whom he called by all the bad names in his copious vocabulary. He had taken a mistress, and he openly favoured her in the face of his wife for her humiliation. By this woman he had three sons. Then he ordered Agnes to visit the Court of Navarre and use her personal influence to obtain the money due. The Countess went, but failed to induce her brother to disburse; and knowing how ungovernable was the temper of her husband, how little he loved her, she shrank from returning to Orthez.

The boy Gaston at the age of fifteen entreated leave to visit his mother at Pampeluna. The lad was distressed at the estrangement, and pined for his mother. Accordingly his father gave him a splendid retinue of gallant youths, and the Bishop of Lescar as his chaplain. Charles the Bad resolved on a diabolical act of treachery. When the boy was leaving he drew him aside, assured him of his distress at seeing the lad's father alienated in heart from his mother, and gave him a bag of arsenic, which he informed him was a love powder. This he was to strew on his father's meat, or drop into his cup, when Phœbus's love for his wife would infallibly revive. But on no account, said Charles, was Gaston to breathe a word of this to any one, and he must be cautious to seize the right moment for the administration of the dose, when unobserved. Gaston, fully believing what his uncle said, hung the bag round his neck under his dress, and returned to Orthez.

Now it happened that Gaston and his half-brother, the bastard Evan, slept in the same room. They were nearly of the same age and size, and dressed alike. Evan did not fail to notice the silk bag and questioned Gaston about it, but was put off with evasive answers.

Three days after Evan and Gaston quarrelled over a game of tennis, and Gaston boxed his half-brother's ears. Evan ran to his father and told him that Gaston carried in his bosom a mysterious pouch of which he would give no account.

At dinner Phœbus was served by his son, Gaston, and looking hard at him observed the string about his neck. Laying hold of him, he tore open his vest, and discovered the bag of powder. He cut the string, and gave some of the white contents on a piece of meat to a dog, that ate it and died. Then in a paroxysm of rage, knife in hand, he leaped over the table, swearing that he would kill Gaston, who had purposed to poison him. He would have slain him on the spot had not his servants interposed and disarmed him.

The Count then ordered the boy to be thrown into a dungeon. At the same time he had all the attendants of the youth who had been with him in Navarre arrested and tortured, and fifteen of them were forthwith hung. "Which was a pity," says Froissart, "for there were not in all Gascony such handsome and well-appointed squires." The Bishop of Lescar had timely warning, and took to his heels.

The Count assembled the Estates of Béarn and laid before them his charge against the boy, and they unanimously decided that the prince must not be executed, but kept in durance for awhile; nor would they separate till they had extorted from Phœbus a solemn undertaking to submit to their decision.

But the poor lad, knowing his innocence, wounded to the quick at the manner in which he had been duped by his uncle, at the blind conviction of his guilt entertained by his father, at the barbarity with which his companions had been racked, and strung up, refused all food. He was confined in a narrow dungeon, badly lighted, and his gaoler at first did not observe that the meals he brought him remained untouched. But on the tenth day—I quote Froissart—

> "The person who served him, looking about the cell, saw all the meat unconsumed with which he had been previously supplied. Then, shutting the door, he went to the Count of Foix and said, 'My lord, for God's sake, look to your son, he is starving himself in his prison. I do not believe that he has eaten a morsel since his confinement.' On hearing this the Count was enraged, and without saying a word went to his son's prison. In an evil hour he had a knife in his hand, with which he had been paring his nails. He held it so close by the blade that of the point scarcely so much as the size of a groat showed.

> "Thrusting aside the tapestry that covered the door of the

dungeon, through ill luck he struck his son on the jugular vein, as he shouted, 'Ha, traitor! why dost thou not eat?' and instantly flung out of the chamber without saying or doing more. The lad was frightened at his father's violence, and was, moreover, weak through long fasting. The point of the knife, small though it was, had severed the artery, and when he felt what had been done, he turned himself on one side on his pallet and expired.

"The Count had hardly returned to his apartment before his servants came running after him to announce the death of his son. 'Dead is he? God help me!' exclaimed the Count. 'Dead he is, my lord.' The Count was greatly affected, and said, 'Ah, ha, Gaston! what a sorry business this has proved for me and thee.'"

This was by no means his only crime. He induced his cousin, Pierre Arnaut de Béarn, governor of the Castle of Lourdes, to visit him, on the plea that he wished to discuss matters with him. Arnaut held Lourdes for the English. Gaston Phœbus desired to acquire this stronghold, which was the key to the Valley of Argelez. He received Arnaut in a friendly manner, and they dined together. For three days he showed him lavish hospitality, and then demanded the surrender of the castle. Arnaut refused. "I hold it for the King of England. It has been confided to my honour," he replied, "and to no other person will I surrender my trust." Gaston Phœbus flew into one of his mad fits of rage, rushed upon him, and stabbed him in five places with his dagger. "My Lord," said the gallant castellan, "this is ungentle treatment, to summon me to your house as a guest, and therein to murder me." The Count ordered him to be flung into a dungeon, where he died of his wounds.

The crime availed Phœbus nothing, for Jean, the brother of Pierre, had been left in charge of the castle, and he refused to give it up.

The Viscount of Châteaubon, the Count's cousin-germain, heir to his lands and titles, after the death of Gaston the younger, was greatly hated by Phœbus. He retained him in prison for eight months, and only released him for a ransom of fifty thousand francs. Froissart gives an account of the end of Phœbus. He had been out hunting near Sauveterre, in the month of August, when the heat was great. He had killed a boar, that was brought to the inn at Riou, where the Count would dine.

"The Count went to his chamber, that was strewn with rushes and green leaves; the walls were hung with boughs freshly cut for perfume and coolness. He had no sooner entered the room than he remarked, 'These greens are agreeable to me, for the day has been desperately hot.' When seated he conversed with Sir Espagne du Lyon (his chaplain) on the dogs that had best hunted. He called for water to wash, and two squires advanced. Ernaudin d'Espagne took the silver basin, and another knight, Sir Thibaut, the napkin. The Count rose from his seat, and stretched out his hands to wash; but no sooner had his fingers touched the cold water than he changed colour, from an oppression at his heart, and his legs failing him, fell back on his seat, exclaiming, 'I am a dead man; but God have mercy on me!' He never spoke after this. He was carried to another chamber, and laid on a bed and well covered.

"The two squires who had brought the water, to free themselves from any charge of having poisoned him, said, 'Here is the water; we have already drunk of it, and will now do it again in your presence,' which they did, to the satisfaction of all. They put into the Count's mouth bread, water, and spices, but all to no purpose, for in less than half an hour he was dead."

No sooner was the breath out of his body than Evan de Foix, his bastard, whom he loved dearly, galloped to Orthez to get possession of the treasure in the tower. On his admission to the castle, before it was known in the town that the Count was dead, he endeavoured to open the chamber that contained the treasure, but failed; it was fast behind three oak doors, and he could nowhere find the key. But in the meanwhile the chaplain had found it upon the body of the Count, and guessing the predicament in which was Evan, he also took horse and raced off to Orthez.

By this time a vague rumour had reached the town that something had happened to the Count, and the townsmen began to assemble in the streets. The chaplain entered the castle, and now that he was provided with the key Evan de Foix was able to reach the treasure. But it was too late for him to make off with it. Before he could pack it up and form plans for its transport, the death of Gaston Phœbus was known, and crowds surrounded the castle and forbade egress. Evan was constrained to show himself at a window and speak the citizens fair. They wished him no ill, they replied, but they would neither suffer him to plunder and carry off the treasure, nor leave the castle, till the Viscount of Châteaubon, the lawful heir, had arrived—this latter was in Aragon at the time. He at once started for Orthez, and a great assembly of the Estates of Béarn was held. It was then determined that of the treasure, the Viscount should have five thousand francs, and the bastards, who had been put in chains till the will of the Estates was known, should be set at liberty and allowed each two thousand francs.

"The Viscount of Châteaubon, on his arrival at Orthez, set at liberty all prisoners confined in the castle. They were very numerous; for the Count of Foix was very cruel to any person who incurred his indignation, never sparing them, however high their rank, but ordering them to be flung headlong over the walls, or confined on bread and water during his pleasure; and such as ventured to speak for their deliverance ran the risk of being treated in like manner."

Gaston Phœbus was born in 1331, and died in 1391. He left three bastards; of these Bernard married Isabella de la Cerda, and became the ancestor of the dukes of Medina-Celi. The eldest son, Evan, he who had unwittingly brought about the death of his half-brother Gaston, met with a tragic fate. A marriage was to take place between a squire in whom the King, Charles VI, was interested and a damsel of the Queen's household, and it was arranged that there should be a masque of savages in the evening, 29 January, 1392–3, in which the King was to take part. There were to be six of these savages in chains, and they were to perform a dance before the wedding party, and one of these maskers was to be the Bastard of Foix. The performers were to be dressed in coats of linen covered with flax, stuck on by means of pitch, and these linen vests were to be stitched on so as to fit the person tight as a glove. Sir Evan de Foix, with some foresight, entreated the King to forbid any one approaching the dancers with torches. Such an order was accordingly issued, and when the maskers entered the room, the serjeants commanded all torch-bearers to withdraw. But, unhappily, whilst the savages were capering, and producing much merriment, the Duke of Orleans entered attended by four knights and six torches, they being not aware of the King's order, and so amused were those present with the dance that this infraction of the royal command was not noticed. No one knew who the maskers were, and various conjectures were offered. Happily for him the King quitted the others, by unhooking his chain, and danced up to the Duchess of Berri, who laid hold of him exclaiming, "You shall not escape me till I have learned your name."

At that very moment the Duke of Orleans, young and thoughtless, ran forward with a torch to examine the savages more closely. In an instant the flax on one ignited, in another moment the flame was communicated to the others, for those five were chained together; only the King was unlinked. The shrieks of those enveloped in flames were awful. Some knights rushed forward and did their utmost to disengage the dancers, but the pitch burnt their hands so severely, and so impossible did they find it to rip away the habits, that they were constrained to desist. One of the five, Jean de Nantouillet, recollected that the buttery was near at hand. Exerting all his force, he snapped the chain, and flying thither, plunged into a large tub of water prepared for the washing of plates and dishes. This saved him, but he ever after bore the scars of his burns.

The Duchess de Berri, the moment that she saw what had occurred, with presence of mind, threw her mantle over the King, and retained him in her arms, as he was rushing off in thoughtless generosity to endeavour to save his companions. "Quick," said she, "leave the room and assume another dress."

Evan de Foix, when enveloped in flames, cried aloud, "Save the King! save the King!"

Of the four that were on fire, two died on the spot. The other two—the Bastard of Foix and the Count de Joigny—died two days after in great agony.

Orthez contains the Calvinist University established here by Jeanne d'Albret, a building of the sixteenth century, now no longer used for the purpose designed.

The bridge over the Gave is picturesque; it has one broad arch spanning the river, and three pointed arches sustaining the road leading to it, raised high to avoid floods. On the main pier is a tower, whence in 1569 the Calvinist soldiery of Montgomery precipitated the priests who would not abjure the faith, upon the pointed rocks below.

Jeanne d'Albret, after the death of her husband, Antoine de Bourbon, threw off the mask, and set diligently to work Protestantizing her dominions. She put one of her pastors in the see of Oloron; her kinsman, d'Albret, Bishop of Lescar, apostatized and married. She found in many places that the people were ready for a change, especially such as had been subject to exactions from the monasteries, which owned much land and exercised extensive jurisdiction. In many, however, there was strong resistance. In 1566 she was about to absolutely interdict the exercise of the Catholic religion in Béarn, Foix, and Bigorre, when the resistance of the Estates and the threatening attitude of the people alarmed her and she withheld the edict for a time. In 1568, finding that Charles IX was about to send troops into her land to protect the oppressed Catholics, and fearing lest she should have her children taken from her, she fled to La Rochelle, the Geneva of French Calvinism.

Charles IX announced his resolution to take possession of Béarn. Bigorre was in revolt against her reforms, and a good many of the seigneurs of Béarn could not endure them. The King commissioned the terrible Monluc to pacify Bigorre, and the Baron de Terride to do the same in Béarn. The Béarnais were in difficulties. They were to a man loyal to their Viscountess, the titular Queen of Navarre, but a considerable number of them were opposed to her religious policy, and did not relish the taste of Calvinism. If they joined the forces of the King they were rebels to their sovereign. If they took up arms for her they fought for a religion that their soul abhorred. Nay, Pontacq, Morlaas, shut their gates against the royal forces, and were reduced. Lescar, Sauveterre, and Salies opened their gates to them.

Béarn was rapidly reduced. Clearly the object at which the King aimed was to bring it completely under the crown of France. Two syndics of Béarn addressed the King in the name of the Estates to declare that for eight centuries the viscounty had been independent, that the King of France was the protector but not the sovereign of the land. The Queen of Navarre now gave commission to the Count of Montgomery to drive the French out of her territories, and to establish throughout them the reform of Calvin as the sole religion permissible. Montgomery was the lieutenant of the Scottish Guard, who, in a tournament, in 1559, had inadvertently killed Henry II, King of France. Obliged to fly the land, he placed his sword at the disposal of any prince who was disposed to smite the Catholics and the Royalists hip and thigh. Obeying the orders of Jeanne, communicated to him from La Rochelle, Montgomery raised a body of sturdy Huguenots and entered Béarn.

Alarmed at the rapidity of his movements, and himself at the head of but a small body of men, the Baron de Terride retreated to Orthez, and shut himself up in the Castle of Moncada.

Montgomery arrived at Pontacq on 6 August, 1562, crossed the Gave, and advanced on Orthez. There, taking advantage of the gates being opened to receive fugitives from the villages round, some of his soldiers thrust in. Simultaneously the walls were escaladed, and the town was given up to indiscriminate slaughter. In the name of their queen, all the inhabitants were put to the sword.

The Gave rolled down the dead and flowed crimson with blood. The Protestant historian Olhagaray says: "The river was full of blood, the streets were heaped up with corpses. The convents were burnt. The cries of the dying and the shouts of the murderers, the lamentations of women and children filled the air with piteous sounds." The Convent of the Cordeliers offered a theatre for barbarities. The friars were made to leap from the windows into the river, and were shot if they endeavoured to gain the bank.

No excuse offered for this massacre will avail. The town was not taken after a siege; it was not stormed by night; it was entered without offering resistance, in broad day. The butchery at Orthez leaves an indelible stain on the brow of Jeanne d'Albret.

A striking incident is remembered. One of the friars was at the altar when the Huguenots burst in. He hastily took the monstrance, folded his arms over it, and to save the Host from profanation, threw himself into the Gave. The river swept his body into the Bidouze, and the Bidouze into the Adour, and it was washed up under the walls of the Cordelier Convent at Bayonne, still clasping in its rigid arms the vessel with its sacred contents.

Terride, accompanied by the principal chiefs, had retreated into the castle, but with such precipitation that they had forgotten to take in a supply of provisions. Consequently in a few days they were forced to surrender, under oath from Montgomery that their lives would be spared.

They were sent to Pau, ten barons of Béarn in all. One evening they were invited by the Calvinist captain to dine with him at his table in the Queen's banqueting hall. During the meal they shook off their despondency, and began to be merry over their cups, when, at a signal from Montgomery, soldiers entered and butchered all the barons about the table where they had been feasting.

"This cruel execution," says Favyn, in his *History of Navarre*, "took place on 24 August, the feast of S. Bartholomew.... The news angered King Charles greatly, and it is supposed that he then formed the resolution of making a second S. Bartholomew's Day in expiation of the first." So one crime draws on another—a Nemesis, which, however, does not fall on the criminals, but on the guiltless. Montgomery was now master of Béarn. How many priests and monks were slaughtered none knew. Nearly all the friars of Morlaas were shot down. The prior of the Carmelites at Sauveterre was hung, and the rest of the brethren thrown into a well till they choked it up. All the priests caught near S. Sever were led to the brow of a precipice and forced at the point of pikes to leap down. At Orthez the prior of the Augustines was ordered to mount the pulpit and recant. He ascended, but it was to profess his adherence to the Catholic faith, whereupon he was shot in the pulpit. All his seven brethren met their fate with like heroism. They were made to walk down a lane formed of Huguenot soldiers with swords drawn, and were hacked to pieces, one after another.

The Calvinist soldiers did not even respect the dead. They broke open the vault in which lay Gaston Phœbus, took his skull, and played skittles with it. Great numbers of gentlemen and their families, Catholics of every rank and sex, fled to the mountains or crossed into Spain.

Montgomery, having finished with Béarn, left the command with the Baron d'Arros, and departed for more active work elsewhere. Jeanne d'Albret now dispatched injunction after injunction, proclamation after proclamation, in one continuous stream, into Béarn from her refuge in La Rochelle. On 28 November, 1569, she required that Calvinistic worship should be established everywhere, in every town and parish, throughout her dominions; and in 1571 she forbade the celebration of the Mass under pain of death. She would allow an amnesty to such as had taken up arms during the late troubles, but only on condition that they adopted her form of religion.

In 1572 Jeanne died in Paris, not without suspicions of poison. She had gone there to negotiate the marriage of her son Henry with Marguerite de Valois, sister of Charles IX.

An excursion may be made to the Castle of Belocq, whose towers are visible from the high road to Bayonne, on the further side of the Gave. It is situated on a height, at the feet of which the green river sweeps past the wooded slopes on the farther bank.

The castle is ruinous. It consists of a large, irregular yard with seven towers in the wall. The entrance gateway is under a donjon. Through a little door one can mount to the top by a flight of stone steps, disturbing the bats. On the same side of the enclosure is a circular tower, octagonal within, with a vaulted chamber in the basement. On the west side is a beautiful little chamber in a tower, also vaulted. One tower towards the river, and commanding it, has been blown up and a great solid mass has fallen into the river below; on it sit the washerwomen of the village beating their linen. On the right bank, opposite Belocq, is the village of Puyôo. Puyôo in patois signifies a tumulus, and the place takes its name from a huge mound hollowed out as a cup at the top. Certainly the substructure of a Frank wooden castle, exactly like the tumps that are found in Southern Wales, and the representations of fortresses in the Bayeux tapestry. The hamlet of Puyôo is occupied mainly by Calvinists.

But that which will mainly interest an Englishman at Orthez will be to go over the ground of the battle fought on 27 February, 1814, in which Lord Wellington defeated Marshal Soult. It was, in fact, one of his most brilliant victories.

Leaving Sir John Hope and Admiral Penrose to invest Bayonne, Wellington, with the main force, had pushed on in pursuit of the French under Soult. These were drawn up at Sauveterre, but whilst Wellington demonstrated upon the front of the line on which Soult rested, and whilst the attention of the marshal was wholly engaged by the movements in his front, Sir Rowland Hill crossed the Gave d'Oloron at Villenave without opposition on 24 February and turned his left. Upon this Soult hastily abandoned his ground, transferred his headquarters to Orthez, and took up a formidable position behind the Gave de Pau.

The position chosen by him was well selected and apparently impregnable. A half-moon of heights of sandstone and rubble, steep towards the west, and with gullies torn in the sides, was occupied by him. His right rested on the bluff above the village of S. Boës. The left flank rested on the town of Orthez. A reserve of two divisions of infantry and a brigade of cavalry were drawn up on an elevated and commanding height by the road to Sault de Navailles. The French marshal disposed of eight divisions of infantry and one of cavalry, but these had been wasted from their former strength, and hardly mustered forty thousand sabres and bayonets, with forty guns.

Wellington was able, unopposed, to cross the Gave in three places, in three advancing columns.

At daybreak on the 27th Beresford, with the left wing, commenced the action by turning the enemy's extreme right at S. Boës, whilst at the same time Picton assaulted the centre. Hill, with the second British and Le Cor's Portuguese brigade, was to endeavour to force the passage at Orthez and attack the enemy's left. There was an interval of a mile and a half between Beresford's and Picton's columns, and here was a conical hill occupied by a Roman camp on the summit, and separated by a marsh from the semilunar range held by the French. On this height in the midst of the camp Wellington took his station with his staff, having the whole battle spread out like a map before him. Beresford, having overlapped the French right, commenced a vigorous attack in front and flank on the village of S. Boës. At length the English reached the top of the hill, and, pursuing the enemy, began to move along the narrow ridge which stretched from S. Boës to the centre of the French position. But they failed to dislodge the enemy, who kept up a rolling fire upon their pursuers, and the artillery raked both flanks, occasioning dreadful carnage, so that the English were brought to a stand-still. At the same time a Portuguese brigade, completely unnerved, turned and fled in disorderly rout, throwing our own men into confusion.

Happily a brigade was moved up to cover the retreat of the Portuguese and allow our own men to recover and re-form. "At last I have him!" exclaimed Soult exultantly. Wellington, from his point of observation, saw that the effort to dislodge the French and roll them back on their centre had failed. He then executed one of those sudden and masterly changes of attack which exhibit the ready resource of a great general. He at once ordered up the third and sixth divisions to assail the centre of the enemy's position, and turn and take the right wing in flank. Simultaneously Picton was to mount the ridge where the French had their right centre, and, breaking the line of formation, drive it back on to the left. The gallant troops crossed the swamp, with the water up to their knees, and mounting the hill through the brushwood unperceived by the foe, amidst the smoke, with a loud shout and a withering fire plunged into the opening at the very moment that the French on the right were pressing their advantage against Beresford, and were driving the fourth division before them.

At the same time Picton reached the summit of the ridge in the middle, drove the French down the slope, and, planting his guns, plunged through the enemy's masses from one end of his position to the other.

Soult saw that the day was lost, and ordered the army to retreat, which it did in regular echelons of divisions, and they held the several positions taken up till the allies closed on their front and moved upon their flank, Hill having by this time crossed above Orthez and cut off the retreat by the road to Pau. Then the French broke their formation, and ran for Sault de Navailles with such speed that the great body of them passed over the bridge in a wild, terror-stricken crowd. However, nearly two thousand prisoners were taken in the pursuit, and several guns. The French loss in killed, wounded, and taken, exceeded six thousand, and some hundreds afterwards deserted, or rather disbanded, and went to their homes. The loss of the allies amounted to 2300.

It is pleasing to know what excellent discipline was maintained by Wellington in his march through the Gascon land from Bayonne to Toulouse. This was due not solely to humanity towards the peasantry, but also as a precaution to obviate insurrectionary movements in his rear. He issued a proclamation, authorizing the people of the country, under the mayors of the villages, to arm themselves, and arrest all stragglers and marauders from the army. Allison says:—

> "Nor did his proclamation remain a dead letter, for on the night of the 25th the inhabitants of a village on the high road leading from Sauveterre, having shot one British soldier who had been plundering, and wounded another, he caused the wounded man to be hung, and sent home an English colonel who had permitted his men to destroy the municipal archives of a small town on the line of march. 'Maintain the strictest discipline; without that we are lost,' said he to General Freyre. By this means tranquillity was preserved in his rear during this critical movement; and the English general reaped the fruits of the admirable discipline and forbearance he had maintained in the enemy's country, by being enabled to bring up all his reserves, and hurl his undivided force upon the hostile army."

# CHAPTER VI

## PAU



THE situation of Pau is singularly favoured, and one can appreciate the judgment of Henry II of Navarre in transferring thither the court residence from
Orthez. Pau occupies the back of a rubble ridge stretching east and west, facing
the south, and drinking in the sunlight and warmth. It does not suffer from cold
winds. The land rises behind it to the north, and one may see the clouds fly over-
head without feeling the air stir at Pau. The calmness of the atmosphere often
persists for weeks together.

In this it has an advantage over some of the towns of the French Riviera, where
the mistral cuts like a knife that has been frozen in an ice-pail. The bitter winds that
sweep down on the Riviera are produced by the snows of the Maritime Alps. But
there are no snows at the back of Pau. When there is no breeding ground for icy
winds, no icy winds are hatched.

But, on the other hand, a good deal of rain is brought up and discharged over
Pau, coming from the Atlantic; and a whole month may elapse without the promenaders on the terrace being able to catch a glimpse of the Pic du Midi d'Ossau.
The Girondin climate is notoriously rainy, especially in spring; but nothing can
surpass the splendour of the days in summer and autumn.

Pau

Mrs. Ellis, who wrote her *Summer and Winter in the Pyrenees* in 1841, says:—

"At the foot of the woody range of high ground forming the promenade runs the broad, shallow river Gave, with a perpetual low murmur that lulls the senses to repose. It is, in fact, the only sound we hear, for there is so little wind in this climate that not a leaf is seen to move, and we therefore distinguish at a greater distance the toll of the matin and vesper bell in the neighbouring villages, and the tinkling sounds which tell when the flocks are led to and from the fields. There appears at first a sort of mystery in this universal stillness. It seems like a pause in the breath of Nature, a suspension of the general throb of life, and we almost feel as if it must be followed by that shout of joy which the language of poetry has so often described as the grateful response of Nature for the blessings of light and life. And never, surely, could this response be offered more appropriately than from such a scene as this rich and fertile land presents."

It was due to this climatic condition that in the first half of last century patients in the early stages of consumption were dispatched to Pau. Now that the treatment of phthisis is revolutionized, it is no longer a resort for such as suffer from pulmonary complaints, but serves as a refuge from the stormy English winters for those who desire pleasant resting places where there are races, fox-hunting, and good company. The climate, however, does not agree with all constitutions. It is enervating, a land of lotus-eaters—

"In which it seemed always afternoon."

Pau, the old Pau, is attached on the north to the dreary *lande* of the Pont-long that has belonged from time immemorial to the inhabitants of the Val d'Ossau, and which is strewn with tumuli. But from this plateau it is in part cut off by the stream Hédas, that has cleft for itself a valley dividing the town into two parts. New Pau has spread and is spreading to north and east, so that its extremities have to be reached by electric trams. Happily, to the west it cannot encroach on the rubble ridge occupied by the park. Between this park and the castle which occupies the extreme west of the town the ridge has been sawn through by the stream, but the gap has been widened artificially, and is now spanned by a bridge.

The Castle of Pau was built at various dates. The four towers and the curtain uniting them, except the south and east faces, are the oldest part, and were erected by Gaston Phœbus in or about 1363. The donjon to the east is of brick, and is furnished with slots. The work begun by Gaston Phœbus was continued by his successor, but the magnificent south façade, the state buildings, and the enrichment of the court within, in the style of the Renaissance, are due to Henry II of Navarre; and the sixth tower was set up by Louis Philippe.

The whole castle, especially the interior, has gone through a complete restoration, for it had been plundered and gutted by the Revolutionists. The tapestries that now cover the walls were collected from various places. The furniture, to a large extent modern, is a clumsy imitation of old work; there are, however, some fine ancient cabinets. In this castle was confined for a while Abd-el-Kader. In 1848 I visited him there several times. He had with him a suite and his wives, all insensible to the stateliness of the castle and the glorious panorama from the windows. They lounged about the rooms silent and smoking, sulky, without occupation and without interests. Their habits were so dirty that the tapestries and rich furniture had all to be removed. Abd-el-Kader had maintained a long and gallant resistance against the French, and when he surrendered to the Duc d'Aumale and General Lamorcière, it was on the stipulation that he should be allowed to retire in freedom to Egypt or into Syria. The terms were accepted and broken. He was removed a prisoner to Toulon, then to Pau, and in November, 1848, he was transferred to Amboise. Napoleon III released him in 1852, and he finally settled in Damascus. In the terrible massacre of the Christians at Damascus in the summer of 1860, by Turks and Druses, Abd-el-Kader acted with such energy to protect the Christians that the Emperor of the French sent him the gold cross of the Legion of Honour. Possibly enough he may have been moved to this intervention on behalf of the Christians by recollecting the kindness that was shown him in his captivity by both English and French residents at Pau, sending him fruit and flowers for the ladies of his harem.

It was during his imprisonment at Toulon that Thackeray wrote his stirring lines:—

> "No more, thou lithe and long-winged hawk, of desert life for thee;
> No more across the sultry sands shalt thou go swooping free;
> Blunt idle talons, idle beak, with spurning of thy chain,
> Shatter against the cage the wing thou ne'er mayst spread again.

> *　　　*　　　*　　　*　　　*

> "They gave him what he asked; from king to king he spake
> As one that plighted word and seal not knoweth how to break;
> 'Let me pass from out my deserts, be't mine own choice where to go,
> I brook no fettered life to live, a captive and a show.'

> "And they promised and he trusted them, and proud and calm he came,
> Upon his black mare riding, girt with his sword of flame:
> Good steed, good sword, he rendered unto the Frankish throng;
> He knew them false and fickle—but a Prince's word is strong.

> "How have they kept their promise? Turned they the vessel's prow
> Upon Acre, Alexandria, as they have sworn e'en now?
> Not so: from Oran northwards the white sails gleam and glance,
> And the wild hawk of the desert is borne away to France.

> "They have need of thee to gaze on, they have need of thee to grace
> The triumph of the Prince, to gild the pinch-beck of their race.
> Words are but wind, conditions must be construed by Guizot:
> Dash out thy heart, thou desert hawk, ere thou art made a show."

With the exception of the castle there is nothing of architectural interest in Pau. The churches are modern, and the predominant feature of the place is hotels, monster hotels that even dwarf the castle.

But the great glory of Pau is the view of the chain of the Pyrenees from the terrace and the park. That from the Schänzle above Berne of the giants of the Oberland is beautiful, but not comparable with the prospect from Pau. All the middle distance in the view from Berne is filled up with rolling hills, and it is over them that one catches glimpses of the snowy heads of the Alps. But from Pau one has in front the broad trough of the Gave, beyond which are the coteaux, not too high, and not obscuring the lower parts of the mountains. It is true that an obnoxious swell to the south-west cuts off the prospect of the range to the Bay of Biscay, but the mountain range can be traced eastward till it fades into vapour, and the mountains on that side are by far the boldest and loftiest. Moreover, one can look from Pau right up the gap of the Val d'Ossau to the roots of the Pic du Midi, an exquisitely beautiful mountain, only surpassed by the Matterhorn; and it has this advantage over its rival, that it can be seen from a great distance, which the other cannot.

Below the terrace of the castle rises the insignificant tower of la Monaye, where the specie for circulation in Béarn and the annexed counties was coined.

In the second chapter I told the story of the House of Foix and Béarn down to the death of Catherine, who ate out her heart with rage because she could not acquire the kingdom of Upper Navarre, to which she laid claim. Her son and successor was Henry II of Navarre.

He obtained the name of Henry in a somewhat singular fashion. At his birth a pilgrim was passing through Pau, of obscure origin, named Henry, on his way to S. James of Compostella. Jean d'Albret, moved by a sudden freak, summoned this man to be godfather to his boy, the heir to the crown of Navarre, instead of inviting a prince to stand sponsor. This occasioned much ridicule among the haughty Spaniards, who said it presaged that the young Henry would be a stranger to his kingdom.

He was brought up with Francis I of France, and the two were warmly attached to each other. He accompanied Francis in his disastrous expedition to the Milanese, and shared captivity with the King at Pavia. His ransom was fixed at a hundred thousand crowns. Henry did not care to burden his little territory with such a charge, and he devised means to escape. A lady in Pavia managed to convey to his prison a rope ladder, and one night in December, 1525, when the moon shone, he slipped out of the window of his cell and descended the ladder. It was too short, and he fell into the moat. Happily this was more full of mud than of water, and without loss of time he scrambled out, plastered with slime, mounted a horse, held in readiness by his accomplices, galloped away, and managed to reach Lyons. On the morning after his evasion the commandant of the Castle of Pavia entered the cell and bade his royal prisoner get up. A voice from the bed replied, "For pity's sake, let me sleep a little longer." He who spoke was a page of the King of Navarre, who had taken his place, so as to deceive the guards and give his master time to escape.

The affection and esteem which Francis I had for Henry were shown in that he gave him as wife his dearly-loved sister Margaret, the "Marguerite des Marguerites, sa mignonne," as Francis called her. The marriage took place on 24 January, 1527. The Court of Paris was inconsolable at the loss of the lively and charming princess. The Parisian doctors remonstrated with her at going to so inclement a place as Pau where, said they, "le gros air du pays lui serait mortel." However, go she would, with her beloved Henry, and on reaching Pau she at once set to work to make herself happy, and to be beloved by the people. She began by studying the patois and worked at it so diligently that she was herself astounded at the progress she made.

> "The newly-married pair," says an old historian, "deliberated how to put Béarn in a better condition from that in which they found it. This land, good and fertile by nature, was in a poor state, uncultivated and sterile through the negligence of the inhabitants. It soon changed its appearance."

Henry devoted himself especially to agriculture; he invited farmers and labourers from Brittany, Berry, and the Saintonge to settle in the land and teach the natives improved methods of cultivation; and the introduction of maize into Béarn was due to him. He set up a linen factory at Nay, and a printing press at Pau. He collected, revised, and edited the *fors* of Béarn, and had them printed at his press in 1551.

One of the most important pages in the life of the Queen of Navarre in the Château of Pau was the part she played in receiving refugee Huguenot preachers. But she never herself became a convert to Calvinism; she entertained great pity for the innovators who were driven from place to place, and subjected to cruel persecution. She offered them an asylum, and listened to their harangues without the impatience shown by her husband, who, when they began to preach, retired to his bottle and his cards.

> "The Queen of Navarre," says Florimond de Rémond, "gave ear to them, received their books at first by the hand of her ladies, has had the Latin prayers of the church translated into French ... out of kindness of heart she throws open her house to the proscribed and banished, and bids them regard it as a retreat and refuge. She exercises marvellous care in protecting those who are in danger on account of their religion, and in succouring the refugees from Strassburg and Geneva.

> "Roussel was received by this good princess into Béarn and given a state lodging in her house. She takes pleasure in listening to him as he discourses on religion. He persuaded her to read the Bible, then very uncouthly translated into French; and this so pleased her that she composed a tragi-comic translation of nearly the whole of the New Testament, and had it acted in the great hall before the King, her husband. For the purpose she secured the best comedians that could be procured from Italy; and as these buffoons are born only to afford amusement, and, monkey-like,

to mimic what may meet the humours of their masters, so these people, recognizing the inclination of the Queen, interlarded the text of these plays with roundelays and virolais on the theme of the clergy. Always some poor monk or *religieuse* was made the butt in one of these comedies or farces."

The Castle, Pau

Florimond de Rémond goes on to say that some of the preachers harboured by Marguerite were not of high character. Among them was Solon, a runaway Carmelite, a "brave et courageux moine," who embraced the doctrines of Calvin, and to make up for wasted opportunities in the past married and buried five wives in succession.

Some of the sacred pieces enacted before the King and Queen were the Nativity, the Adoration of the Magi, the Flight into Egypt; and into these plays scurrilous and indecent songs were introduced, without a word of protest from the preachers.

Marguerite took as her valet Clement Marot, who had not the best of characters, and scandal said that she liked him a little too well.

Unsuspectingly Marot did a great work for Calvinism in France.

He had translated the Psalms of David into popular rhythm. His metrical version became the rallying songs of the Huguenots, and formed the basis of their liturgy. They were set to popular folk-airs.

The French ladies, as he said himself, placed

> leurs doigts sur les espinettes
> pour dire saintes chansonettes.

So little heretical was his version regarded that in 1540, before it was printed, Francis I made a present of it to Charles V. Florimond de Rémond says:—

> "Each of the princes and courtiers adopted one or other of the psalms for himself. King Henry chose as his own Psalm XLII., *Ainsi qu'on oyt le cerf bruire*, which he sang when hunting. Mme. de Valentinois (Diana of Poitiers), his mistress, took as hers Ps. CXXX., *Du fond de ma pensée*, which she sang when galloping. The Queen had selected V.; *Ne veuillez pas, O Sire*, set to a buffoon melody. The King of Navarre, Antoine de Bourbon, chose XLIII., *Revenge moy, prens la querelle*, which he sang to a branle (a dance tune) of Poitou; and so with the rest."

But little by little these metrical psalms assumed an aggressive tone; passed among the people, and these took them to heart more seriously than did the courtiers.

Bordier, in his *Chansonnier huguenot*, says:—

> "It was soon seen with what energy the Huguenots assimilated this poetry, which responded so well to their burning faith. They knew the psalter by heart. It became one of the tokens by which they recognized one another at long distances, before coming in sight, when certain familiar melodies were borne to their ears. From the windows of the Louvre Henry II more than once saw a crowd flushed with enthusiasm fill the Pré aux Clercs, promenading in the evening with gravity, trolling out these psalms."

The Queen of Navarre was certainly a strange mixture; she wrote treatises of piety, composed a *Mirror of the Sinful Soul*, wrote songs, and in her old age was the authoress of that book of indecent tales, the *Heptameron*, which is still read, whereas the *Mirror of the Sinful Soul* is forgotten.

She took as her device the marigold turning to the sun, and as her motto, "Non inferiora sequor," hardly appropriate to the compiler of the *Heptameron*.

A pretty story is told of her by Brantôme. She had as one of her ladies-in-waiting Mlle. de la Roche, who had been the mistress of Captain Bourdeille, but whom he had cast aside and forgotten. Mlle. de la Roche died in the Queen's service at Pau, and was buried in the church of S. Martin. Three months later Bourdeille came to Pau, and was received by the Queen, who invited him to attend her to the church. When there, standing in a certain place, Marguerite said to him, "Do you feel the ground heave under your feet?" "Not in the least," he replied. "Surely you do?" "Madame, I assure you that I do not." "That is strange," said the Queen, "for beneath your feet lies your poor, deserted Mademoiselle de la Roche, sighing because that above her stands the man who deceived her. I leave you now alone to your reflections."

Marguerite entertained a horror of death, but on hearing that her dearly-loved brother Francis was no more, her joy of life, her spirits left her, her health failed, and she died at Odos in Bigorre in 1549.

Her daughter, Jeanne d'Albret, was left heiress of Navarre, Béarn, Bigorre, Foix, and Armagnac, which had been part of her mother's dower. Jeanne was born in the Castle of Pau in 1528. At an early age she was removed to the Court of the King of France, and was betrothed at the age of twelve, and married in 1546, when eighteen years old, to the Duke of Cleves, who was twelve years her senior. She was so burdened with pearls and embroidery over brocade and gold lace at her wedding that she was unable to walk, and had to be carried into the church from the carriage in the arms of the Constable of France. But she did not relish the union, and it was annulled. In 1548 Jeanne married Antoine de Bourbon, a feeble, voluptuous, irresolute creature, "to one thing constant never." He was first a Catholic, then a Huguenot, under the influence of the commanding intellect of his wife, and then a Catholic again; it mattered not to him, for he had no fixed principles. But Jeanne never forgave his rejoining the Church, for she was a bigoted Calvinist.

Jeanne was nearly deprived of her husband. Antoine de Bourbon, who was suspected of taking part with his brother, the great Condé, in the conspiracy of Amboise, 1550, was marked out for destruction. The two brothers were arrested by Francis II. Olhagary, a Protestant writer, gives what follows. He had it from the recital of Queen Jeanne herself; but how far coloured by her prejudices we are unable to say.

> "The Prince of Condé was sentenced to have his head cut off before the King's residence, on 10 December. Antoine de Bourbon was to be stabbed by the King himself. For this he was ordered to attend in the chamber of the King, who pretended to be ill. Francis was to stab him with his own hand, aided by the Guises who were hid behind the arras."

Antoine was on the point of entering the presence chamber when the Duchess de Montpensier caught him by the arm and revealed to him the plot. He then withdrew. But again a messenger arrived from the King ordering him to appear. Then he summoned to him Reuti, the captain of his guards, and said—

> "I am going to where my death is planned, but never shall skin be sold so dearly as I will sell mine. I beseech you to render me this last service. If I die, take my shirt soaked in my blood, and carry it to my wife and son, and charge her—for my son is too young to be able to avenge me—to send the pierced and bloody shirt to all the foreign princes, and call on them to avenge my death."

Antoine then entered the room where was the King, but his behaviour, the frankness with which he met the charges laid against him, caused the heart of Francis to relent, and he dismissed the King of Navarre unhurt. It was then that the Cardinal of Lorraine exclaimed, referring to the weakness of the King—"There is the heart of a poltroon!"

Jeanne had been the mother of two sons; the elder died of over-coddling, the second of an accident. When she was again expecting her confinement, her father, Henry II, roughly told her that she did not know how to manage her children, and insisted on her coming to the castle at Pau for confinement, under his eye. She obeyed, and arrived on 4 December, 1553. Then the old King showed her a casket of gold, attached to a chain long enough to go thrice round her neck. "Do you see this?" said he; "I will give it you along with my will, that is in this box, if you will sing a Béarnais song whilst in your pangs, so that the child may not be a squaller." She promised, and on 14 December, feeling her hour approach, sent for her father, and began to sing a Béarnais hymn to Our Lady at Bridgend; for there was a chapel to the Blessed Virgin on the ancient bridge over the Gave. Her song was:—

> "Nousté Dame deii cap d'eii poun
> Adjudat me à d'aqueste ore," etc.

But as many of my readers do not understand the patois, I will give it in English:—

> "Our Lady at the head of the bridge, assist me in this hour.
> Pray to God in Heaven, that He may deliver me, that the fruit of
> my body may see the light.... Our Lady at the head of the bridge,
> assist me in this hour."

She gave birth—some say on 13 December, some on 14 December—still singing, to a boy. Henry II took it from her, gave her the casket, saying, "This is for you," and as to the boy, "this is for me." Then he rubbed the child's lips with garlic, and poured into its mouth some drops of Jurançon wine, and said: "Va, tu serras un vrai Béarnais."

When Marguerite had given birth to Jeanne the Spaniards had remarked, "The cow has littered a lamb!" in reference to the cow in the Béarnais arms. Now Henry d'Albret, taking the child in his arms, showed it to his nobles and exclaimed: "See, the lamb has littered a lion!"

In the castle is shown the cradle in which the future king of France, Henri Quatre, was rocked. It is a large tortoise-shell, inverted, and suspended by silken cords. When the Sansculottes burst into and sacked the château in 1793, they purposed to destroy this relic of royalty. But the commandant of the castle had foreseen this, and had substituted for the original another tortoise-shell, obtained from the cabinet of a naturalist in the town. This latter was destroyed, but the original was preserved in the attics of the castle.

At Bilhère, a little way out of Pau, on the road to Orthez, is the cottage in which Henry was nursed by a peasantess. That cottage remains much in the same condition as it was then, and is pointed out to visitors with pride.

When only five years old his mother took him to Paris to present him to Henry II, King of France. The King took the little prince in his arms and asked him, "Veux-tu être mon fils?" The child, unable to speak other than Béarnais patois, pointed to his father and answered, "Aquet es lou seignou pay" (This is monsieur, my father). "You are right," said the King, "but as you will not be my son, will you be my son-in-law?" To which the boy promptly replied, "Obé." Marguerite de Valois was then eighteen months older than Henri.

After a while in Paris he was taken back to Pau and committed to the care of Suzanne de Bourbon Busset, Baroness Miossens, who was sent with him to the Castle of Coarraze, near Nay, with instructions that he should be reared among the children of the mountains on simple, wholesome diet.

Accordingly he was treated like the peasant children—was clothed in the same garb, and partook of the same athletic sports. His food was often dry bread. Frequently he trod the mountain paths with bare feet, or clattered about in sabots. For many years he knew no other tongue than the patois, and in after life a bon mot, or a lively sally in his maternal language, served as one of the most powerful means by which to influence the young Gascons whom he led to battle.

Antoine de Bourbon fell at the siege of Rouen in 1562, fighting against the Huguenots, and Jeanne was then left free to force Calvinism on her subjects. Thenceforth she was able to rule despotically in her own dominions, till interfered with by the French king. Beza, with approval, records her declaration: "Sooner than ever again attend Mass, or suffer any of my subjects or my children to do so, I would, if possible, cast them into the depths of the sea." And to Henry, when young, she said passionately that should he at any time attend Catholic worship, she would repudiate and disinherit him.

She began by confiscating Church property and appropriating to herself monastic lands. Commissioners were appointed to go through the country, wreck the churches, and sweep into her mint all the gold and silver chalices, candlesticks, and crucifixes, to be coined into money. She expelled the priests and put ministers in their place. At Pau she hung two of the canons of S. Martin's, and sent a Huguenot preacher into the pulpit. The town council remonstrated. The Queen's reply was that she would with her troopers drive the councillors to be present at his predications. She made it punishable with death as high treason not only for a priest to say Mass, but for man, woman, or child to attend at one.

**Room of Jeanne D'albret, Castle of Pau**

Charles IX of France went to Nerac, in Gascony, to visit Jeanne.

"In some respects," says Mr. White, "the province of Gascony through which the Court was now travelling, had suffered more than any part of France from the effects of the war. The Protestants had succeeded in putting down Romanism, and at every step he took Charles was reminded of the outrages offered to his religion; he restored the old form of worship, but the scenes he then witnessed appear never to have been forgotten. As he rode along by the side of the Queen of Navarre he pointed to the ruined monasteries, the broken crosses, the polluted churches; he showed her the mutilated images of the Virgin and the saints, the desecrated graveyards, the relics scattered to the winds of heaven."[6]

Jeanne looked with sparkling eyes and with a heart that swelled with exultation at this wreckage, but she noticed the pain it caused to the young king, and thenceforth regarded him with distrust.

A Béarnais named Gondin ventured to remonstrate with Jeanne at her high-handed dealings. "The King of France," said she, "choses to have but one religion in his realm. I am a queen, and I choose to have but one." "The King of France!" echoed Gondin; "that is another matter. I could cross your majesty's kingdom in a hop, skip, and jump." "Then I will trouble you, sir, to hop, skip, and jump out of my realm, and that smartly," was her prompt reply.

At the same time that Jeanne issued her order for the change of religion, she forbade the dances of the peasantry and wailing at funerals.

Of Jeanne d'Albret it might be said in the words of Quintus Curtius: "Nihil præter vultum fœmineum gerens." Marguerite de France, sister of Francis II, Charles IX, and Henry III was married in 1572 to Henry of Navarre. The union was not happy, neither cared for the other; and when Marguerite came to Pau she was affronted at her treatment.

> "We came to Pau," she wrote, "where no exercise of the Catholic religion is tolerated. However, I was allowed as a favour to hear Mass in a little chapel three or four paces in length, and so narrow that seven or eight persons filled it. At the hour of Mass, the drawbridge was raised to prevent the Catholics of the place from attending; for they were most desirous to do so, having been debarred from it for several years. But, it being Whit-Sunday, some of the citizens succeeded in slipping in before the drawbridge was raised. They were not detected till the end of the service, when some Huguenots who were spying perceived them. They instantly informed the king's secretary, and in my presence were dragged out, whipped, and cast into prison, and were not released for long, and then not till they had paid a heavy fine."

When Henry IV came to the throne of France the care of his hereditary dominions in Gascony was confided to his sister Catherine. In the Castle of Pau at that time was brought up Antoine de Bourbon, Count of Moret, Henry's son by Jacqueline de Bueil. There he studied, but proved a sorry scholar. In later days he ventured on criticizing the works of Gombaud, whereupon this latter retaliated

---

[6] White (H.), *The Massacre of S. Bartholomew*. London, 1868.

with an epigram.

> "Vous chocquez la nature et l'art,
> Vous qui n'êtes né que d'un crime;
> Mais pensez vous que d'un bastard
> Le jugement soit légitime?"

Antoine fell in the battle of Castelnaudary, in 1631. Half a century later, there appeared in Anjou an old hermit, who called himself John Baptist, and whose face resembled Henri Quatre markedly. Moreover, he admitted having been in the battle of Castelnaudary, and showed himself to be intimately acquainted with Pau and with every part of the castle; but he would never say who he was. Louis XIV, having heard of him, sent to demand whether he was the Antoine de Bourbon, son of Henry IV, who had been reported dead. He refused to answer, and on his death-bed, when again questioned on this point, returned an evasive answer.

In matters of religion Henry IV was tolerant. He wrote in 1594:—

> "I have in my kingdom of Béarn two parishes separated only by a river. In one of these there has never during my reign been any (Calvinist) preacher; in the other, never a Mass said, yet the inhabitants of these parishes have not wronged one another to the value of a sou. You will see, that I will bring about such concord in my kingdom that there will be no further squabbles."

But before this, when in Paris, under the surveillance of Catherine de Medici, he was obliged to send the Count de Grammont and a commission into Béarn to restore Catholic worship. D'Aubigné relates an incident relative to this attempt that is characteristic of the temper of the times. When the Baron d'Arros, who had been appointed after Montgomery, by Jeanne d'Albret, to enforce the sole exercise of Calvinistic worship in her states, heard of the coming of De Grammont, he happened to encounter his father, aged eighty, and blind, coming out of the Huguenot meeting-house. The old man led his son home, placed in his hands a drawn sword, and bade him slay and spare not the Lord's enemies. Arros and thirty-seven followers went to Hagetmau, where Grammont and the commission-ers were, and entered the castle unperceived. Then they fell upon and slaughtered officers, soldiers, and servants, indiscriminately. De Grammont alone was spared. His wife—Corisande d'Andouins, one of the loveliest women of the time—threw herself between her husband and Arros, and with tears implored the latter to spare Grammont.

When the Baron d'Arros returned to his father to receive a blessing after this exploit, the old man bitterly reproached him for having spared even one. "My son," said he, "how, as a valiant Maccabee, have you allowed this Nicanor to live? The crow you have spared will pluck out your eyes."

Calvinism, after having had complete mastery for over half a century, seems not to have taken firm root. At the present day, out of a population in Béarn of 426,350, there are but 5000 Protestants.

In one of his bear-hunting expeditions, when a lad, Henry of Navarre had visited the church of Bielle in the Val d'Ossau, and had noticed the columns of Italian marble in the church, the spoils of a Gallo-Roman villa. When he was king he sent to Bielle to have these pillars forwarded to him in Paris. The reply of the villagers was: "Sire, our hearts and our properties are yours, dispose of them as you will; but as to these columns, they belong to God. *Entendez vous-en avec lui.*"

As king, Henry said that his ambition was that every one of his subjects, every peasant in Béarn, should be able every Sunday in the year to put *la poule au pot!* A couple of centuries later an epigram was written thereon.

> "Enfin, la poule au pot sera donc bientôt mise;
> On doit du moins le présumer;
> Car, depuis deux cent ans qu'on nous l'avait promise,
> On n'a cessé de la plumer."

He did not forget the good things he had eaten in his native land when far away in Paris, and he wrote to Pau to have sent to him "some good melons, muscat grapes, figs, and peaches"; and again, "a dozen geese of Béarn, the fattest that can be found, such as will do honour to my country."

The old cathedral church of Lescar occupies a very ancient site—a Roman town, Beneharnum, on the great Roman road that ran from Narbonne to Dax. The church deserves a visit. Although not large it is fine, dating from the twelfth century. It was erected apparently on the site of some Roman building, for the mosaic that surrounds the high altar, and marks where stood the original apse of the first church, is Roman work, and represents a tiger hunt. It was formerly covered by the floor of the stalls; but these have been removed, and the mosaic, that was much injured, has been restored carefully.

The whole of the low country, and the bottoms of the mountain valleys, were occupied by Romans. Gallic nobles had their villas that studded the land. At Bielle, already mentioned, is a mosaic pavement, and an evidence of the luxury of the period is seen in this villa having had pillars of marble brought from Italy. Other mosaic pavements have been found at Biellan, near Lescar, and at Taron-Sadirac, in the garden of the *presbytère* and in an adjoining field. The high altar of the church there is entirely formed of slabs taken thence. In 1847, when I was a boy, I heard peasants romance about a "Palais des Fées," that lay underground in a field by the Lyss, in the commune of Jurançon. I visited the spot and found numerous cubes of mosaic of diverse colours in a ditch. I then saw the peasant proprietor and asked him whether he had discovered anything when ploughing. "Mais oui!" he said; "five years ago I uncovered a picture that represented men sitting about a table drinking and playing cards." I knew how to make allowance for a Gascon's imagination, so I bargained with the man to allow me to institute a search. We cut a trench parallel to the stream and crossed walls and mosaic pavements through a length of 150 feet. I then came to terms with the owner of the field. He was to allow me to dig, and he was to charge two sous at the gate for admission.

In a fortnight we had cleared out several rooms, and then, as my pocket-money was exhausted, the English of Pau raised a subscription to pay for the prosecution of the work. In the end we uncovered eleven chambers with well-preserved mosaic floors, and two more of which the floors had broken in upon the heating apparatus underneath, but which had been very richly patterned. The villa consisted of a suite of winter rooms and another for summer residence. In the former all the floors and walls were warmed by a hypocaust. The villa was, moreover, well furnished with baths.

In the middle, between the winter and the summer quarters, was the atrium, a court with a tank, in the midst, of pure water, conducted into it by a lead pipe from a well in the hill above. The bottom of the tank was paved with mosaic, representing marine animals, fish, crabs, etc., and the two containing walls were cased in slabs of coloured marbles. Opening out of the atrium was the *tablinum*, the reception room of the house; the walls skirted with alabaster, above which they were painted. The most remarkable of the representations on the floors was in the hall next the entrance porch; it showed a cross in mosaic, with a monstrous bust of Neptune at the intersection of the arms, surrounded by fish and lobsters.

When the villa was almost wholly excavated, the municipality of Pau purchased the field, and built a shed over the foundations, but, penny wise and pound foolish, neglected to cut a drain around the remains. The consequence was that each room became full of water in the winter, and, frost ensuing, split up the mosaics. When I revisited Pau two years later most of the pavements were ruined. Now, shed and every trace of the villa are gone; the whole is ploughed over, and the only token that there was anything of interest in the field is a notice-board set up to forbid trespassers invading it. On the farther side of the stream is another villa, which I began to dig out, but found the pavements nearer the surface and not so well preserved. Moreover, the proprietor got it into his head that I had discovered and appropriated a pot of gold coins, and he peremptorily forbade further research.

The bridge over the river, some quarter of a mile down, is called le Pont d'Auly (*pons aulæ*), and on the height of Guindalos above are the earthworks of a Roman camp.

Pau has produced several eminent men. Hardly had Henri Quatre closed his eyes before the town gave birth to Gassion, born in 1609. His father purposed making of him a lawyer; but, as a lad of sixteen, rather than be chained to a desk, he started barefoot from Pau, with his shoes slung to a stick over his back, and with twenty sous in his pocket. He entered the army, and his life was spent in warfare, beyond the Alps, on the Elbe, on the shores of the Baltic. He was wounded seventeen times, and fell on the field of battle at the age of thirty-six, a marshal of France and the greatest captain of his age.

More fortunate than he was Bernadotte, also a soldier risen from the ranks, who became King of Sweden and Norway. He was born in the little house, No. 6 Rue de Trau, and was the son of a needy scrivener. His name in full was John Baptist Julius Bernadotte, and he was born on 26 January, 1764. He became a drummer-boy in the marines at the age of seventeen.

He came to the front at an opportune time. The Revolution had turned France topsy-turvy. The officers had fled the country to escape the guillotine, and the corporals and serjeants stepped into their places. The regiments elected their captains, and the history of the Republican wars shows that the soldiers exercised their electoral rights with discretion. In 1792 Bernadotte was a colonel.

The Directory appointed him ambassador at Vienna. The choice was not happy; he had not the breeding of a gentleman, and behaved with insolence in the most punctilious of courts. On the day upon which the volunteers were enrolled for the defence of their country, Bernadotte ostentatiously hoisted the tricolour, which the mob tore down. The ambassador in vain demanded satisfaction. He quitted Vienna, but the Directory disavowed him. Soon after his return to France he married Eugènie, the daughter of the soap-boiler, Clary, of Marseilles, and sister of the wife of Joseph Bonaparte. He lived for a while in retirement, but was summoned by the Government to Paris and was given the command of the army of observation in Germany.

After the revolution of the 30th Prairial, in the year VII (18 June, 1799), Bernadotte was appointed Minister of War; but the astute Siéyès was meditating a *coup d'état*, and mistrusting Bernadotte, deprived him of his portfolio. He accepted the title of Councillor of State from the First Consul, and the command of the army of the West.

In 1804 Napoleon raised him to the dignity of Marshal of the Empire, and gave him the command of the army in Hanover. In June, 1806, he created him Prince of Pontecorvo, and employed him in the war that broke out with Prussia. It is unnecessary here to follow his career in the wars of Napoleon. The Emperor never liked him, and even thought of depriving him of the title he had conferred upon him. He dispatched him in disgrace to Rome; but before he reached it a deputation from Sweden arrived (September, 1810) with the tidings that King Charles XII had named him Crown Prince, and that the Estates of Sweden had unanimously ratified the appointment, with the condition that he should resign his French citizenship and adopt the Lutheran religion. To this he consented, and landed at Helsingborg on 20 October, 1810, and on 5 November was recognized as Crown Prince, and adopted the name of Charles John. By arrangement with Russia Norway was detached from Denmark and annexed to Sweden, much to the dislike of the Norwegians.

In 1813 Sweden declared war against France, and Bernadotte led 20,000 Swedes to join the allies; but his dilatoriness caused him to be too late to take part in the Battle of the Nations at Liepzig. He was naturally reluctant to cross swords with his old master.

In 1814 he marched in the same leisurely manner into France, and arrived in Paris after it had been occupied by the allies. On 5 February, 1818, he succeeded his adoptive father, and was crowned King of Sweden and Norway at both Stockholm and Drontheim. He was succeeded by his only son, Oscar, in 1844.

It is a curious fact that both the two kings born at Pau abjured their religions to obtain a crown. Henry IV abandoned Calvinism to become a Catholic and receive the crown of France; John Baptist Julius Bernadotte threw overboard such Catholicism as he had—a light cargo—and accepted Protestantism to obtain the crown of Sweden and Norway.

Morlaas, six miles to the north-east of Pau, reached by a light railway, was the ancient capital of Béarn. It has dwindled to a poor village, but retains portions of its old fortifications and an interesting church, founded in 1089, that has a Romanesque crypt and west front. The church had fallen into decay and the portal was much mutilated, but it has been restored. A side chapel contains one of the very few specimens of church furniture spared by the Huguenots, because overlooked—an altar-piece of the sixteenth century.

The Pont-long I have already mentioned, an elevated moor to the north of Pau, beyond the racecourse, that belongs to the peasantry of the Val d'Ossau. On it may be seen the shepherds pasturing their flocks in winter, when the mountain herbage is buried under snow. These men formerly wore their characteristic costume—a dark blue or brown *beret*, like a tam-o'-shanter cap, a jacket of brown or scarlet, a waistcoat of white wool, brown knee-breeches, and a bright-coloured sash about the waist. They wore their hair long in curls flowing over their shoulders. Now compulsory military service has deprived them of their flowing locks, and the blouse is gradually displacing the handsome traditional costume.

These men spend their time in knitting stockings whilst watching their flocks. The sheep are horned, and have pronounced Roman noses. A curious usage is for the dog to precede the sheep instead of driving them.

There are numerous tumuli on the Pont-long. I opened two in 1847, and found that they pertained to the Iron Age, and were undoubtedly Gaulish. The floor was formed of rolled stones, and on this were placed urns, some of great size, containing burnt bones; they were red outside, black within, and the clay was coarse; but with them was one beautifully moulded little black vessel of the finest paste. Beside two of the cinerary urns were hones of grit, rounded on one side and flat on the other, with a groove running down the middle.

The peasants had a legend anent the larger of the two that I opened. Three men resolved on digging into it, and chose for the purpose a stormy day when no one was likely to be abroad and observe them.

They had not dug far before Pierre observed, "But we shall surely find plenty of sous."

"Des écus," said Jacques.

"Des napoléons," suggested Baptiste.

After some hours' work they came on a flat slab, on raising which a treasure of gold pieces was revealed. The men plunged their arms in and could not reach the bottom of the store. Gold, gold, ever more gold.

It was decided that a cart must be procured to remove the treasure, and lots were cast as to who was to remain on the tumulus, whilst the other two returned to Pau for a cart. The lot fell on Pierre, and the others departed.

Evening had settled down when they returned with a vehicle drawn by two oxen. Jacques and Baptiste discerned a dark figure on the mound, which they assumed to be that of their companion left to guard the treasure.

Then, mounting the tumulus, they asked whether any one had been there during their absence. The dark figure said, "Look up!" The men turned, the figure threw back his cloak, and they knew it was the devil, horns and hoof complete. Before they could recover from their astonishment and terror, with a switch of his tail he had whisked them into the cart. He mounted himself, and instantly the oxen—their own oxen—rose in the air with the vehicle, wheeled thrice about the mound, and then suddenly descended, carrying cart, men, and Satan into the pit. The earth closed over them and they were seen no more. Only Pierre lived to tell the tale. At the first appearance of the Evil One he had crossed himself. He was flung from the tumulus, and lay sprawling and blessing himself till after his comrades had vanished.

Nay may easily be visited, as it is on the main road to Tarbes. It has a church of the fifteenth century, and the frontage of a Renaissance house in which Jeanne d'Albret delighted to reside.

Farther on is Coarraze, where are the remains of the château in which Henri Quatre spent his early boyhood. Only the tower and the portal are of the sixteenth century, the rest is a structure raised in the eighteenth century. Over the doorway may be read the Spanish inscription: "Lo que ha de ser no puede fallar."

The church is early and fortified. The terrace in front of the castle commands a beautiful and extensive prospect of the Pyrenees in their ever-changing tints and lights and shades.

At the extreme limits of the department is Betharam. The name has been supposed to be derived from the Arabic *Beit-Haram*, the Holy House, and the place to have been a sacred spot during the Saracen occupation of the land. If so, then they bequeathed their veneration for the locality to the Christians, who drove them from it, for Betharam has been esteemed a holy house for centuries, owing to the possession by it of a miraculous statue of the Virgin, about which one of the usual childish tales is told that have such a family likeness, and show such lack of variety. A shepherd saw a blaze of light at the foot of a rock, and discovered that it proceeded from an image. When the figure was removed to the farther side of the Gave, with a leap into the air like a field cricket it recrossed the river and returned to its station under the rock. Then it was transferred to the high altar of the parish church of Lestelle and locked in. But bolts and bars could not restrain it; out it came through the key-hole and made for its rock shelter again.

A church and convent were erected under the rock. In 1569, by order of Jeanne d'Albret, both were burnt; but were rebuilt in 1614. The church is a barbaric structure, immediately below a hill, surmounted by a Calvary. Here formerly dwelt a hermit, who maintained himself by selling tooth-combs of boxwood that he had made. But he is gone, and has left no successor. The bridge at Betharam is greatly admired, wreathed as it is with ivy, which falls in long tresses and almost touches the Gave.

I have spoken of the view from the park at Pau. Finer views may be had from the heights on the farther side of the Gave, from Guindalos and Gelos; and in early spring, when strolling among these hills, one may gather handfulls of cyclamen, anemones, violets, and the white spires of the asphodel.

**Betharam**

On market-days at Pau may be purchased clumps of the beautiful little scarlet anemone that formerly grew wild in the vineyards, but has been so much in request that it has disappeared, except under garden cultivation. And finally, we must taste the wine of Jurençon and S. Faust, not in the hotels at Pau, but in the village cabarets. It is much in request, and is largely bought up by the Bordeaux wine merchants, who mix it with thinner wines to give them richness and body. It is of an amber colour, is strong, heady, and delicious.

# CHAPTER VII

## OLORON

Iluro—Road over the port—The *beret*—Three parts to the town—
How the bishop got a cathedral—The porch—Ste. Croix—Bish-
op Roussel—Frightened to death—Escot—Independent Repub-
lic—Emigration—Sarrance—The *Heptameron*—Accous—Story of
Loustaunau—Osse—Urdos, the French Gibraltar—Mauleon—
Espadrillos.

OLORON is the ancient Iluro, in Gallo-Roman times one of the twelve cities of
Novempopulania, and of importance as the key to the passage of the Pyrenees by the Val d'Aspe over the Somport.

The Roman road branched off from the Via Aurelia at Lescar, crossed the Gave
de Pau, and struck direct for Oloron, where, doubtless, soldiers and merchants
and travellers in general rested before undertaking the passage of the mountains.
The Roman road, after crossing the chain, descended to the plains, and ran straight
as a bird-line for Saragossa. At Escot a Latin inscription remains, cut in the rock by
the wayside, commemorating the remaking of the road under the direction of one,
Valerius Vernus.

Oloron is a busy town, carrying on the manufacture of the *beret*, the tam-o'-
shanter, wherewith every Basque and Béarnais covers his head.

The town is prettily situated at the junction of the Gave d'Aspe and the Gave
d'Ossau, which divide it into three parts. One, Ste. Marie, was for long the communal centre and the residence of the bishops of Oloron. The old feudal city is
staged up a hill between the two rivers. In it is the church of Ste. Croix, built in
1080 by the Viscount Centule IV. Centule had married a distant cousin, Gisela. But
he coveted the fair lands of Bigorre, to which Beatrix, daughter of Count Bernard
II, was the heiress.

Amatus, Bishop of Oloron and the papal legate, was in want of a cathedral; so
they put their heads together, and Amatus undertook to obtain the annulling of
the marriage with Gisela by Pope Gregory VII. The Pope wanted money, Centule
wanted Bigorre, and Amatus a cathedral. Gregory made no difficulties, so Gisela
was repudiated, and sent to end her days in a convent, as though she were the
guilty party. Amatus was paid for his help in this scandalous job by being given a
cathedral, and Centule, in the exuberance of his delight at becoming possessed of
the rich heiress, built as well the church of Ste. Croix.

It was easy for any man with means in those days to wriggle out of an union that was inconvenient. The Popes had drawn up a catalogue of relationships within which degrees marriage was prohibited, unless a dispensation had been procured *argent comptant*. Kinship to the seventh degree, affinity as well as consanguinity, could be pleaded. Spiritual relationship through sponsorship at the font also served. Right or wrong in the matter was not considered. It was a contrivance of the Papacy for extortion of money.

The church of Ste. Marie is the ancient cathedral. The most ancient portions belong to the eleventh century. Externally it is not a striking edifice; nevertheless it is one of the most curious in the South, and has just one splendid feature— the sculptured porch, which is the basement of an enormous and massive tower, pierced by arches. Beneath this is a beautiful portal, round-headed, containing a double entrance, the doorways parted by a pillar. The sculpture of tympanum and archivolt are excellent for their period. A man once caught, plucked, and cooked a nightingale. With such a voice it ought to be excellent eating, he argued. But when he set his teeth in it, his judgment on the nightingale was, "Vox et præterea nihil." So, with such a throat one might reckon on a magnificent interior, but within the church responds not at all to the conceptions raised by the portal, and answers little to the idea formed of a cathedral.

But the diocese of Oloron was one of the poorest in all France, and was just half the value of that of Lescar.

The quarter of Ste. Croix has narrow streets, with old houses, some Romanesque, some Gothic, and others Renaissance. It had been cramped within its walls, and could expand upwards only. Now the fortifications have been demolished, and but a single flanking tower remains.

The church is remarkable only for its Byzantine cupola. In many points it recalls the Romanesque structures of Auvergne. Anciently the only access to the nave was through a richly ornamented door at the side. The western entrance is a modern addition.

The third quarter of Oloron is modern, bright, and cheerful, but uninteresting. In this quarter some houses bear the escutcheons of foreign powers, for three states speaking Spanish have their vice-consuls here—Spain, that entertains active relations with the valleys of Ossau and Aspe; and the Argentine and Uruguay republics, that are draining Béarn of so many of its natives for settlers. Moreover, Oloron is the principal centre for the making of the *beret*, as already said, also of bright-coloured handkerchiefs much affected by Spanish women in the New as in the Old World.

Oloron was a bishopric as early as 506. Marguerite de Valois, Queen of Navarre, appointed to it Roussel, the reformer, who began as a disciple of Calvin, and finished by entering into unseemly wrangling with him over some petty question in theology in a series of acrimonious letters. Marguerite had to interfere, and entreat both to cease their scurrility as an offence to religion. Roussel, as bishop, did his utmost to detach the people from their ancient faith, which he had sworn to maintain when consecrated, but which at the very moment when he took oath he had resolved on overthrowing.

He was preaching one day at Mauleon, assailing Catholic doctrine with vehemence. A gentleman named Matye was present, and unable to endure this without a protest, and being armed with an axe, struck at the slim pedestal of the pulpit with the butt-end, and with such force as to send Roussel a bound into the air. When he came down, again descended the axe, sending the bishop another leap, like a pea on a drum. Roussel's nerves were so shaken that he fled the church, and galloped off to a Pyrenean watering-place, there to recover the shock. But instead of recovering he died, 1549. A suit was brought against Matye in the Parliament at Bordeaux, for having frightened the bishop into his grave; but nothing came of it.

Under Jeanne d'Albret the bishopric was suppressed; however, a bishop was appointed in 1599. Oloron ceased to be an episcopal seat at the Revolution.

The Val d'Aspe begins at Escot. At the foot of the mountain of Narpayt stands up a rocky needle, named after S. Nicolas, separated from the road by a belt of tillage. From this point the valley narrows; a bridge crosses the river, over which runs the road to the Val d'Ossau. Pinnacles of rock and bare precipices pierced with caves border the Gave, that flows between the green lips of rich pastures. A fine peak, the Trône-du-Roi, stands up on the left bank. For the most part the mountain slopes are bare, growing nothing but box shrubs, and yet at one time hence came the tall pines that furnished the navy of France with masts. They were improvidently hewn down, and floated in rafts to Bayonne, and no thought was given to replanting, so that they were completely exhausted in 1780.

At Sarrance the valley expands. The village borders a sweep of the Gave, under the Signal de Sarrance, rising to the height of 4210 feet, cleft by a ravine well wooded, and with sweet green pastures. To the south is another peak, clothed in forest, rising to 4380 feet.

The Val d'Aspe formed one of those independent commonwealths of which in the Middle Ages there were so many in the Pyrenees. It was under the suzerainty of the viscounts of Béarn, but enjoyed complete self-government. In 1477 the Procureur-Général of Béarn claimed the forests as the property of the viscount, but the inhabitants protested that the Val d'Aspe existed before the viscounty had been constituted. The case was tried in the court at Pau, and judgment was given in favour of the little republic. The Aspois always were proud and independent. But unhappily a fever for emigration to South America has set in and has depopulated the valley seriously. In 1862 the inhabitants numbered 11,368, but in 1901 they had fallen to 7977. And this is not due to poverty, for there is not a beggar to be found in the valley.

Sarrance takes its name from the situation—*sarrada* in Béarnais is "narrow" and *ance* is a "passage." A bridge wreathed with ivy spans the stream, near a chapel. A terrace shaded with plane trees has its walls ablaze with snap-dragon, sprouting out of every crevice. From the chapel a stair leads down to the riverside, where is a niche containing a statue of the Virgin and Child, indicating the spot where, according to tradition, the image of N. D. de Sarrance was found.

The old monastery stands on an elevation at the southern extremity of the village. There is a little grass-grown square with a fountain in it. On one side of the square are untenanted houses, formerly guest-rooms of the convent; on the other is the monastery with its church. This latter is of no interest, as the old church, considered to be the finest in Béarn, was completely destroyed by the Calvinists. The tower is absolutely hideous. In a side chapel is a rude black Madonna, an object of superstitious devotion.

It was here that Marguerite, sister of Francis I and Queen of Navarre, composed her *Heptameron*. This is what she says in the introduction:—

> "On the first day of September, when the baths of the Pyrenees begin to have their virtue, several persons—some of France, some of Spain, and others from elsewhere—were united at Cauterets, the marvellous waters of which have cured sick who were given up by the doctors. When the party was about to separate it was found that the floods were out so that there was no reaching Tarbes. So, having halted awhile at the Abbey of Saint Savin, the whole company met again at the monastery of Notre Dame de Sarrance, in Béarn. In order to reach Pau it was necessary that the bridge over the Gave should be repaired, and this occupied ten days. In order to relieve the tedium of our stay in the convent of monks, the company arranged a time-table for proceedings. In the morning we met in the rooms of the Lady Oysille, the eldest present. An hour was spent in reading the sacred Scriptures. Then we heard Mass. At ten o'clock came dinner; after that every one retired to his or her chamber about their own affairs. At noon no one failed to go to the beautiful meadow, by the side of the Gave, where the trees are so covered with foliage that the sun cannot pierce through nor take the freshness out of the air. There, seated at our ease, every one relates tales, either true or invented to amuse, as did Boccaccio. At four o'clock the merry tales are interrupted in order that we may pray; and no one fails devoutly to attend vespers."

There are certain points to be noted in this. In the first place, neither here nor anywhere else, does the Queen let fall a word by which one can see that she appreciated the beauty of the mountain scenery through which she travelled. Yet the localities for some of her tales are Cauterets, Sarrance, Odos, and Pau.

In the next place, the stories that these ladies told, and which the Queen of Navarre collected, are so indecent, and contain such foul expressions, that we are amazed to think that any woman, however corrupt may have been the times, should not blush to hear, and be ashamed to write them down.

And lastly, what a jumble of occupations! Bible-reading in the morning, obscene stories in the evening, and then—prayers.

The meadow is there still, and one may sit in it now as then; but now it is with thoughts of thankfulness on the change that has been accomplished in manners and in sense of decency. A little above Sarrance, on the east, opens the entrance to a cirque. The southern wall, which is most precipitous, supports a plateau strangely regular in form, like a cone with its head sliced off, 4700 feet high. On the right bank of the Gave opposite Bedous are four little heights, two pointed, one rounded, the other flattened at top. They are eruptive dykes of ophite, a rock somewhat abundant in this valley.

Bedous is now the most considerable place in the valley, much more busy and fuller of inhabitants than the cantonal capital Accous.

At Accous is an obelisk erected to the memory of the Béarnais poet, Despourrins (1690–1759), who was a native of the place.

One day an English general, crossing from Spain and descending the Val d'Aspe, encountered a little shepherd boy with quick eye and intelligent face, whom he questioned about objects of interest in the neighbourhood. Pleased with the lad, he invited him to enter his service as valet, and the youth, who had a rough time at home, without more ado clambered on to the box to travel to distant and unknown regions. This little shepherd was called Loustaunau, and he followed the officer to India. When his master died he sought to make his fortune by starting a house of commerce in the territory of the Mogul. Then war broke out between the Emperor of Delhi and the Nabob of Lahore.

Chancing to witness a battle between them from an eminence, Loustaunau remarked to a Banian that the disposition of the Mogul army was faulty. "If," said he, "I had the command of 1200 horsemen, and had a couple of cannon, I would soon determine the battle." What he had said was reported to the Great Mogul, who at once gave him what he desired. The Béarnais jumped on the back of a horse, took the command of a troop, and ranged it behind a bit of rising ground, placed his guns where he could rake the enemy, and charged the centre of the enemy, and broke it, whilst his cannon pounded the troops of the Nabob. The victory was complete.

Loustaunau was richly rewarded, and given a princess to wife, by whom he had several children. In a battle fought against the Maharattas he lost his left hand, and had it replaced by one of silver.

A quarter of a century had elapsed since he left the Pyrenees; he had amassed a fortune, and a longing came over him to revisit his native valley. Accordingly he returned to France and invested his money in factories, and in châteaux that he purchased within Béarn and in Bigorre.

But disaster came. His factories were burnt by the Spaniards, and his fortune melted away. He meditated a return to India, and started for the East. But unhappily he made the acquaintance of Lady Hester Stanhope, who gained complete possession of his mind. Forgetting the needs of his family, and the object of his journey, he stayed with her at the foot of Lebanon, where he led the life of a prophet and *illuminé*. Lamartine met him there, and there he died. He had left his children at Tarbes. Three of his daughters were alive in 1860, living in poverty, maintaining themselves by needlework, and looking back sadly on their early days as a dream out of the *Arabian Nights*.

The village of Osse, planted between strangely shaped hills of ophite, facing the south, is the last refuge of Protestantism in the valley. The population is 560, the majority of whom are Calvinists, and they maintain a pastor and have a "Temple."

Urdos, the Forum Ligneum of the Ancients, is the last town in France. The fortress commanding the pass is hewn in the natural rock, in a buttress of the mountains rising in stages from the road to the height of 500 feet. Externally the mountain gives little token of what it is, honeycombed with galleries, batteries, stairs. A façade of masonry battlemented and flanked by turrets at the foot of the rock, and a few loopholes and embrasures for cannon, pierced in the face of the cliff, are all that show that this is a French Gibraltar, capable of containing a garrison of 3000 men.

Mauleon, the ancient capital of the little viscounty of Soule, that passed to Béarn, is prettily situated on the banks of the Saison, at the foot of a hill that is crowned by a castle reached by a bridge over the moat or chasm artificially cut in the rock.

The huge roofs of the Hôtel d'Andurrain form the hat to a Renaissance building.

Mauleon, after remaining stagnant for centuries, has begun to stir, and has become the centre of manufacture of the espadrillos, or shoe with canvas top and twisted rope sole, so much in use in the Pyrenees and in Spain.

A dozen years ago the whole population of Mauleon was a thousand, and now two thousand men and five hundred women are engaged in the factories; for in Senegal the natives have all at once taken a fancy to the espadrillos, and the fashion is spreading from Senegal; there is no saying where it may end in wide Africa.

The workmen and women employed are not, however, Basques or Béarnais, but are Spaniards. Here is trade, and that a growing trade, in their midst, and the native population shrug their shoulders, leave it to foreigners to carry on, and depart for South America in shoals.

# CHAPTER VIII

## THE VAL D'OSSAU

The gap of the Val d'Ossau—Gan—Original course of the Gave—
Buzy—Gorges de Germe—Arudy—Destruction of forests—
Boxwood—Cromlechs—Bielle—Independence of the Republic
of Ossau—Costume—Dances—Laruns—Eaux Chaudes—Beg-
gary—Gabas—Eaux Bonnes—Death of the Rev. Merton Smith.

LOOKING south from the terrace at Pau one sees a noble portal in the mountain
chain apparently leading to the roots of the Pic du Midi d'Ossau. But it is a
mistake to suppose that the drainage of those snowy crests can descend at once
into the Gave at one's feet. Between the Val d'Ossau and that of the Gave de Pau a
region of hills intervenes. Moreover, the valley that gapes does not lead to the foot
of that noble pyramid. It leads to Laruns only, and there the broad trough ends,
and above that the Gave descends through a cleft painfully cut through intervening strata.

On the railway from Pau to Laruns the first station is at Gan. In this village, as
I remember it fifty years ago, there were but two houses with glass windows, the
parsonage and a Renaissance dwelling that belonged to Corisande d'Andouins,
one of the many mistresses of Henri Quatre. When cold weather arrived, then the
peasants closed their shutters, perforated with a few holes—a heart, a cross, an
S—and through this opening derived their light. The train clambers up the heights
past Buzy, and then all at once bursts on the sight the broad Val d'Ossau—rich,
fertile, smiling with maize and vines, and villages, and beyond the Pic du Midi.
The Gave d'Ossau descending from the snowy range on the frontier of Spain ran
due north, as if to reach Pau in one direct channel, but was arrested by the hills,
and turned along the depression at Buzy and turned westward where now goes
the branch line to Oloron. But dissatisfied with this bed, it tore at the rocks near
Arudy, and sawed for itself the Gorges de Germe, a savage ravine, very tortuous,
cut through hills covered with woods. The abandoned bed was taken possession
of by man. It lies at a lower level than the actual channel, and the river must have
been deflected by immense piles of rubbish brought down from the mountains. At
the west end of the church at Buzy may be seen a huge boulder rounded by rolling,
used as the pedestal to the village cross. The ancient channel furnishes turf for fuel,
and in it are grown beds of rank bulrushes.

Beyond Buzy, on the way to Arudy, is a dolmen already referred to, but not on
its original site. When the road was altered it was removed and re-erected.

The train halts again at Arudy, only interesting for the view, and for the tomb of a bishop, and a fifteenth-century church with a reredos.

The Val d'Ossau in its lower parts is a wreck. The mountain spurs on each side were once clothed with magnificent forests of pine.

"The Pyrenees," says Michelet, "exhibit to us the disappearance of the Old World. Antiquity is no more, the Middle Age is at the point of death. The mountains themselves, strange as it may seem, have their very existence attacked. The fleshless peaks reveal the fact that they are in their senile decay. It is not that they have failed to withstand the blows of the storm, it is man who has assisted in their ruin from below. That deep girdle of forests which veiled the nakedness of the ancient mother, has been plucked away by man. The vegetable soil, which the herbage retained on the slopes, is now carried below by the waters. The rock stands up bare; chapped, exfoliated by the glare of the sun, by the tooth of frost, undermined by the melting snow carried down by avalanches. In the place of succulent pastures nothing remains but a dry and ruined soil. The agriculturist who has driven away the hunter, gains nothing thereby. The water which formerly trickled down gently into the valley athwart pastures and forests, now roars down in devastating torrents, and covers the fields with the ruins it has made. A vast number of hamlets in the high valleys have been abandoned, through lack of fuel, and the inhabitants take refuge in the lowlands, flying from the results of their own improvidence.

"In 1673 the mischief done caused alarm. Orders were issued by Government that every inhabitant should annually plant at once one tree in the domain, and two in the communal lands. In 1669 and 1756 and still later new regulations made give evidence to the panic caused by the progress of the evil. But, at the Revolution, every barrier gave way, the population being poor, set to work to enrich itself by completing the destruction of the forests. They climbed, axe and firebrand in hand, to the nests of the eagles, they swung over abysses, hacking and destroying. Trees were sacrificed to the most trivial needs. Two pines were cut down to make one pair of sabots. At the same time the sheep and goats, multiplying, fell on the forests, gnawed the trunks, devoured the young trees, destroyed the shrubs, killed the future. The goat above all, that most destructive of all creatures, and the most daring of all, introduced a reign of terror into the mountains. That was not one of the least of the labours of Bonaparte, when he set to work to control the ravages of this beast. In 1813 the number of goats had been reduced to a tenth of the number that they had been in the year X. But he was not powerful enough to put a finish to the war against Nature."

The pines have been succeeded by boxwood that brings in a certain revenue. It is not cut till the stem has attained a girth of three inches; but it would be well if it were allowed to reach a girth of four or five, as it serves as a valuable cover for young pines where attempts are made to replant. The box never grows very high, but some bushes arrive at the height of fifteen feet, and a girth of trunk of fifteen inches. The wood is made use of for the turning the beads of the rosaries, made at Betharam, Saumur, and Lalouvesc in the Boutières. It cannot be utilized till the stem has arrived at the diameter of a two-franc piece. In 1892 the boxwood from Laruns sold for 3185 francs, but in 1895 for not more than a thousand francs.

At Louvie Juxon and above Bielle and Bilhères, near the entrance of Benon, are what the French call cromlechs, circles of stones, supposed to be prehistoric monuments. These are, however, very small, the stones insignificant, and the shepherds of the district state that precisely similar stones are planted by themselves about temporary huts of branches and turf that they erect when obliged to spend nights as well as days on the mountain.

Bielle was the ancient capital of Ossau. This valley was a republic under the suzerainty of the viscounts of Béarn. It governed itself, and had its own courts of justice, and absolutely refused to suffer the soldiers of the viscount to enter their little republic. He himself was not recognized till he had sworn to respect its rights and privileges as contained in the ancient *fors*.

At the present day a candidate for election to the Assembly addresses the electors always as "Messieurs d'Ossau." It was by this title that the princes of Béarn spoke to them. In Ossau there were no nobles; there was no appeal from the judgment of their court to Viscount of Béarn or to the King of France.

The constitution of former days still exists in regard to communal property. This is divided into two categories: the particular mountains belonging to each separate commune, and the general mountains in the canton of Laruns pertain to a syndicate formed of representatives of seventeen parishes. In addition the Ossalois own the lande of Pont-long, of which I have already spoken. In recognition of their having ceded to Gaston Phœbus, or before him to the first viscount who built a castle at Pau, sufficient ground for his castle and park, they obtained the privilege to sit at table with their viscounts.

The valley bottom is fertile, but tillage is pursued only there. Cattle and sheep spend the summer on the high pastures, and the sheep are driven in winter to the Pont-long.

Costume is fast disappearing. On Sunday at Bielle and Laruns may be seen the old women still wearing their scarlet *capulets* lined with silk and edged with black velvet; the black corset is faced on the breast with crimson silk. A woollen skirt descends in symmetrical folds to a little way below the calf; the leg is clothed in white stockings, unfooted, that widen over the foot. The male costume is quite gone. The only part retained is the *beret*. It is a pity, for the costume was admirably adapted to the men's life in the mountains. The thick, red, brown, and white jackets, waistcoats, and breeches were of home make and handloom weaving, from the wool of their own sheep, and lasted for years without becoming threadbare.

Even the musical instruments general when there was a dance have gone, the *tambouri* of six strings, struck by a fiddlestick, whilst a piper played a flageolet of four holes, from which he could draw six or seven notes. The great fête at Laruns is on 15 August, and if the charm of this is gone with the abandonment of the pretty costumes, it is still an animated and gay scene.

At Laruns the broad trough of the Val d'Ossau comes abruptly to an end. Here from the left comes down the Valentin of Eaux Bonnes in a series of cascades, the drainage of the snows of the noble mountains at the head of the Val d'Azun, where they spill westward. But the Gave d'Ossau, that has its source under the Pic du Midi, has sawn for itself a way through rocks, and gushes forth through a notable chasm directly above Laruns. This, the ravine in which lies the thermal establishment of Eaux Chaudes, is by far the most interesting, it gives access to the elevated village of Gabas, and to the Col d'Aneou, by which one can pass into Spain. All the upper part of the course of the Gave is of surpassing beauty, and the Alpine pastures yield rich spoil to the botanist, owing to the variety of geological formation, limestone, schist, granite, and porphyry.

The road to Eaux Chaudes, made in 1847, has been in part superseded by one made later, but for pedestrians it is the most pleasant, as it is the shortest. It enters the Gorge du Hourat, and runs the whole way between precipitous walls of rock, beside the torrent which roars down with tremendous velocity. At one point the road has had to be built up against the side of the precipice as a bridge, to allow a torrent, which falls from a height of several hundred feet, to pass under it, and so join the Gave, the river that has formed the cleft of the valley. At Eaux Chaudes there is little space; in winter hardly any sun, in summer there is a sense of oppression from the contraction of the mountains and the exclusion of distant view. But many delightful excursions may be made from it. Eaux Chaudes owes its origin to Henri Quatre, who required his chancellor, the Bishop of Oloron, to build there an establishment for one of Henri's many mistresses, la Fousseuse, that she might there drink the waters.

The sturdy independence and self-respect of the peasantry of Ossau have been broken down sadly by the influx of visitors. Mr. Blackburn observes truly enough:—

> "It is said that English visitors have completely demoralized the Valley of Chamounix, and that the *curés* are in despair; but whatever sins we have committed in Switzerland, the French people have done worse, the difference between the two nations being this, that the latter enjoy indiscriminate almsgiving, and we do not. The result in this valley is demoralizing to an extent that would scarcely be credited excepting by eye-witnesses. As we drive along we see the peasantry leaving their work in the fields at the sound of approaching wheels, and crouching at the roadside in attitudes of pain and misery; girls and boys leave their play to follow the carriages, and whine for *quelquechose*; crops are half-gathered, and work of all kinds is neglected during the season of the sous; the cry is everywhere, 'Give, give!'

"A girl of sixteen, well dressed and evidently well-to-do, comes up with a bouquet of wild flowers; she asks ten sous for it (about the wages of a day's work), but will take no less; and on receiving the money will immediately ask for the bouquet back again, to sell to some one else.

"And this is not all, for those of the inhabitants who have not brought up their children to the liberal profession of begging, have invented another ingenious and profitable mode of life, that of turning the cascades in the neighbourhood into penny peep-shows, shutting them off so that they can only be approached by a wicket gate kept by one of themselves."[7]

One of the pleasantest short walks is to the Grotte des Eaux Chaudes, passing before a little cave from which issues a stream that proceeds at once to dash headlong down the crags into the Gave. Beyond this is the large cave opening in the face of a cliff. This grotto is traversed by a stream which may be crossed by a bridge of wood to where, in the depth of the cave, it leaps down out of a fissure in the wall in a cascade. It is probably fed by the drainage of the Plateau d'Anouillas, where the water descending from the Pic de Gers disappears. When the stream has left the cavern it again dives underground, and flows below the rocks in stages that descend to the bottom of the valley, and reappears only just before it enters the Gave. But the finest excursion from Eaux Chaudes is to Bious-Oumettes, a plateau whence a superb view is obtained of the Pic du Midi d'Ossau. This peak is 9800 feet high, of porphyry and granite, cleft by a profound vertical fissure, and is perhaps the finest, certainly the quaintest, of the Pyrenean mountains.

Gabas, the last village on the French side of the chain, is a halting-place for travellers and for muleteers conveying goods from Spain. It is a cantonment of custom-house officers; and here may be seen picturesque groups of shepherds in their fleecy jackets, Spaniards in their richly-coloured blankets, and the uniformed douaniers. The path leading to the plateau is lined with fir trees, but on all sides may be seen the ravages of fire, the axe, and winter storm, in charred stumps, twisted or hewn-down trunks, thrown down to be floated by the Gave through its stages to the lower valley.

The distance from Laruns to Eaux Bonnes is much the same as it is to Eaux Chaudes. On reaching the former watering-place—"Je comptais trouver ici la campagne," wrote M. Taine. "Je rencontre une rue de Paris et les promenades du Bois de Boulogne!" It is a place of big hotels, baths, pensions, shops where toys, trinkets, and trumpery are displayed for sale, and, of course, a casino.

"In whichever direction we turn," says Mr. Blackburn, "there are houses built into and often forming part of the mountain, resting on ledges of rock, like to eyries; but so cleverly contrived is the arrangement of the place, so admirably has space been economized, that there is a feeling of freedom about it, quite inconsistent with living in a bird's nest.

[7] Blackburn (H.), *The Pyrenees*. London, 1867.

"Thus, with the mountains several thousand feet above our heads, and the Val d'Ossau stretching away for many miles at our feet, with rocks overhanging and tree-tops waving, through which we can see the blue sky—with scarcely a foot of level ground anywhere, save the Promenade Horizontale, with cascades and waterfalls at our windows, we find ourselves as comfortably and luxuriously housed as in any modern city."

Speaking of the church Taine says: "Cette église est une boïte ronde, en pierre et plâtre, faite pour cinquante personnes, ou l'on en met deux cents." This box of stone and plaster has disappeared to make room for one of more suitable dimensions in what is caricature of Romanesque.

There is a good carriage road from Eaux Bonnes over a fine pass into the Val d'Aruns and to Argelez. The chief excursion is to the Pic de Gers, 8570 feet high.

The Eaux Bonnes springs have been known for centuries. The Béarnais soldiers wounded in the battle of Pavia in 1525, were sent here to be healed; and for some time after that the springs went by the name of les Eaux d'arquebusades. But they owe their modern renown to the works of Théophile Bordeu. There are seven sources of sulphurated waters, which are good for throat disorders, wounds, sores, and morbid maladies.

The Eaux Bonnes was the scene of a sad accident in 1883, that happened to the Rev. Merton Smith, vicar of Plympton S. Mary, in Devonshire. He had gone to the Pyrenees for his month's holiday, and visited this watering-place. On 8 August he left his hotel at 3 p.m., in his usual spirits, to walk to Eaux Chaudes, and never returned. He had intended to return the same evening.

Nothing could be heard of him. Inquiries were made in all directions, search parties were organized; he could nowhere be found. Months passed, and his disappearance remained unexplained. The Bishop of Exeter was in perplexity what to do. He could not institute to the living without certain knowledge that Mr. Merton Smith was dead, and this knowledge could not be obtained.

Uncharitable tongues wagged. Some said that he had fallen a victim to the fascinations of a Pyrenean shepherdess, and that he was picking edelweiss and playing a flute on some high Alp to the delectation of the damsel. Some said that he had been captured by Roman Catholics and interned in a monastery. Some said that he had been murdered by Ossau mountaineers for the sake of his money.

Not till eighteen months after his disappearance was the mystery cleared up. His body was found on the mountainside, buried among thick bushes of box that had concealed it. He had apparently been stooping to pick a flower and had fallen over a precipice and been killed instantaneously. His watch and purse were intact. It was by chance only that a woodcutter discovered the remains whilst clearing the boxwood.

# CHAPTER IX

## LOURDES

Line from Lourdes turns north—Argelez glacier—The Lavedan—
The Seven Valleys—Lourdes of old—The castle—Held by the
English—Attacked by the Duke of Anjou—Held by Saracens—
Besieged by Charlemagne—The Grotto—Bernadette Soubirous—The *curé* Ader—The apparition expected—The vision—Repeated—Crowds attend Bernadette—The spring—Mud—Price
of the water—Je suis l'Immaculée Conception—Explanation—
Compromising pamphlet suppressed—The Abbé Ader removed—La Salette—Similar visions seen by Huguenots—Doctor
Dozous—The Empress and Prince Imperial—The Emperor pa-
tronizes the Grotto—Disappearance of documents—Laserre—His
book a romance—The Jesuit Cros exposes it—The water of the
spring—Drawn from the Gave—The Bishop's commission—Pius
IX appoints a festival in honour of the apparition—Removal of
Bernadette to Nevers—Her brother refused permission to see
her—Forces his way in—Last scene—The procession—Where the
natural ends and the supernatural begins—No guarantee that the
cures are permanent.

As the train sweeps into the station at Lourdes, on the right side, a few feet
above the Gave, may be seen the twinkling lights of the Grotto of Massabielle,
about which presently.

From the station of Lourdes the line turns north to Tarbes and Toulouse, along
what was the ancient course of the Gave, a course that is patent to the eye, till the
Argelez glacier threw up a barrier of morraine that deflected the river, and sent it
careering to the west.

Lourdes stands at the entrance to and is the key to the Lavedan, so called
from *abies*, the pines that once clothed the mountain-sides. The Lavedan is fertile.
It is the trunk whence branch out numerous valleys that run up to the roots of the
mountains and receive their water. But Lavedan formed a republic of seven of
these valleys—Batsouriguère, Castelloubon (through which flows the Nès), Es-
trom de Salles, Azun, Saint Savin, Devantaïgue, and Barèges.

The Basilica, Lourdes

"Count" Henri Russell-Killough, in his *Fortnight Among the Pyrenees*, describes the Lavedan.

> "Vine, fig trees, cherry trees, poplars, willows, elms, walnuts, maize, all meet here, and vegetation rises nearly to the tops of the mountains. On a fine day the whole thing looks like a modern Eden."

I remember Lourdes before it was "invented" by Bernadette Soubirous and the *curé* Peyramale. It was a dead place, with narrow streets, very dirty, clustered about the rock on which stands the castle. Although the true capital of the Lavedan, the market for all the produce of the Seven Valleys, yet it seemed to be tenanted only by beggars.

Lourdes commands the roads which here unite from Argelez, Tarbes, Pau, and Bagnères. It was a place of great military importance, and was the last stronghold in Guyenne retained by the English. It did not surrender till 1418. The castle had been given to the English by the French king John as part of his ransom, in conformity with the Treaty of Bretigny, 1360, when the towns and barons of Gascony were required to swear allegiance to the Black Prince, as representative of the English king. After awhile the country rose in revolt, exasperated by the exactions of the English, and the Duke of Anjou, brother of Charles V, supported the Bigorriens.

After that all the plain had been recovered by the French, nothing remained to the English but the Castle of Lourdes, the Lavedan to Barèges, far removed from their base at Bayonne. The Duke of Anjou took the town easily, as it was defended merely by a pallisade, but could not capture the castle, which bade defiance to him during six weeks. He vainly endeavoured to buy the governor, and was forced to retire discomfited. The attempt made by Gaston Phœbus and the murder of Pierre Arnaut de Béarn by him has been already related.

But the castle has an earlier history. It is supposed to have been a Roman castrum. It was occupied by the Saracens, who retained it after their defeats at Poitiers and Tarbes, till the reign of Charlemagne. He besieged it. According to legend an eagle, flying above the highest tower of the castle, dropped a fish on the battlement at a spot still called Pierre de l'Aigle. Thereupon the Moorish commandant Mirad sent a messenger to Charlemagne to say that he might understand how vain were his expectations of reducing the garrison by famine, as the Prophet himself provided it with food.

Charlemagne did not accept this view of the incident, and continued the investment till the castle surrendered. The Bishop of Le Puy had promised Charles the aid of Our Lady of Puy, if properly considered. "Give her something," said he, "if it be but a tuft of grass from the castle wall."

Mirad and the garrison put wisps of hay about the points of their lances, in token of submission. Then Charles bade the bishop open his lap and threw into it all the hay from the spear-heads. This was in 778.

In the eighteenth century the castle (Mirabel is its name) was converted into a state prison, and it became the Bastille of Gascony. Since the empire it has served as a barrack for a small garrison.

But it is not the castle that now attracts visitors to Lourdes, but the Grotto of Massabiel, the story of which must be told briefly.

Bernadette Soubirous was the daughter of a drunken, dishonest miller, who had lost his mill through speculation, and had been imprisoned. He and his family were living as pensioners on the Abbé Peyramale, *curé* of Lourdes, in a wretched cottage in a back street—five persons huddled into one room. Bernarde, afterwards called Bernadette, was an under-sized, ill-fed, unhealthy child of limited intelligence and utterly uneducated. For some reason never explained she was sent to Bartrès, where she was employed in tending sheep. There she attracted the attention of the *curé* Ader, who repeatedly declared his conviction that she was just the sort of person to be vouchsafed a vision like that seen by the shepherd children of La Salette.

At the end of January, 1858, the Abbé Ader sent Bernadette, then aged fourteen, back to Lourdes, where she was at once taken in hand by one of the *vicaires* of the place, the Abbé Pomian, who became her confessor and director.

Singularly, perhaps significantly, on 28 December, 1857, M. Falconnet, *procureur général* at Lourdes deemed it expedient to send a report to the *procureur impériale* at Pau, that something was brewing in the place. This is his letter:—

> "I have been informed that manifestations of a supernatural character and of a miraculous aspect are being prepared for the end of this year. I would advise you to take measures that the facts should be closely watched. I must know the details so as to be aware under what articles of the penal code prosecution is possible. I fear that little help can be gained from the administration civil or religious. Our duty is to do all in our power to stop the recurrence of such scandals as those of La Salette, the more so as the religious intrigue is a means of hiding one that is political."

It is evident from this letter that something was expected at Lourdes. The magistrate was mistaken only as to when it would take place, which was forty-five days after this letter was written. On 11 February, 1858, a cold day, Bernadette was dispatched along with her younger sister, Marie, and a companion, Jeanne, to collect sticks for fuel beside the Gave, under the rock of Massabielle. Bernadette suffered from asthma, had a bad cough, and scrofulous sores on her head. To reach their destination a small stream had to be crossed. Marie and Jeanne slipped off their sabots and went through the water, which was so cold that it made them cry out. Bernadette stopped to remove her wooden shoes and thick stockings. Beyond the stream rose a limestone rock with a cave in the face, the floor of which was level with the bank of the Gave. An oval opening above it allowed light to penetrate from aloft into the recesses of the grotto. At the entrance to this hole grew a rose bush.

Whilst stooping to take off her stockings, the rush of blood to her head made the child fancy that she heard a sound as of wind, and looking up she imagined that she saw a light in the upper hole, and a lady standing in it, robed in white, wearing a blue sash, a veil over her head, with a rosary in one hand, and golden roses on her feet.

To her excited fancy it seemed that the apparition smiled and made the sign of Redemption with the cross of the rosary. Bernadette uttered an exclamation, traversed the stream, told her companions what she had seen, and asked them if they observed the lady. "No," they replied, "we have seen nothing." Then Bernadette said, "No more did I, either."

On their return to Lourdes, Marie told her mother what Bernadette had stated, and Mme. Soubirous treated it as idle fancy.

The matter, however, was noised about and provoked attention, the more so as from the magistrate's letter we are made aware that something of the sort was expected in the place. On Sunday, 14 February, a party accompanied the girl to the spot; whereupon she knelt down, fell into an ecstasy, and declared that she again saw the apparition. All Lourdes was now stirred. Three ladies next took Bernadette in hand, and were almost constantly in attendance on her—Mme. Millet, Mlle. Peyret, and Mlle. Pène, sister of one of the curates of Lourdes. In their presence Bernadette had other visions. Peasants now came in crowds, surrounded the girl, and accompanied her on each expedition to the grotto. At the suggestion of her confessor she put questions to the figure, and it replied, so Bernadette asserted, enjoining penance, and the building of a chapel on the spot.

One day "Madame," said the child, "if you have something to communicate to me, have the goodness to write it down."

"There is no need for writing what I have to tell you," replied the mysterious lady; "but do me the favour of coming here during fifteen days."

On one occasion the apparition bade the girl go into the grotto, grub for water, wash in it, drink it, and eat a mouthful of grass.

> "The Grotto at this period," said Mlle. Lacrampe, who was present on this occasion, "had not the depth that it possesses now. Pebbles and sand were heaped up in it to a considerable height, so much so that one speedily reached a point where it was necessary to bend double to get further. Bernadette, after having raised her eyes to the niche, put her hand to her hood to arrange it, and lifted her gown a little so as not to soil it. Then she stooped to the earth, and when she raised her head and turned her face towards the apparition, I saw that her face was all smudged with dirty water."

Bernadette herself related:—

> "The lady told me to drink of the fountain and to wash in it. Not seeing any spring, I was going to the Gave, but she signed to me to enter the cave. I entered and saw only a little dirty water. I put my hand to it, but could collect none, so I scratched, and the water came, but it was muddy. Thrice I rejected it. Only on the fourth attempt could I swallow any."

The Jesuit father Cros says with regard to this exhibition: "Mademoiselle Lac-rampe se retira si défavorablement impressionée, qu'il a fallu des années et des miracles pour la convaincre." M. Estrade, receiver of indirect taxes, says with re-spect to this affair: "Je commerçais à être dérouté, et ne savais que penser de tout ceci."

Thus was the miraculous spring discovered, the water of which, or what is supposed to come from it, is sent throughout the world, a case of thirty bottles carriage paid to the station 7 fr. 45 c. One bottle, "franco à domicile," in France 1 fr. 80 c.

Now it is absolutely certain that the water was there before Bernadette Soubi-rous scratched till she reached it. The Abbé Richard, a geologist, says that it was there and it was known to be there by many individuals in Lourdes.

On 25 March Bernadette made her seventeenth visit to the grotto. The *curé* Peyramale had been at her repeatedly insisting that she should ask the apparition who and what she was.

Accordingly on this occasion she said: "Madam, kindly inform me who you are?"

Then the figure crossed its hands over the breast, lowered the eyes, and said: "Je suis l'Immaculée Conception, et je désire une chapelle ici."

It is deserving of notice that the apparition did not state that she was the Bless-ed Virgin, but that she was an abstraction, the manifestation in visible form of a dogma.

Now Bernadette had been subjected for some time to strong suggestion. She had been influenced by the Abbé Ader at Bartrès, who had announced that she was just the sort of person to be chosen by the Blessed Virgin to see her; then she had been under the direction of the *vicaire* Pomian, and the strong personality of the *curé* Peyramale, who could mould such a feeble creature as wax. I do not im-ply that they consciously provoked a fraud; far from it. I think that these clergy had made up their minds that Bernadette was a suitable subject to be favoured by a vision, and had let her understand what their opinion of her was. Indeed, the schoolmaster at Bartrès, in his simplicity, wrote as much in the *Guide du Pèlerin à Lourdes*. The fathers of Garaison, who "ran the show," to use a vulgar expression, were so alarmed at this revelation, that they brought up and destroyed every copy of the *Pèlerin* on which they could lay their hands. According to J. de Bonnefon, *Lourdes et ses tenanciers*:—

> "Somewhat later, the Abbé Ader, dissatisfied, neglected, for-gotten, was filled with scruples, and told everything."

What his authority for this statement is I do not know, but this is certain, that Ader was hurriedly removed from his *curé*, and sent hastily to the Benedic-tines, and kept in the abbey of Saint Benoît for two years, without occupation, but lodged and fed and entertained, not at his own cost. At the end of that time he was thought to be no longer dangerous, and was appointed *curé* of Oroix, a little place with not two hundred inhabitants, in a remote corner of the diocese, miles from every highroad. That Bernadette had heard of the apparition at La Salette is certain, even if she had not heard Ader liken her to one of those who saw that apparition, which took place in 1846, and was preached about and talked of everywhere. I spent a summer in a château in the valley of Argelez in 1850, and the *curé's* mind was full of it. He lent me a book concerning it, and became hot in defence of the veracity of the children.

Representations of the vision of La Salette were set up in churches—statues and pictures and stained glass. Bernadette was a constant attendant at church, and must have heard of this event.

Again, but three years previously, Pius IX had proclaimed the doctrine of the Immaculate Conception as *de fide*, and every pulpit was ringing with it. What it meant Bernadette did not know. But in her narrow, uncultivated mind it took form as a prime verity of the faith which was disputed by those who were weak in their belief—who were not good Catholics.

What could have been expected under such influences, but that if the child fancied she saw a vision, that vision would proclaim the doctrine recently promulgated. Can it for a moment be doubted that if she had heard the efficacy of a certain medicine vaunted, seen it everywhere advertised, had it urged on her from the pulpit and in the class and in the confessional, she would have heard the apparition say, "Je suis l'infallible pilule pink."

That Bernadette was an impostor cannot be admitted; no one who knew her, none even of those who disbelieved in the apparition, had any doubt on that score. But she was epileptic, hysterical, and subject to hallucinations. She was very different from Melanie and Maximin Mathieu of La Salette, whom the saintly *curé* d'Ars saw, and was at once convinced that they were liars. Very similar visions to that seen by Bernadette had been seen by Huguenots. In the spring of 1668, near Castres, a young shepherdess of La Capelle, aged ten, beheld an angel who forbade her going to Mass. The news spread through the country, and, just as at Lourdes, so at La Capelle, crowds assembled to see her in an ecstasy, and hear her converse with the angel, who bade her announce to all to avoid entering Catholic churches.

Roman Catholics would say that the girl was deceived by the devil, and that Bernadette's visions were from heaven. But in fact one was as genuinely a delusion as the other.

Unfortunately the case of Bernadette was not examined coolly and impartially. Very soon a doctor, Dozous, took up the cudgels for the miracle. Here is what the *procureur impériale* says of him, and from that one can judge of the worth of his evidence.

> "Doctor Dozous was formerly physician at the hospital of Lourdes, but was dismissed his post two years ago. He has resented this bitterly, I understand. Nor was he pleased that he was passed over and three of his confrères were nominated by the prefect to report on the physical and moral condition of Bernadette Soubirous. Be that as it may, he has made a change in his opinions since then. He did call these visions farces, now they are

something beyond the power of human nature to explain. On 7 April he was for the first time struck with a circumstance that had previously not struck him or any one else. Bernadette, during her ecstasy, held a lighted candle between her hands, and the flame licked her hands without burning them. Other spectators, quite as well situated as M. Dozous, assert that he saw incorrectly, or ill appreciated what he did see."

On 12 March, 1858, the Emperor Napoleon III demanded information relative to the affair of Lourdes. Somewhat later the Empress was at Biarritz, and had with her as attendant Mme. Bruat, who had just returned from Lourdes, bringing with her some of the grass that grows in the grotto. It fell out one night that the Prince Imperial was ill, and croup was feared. Mme. Bruat urged the application of the herb from Lourdes. The Emperor was roused, and in his presence the bit of dried grass was applied to the lips of the child, and he became easier.

The Emperor and Empress at once extended their protection to the grotto, and all serious examination into the matter was at an end. This was on 2 August. The consequences were immediately felt. None of the civil authorities at Tarbes or Lourdes dared thenceforth express doubts in the genuineness of the apparition. It had a further effect. There existed a good number of documents in the *dossier* at Tarbes relative to what had been going on at Lourdes, very candid accounts — perhaps too candid. One compromising packet disappeared, and was offered privately for sale to several persons. The police were at once set to work, and secured the stolen packet, which was *not* restored to its place, but totally and irretrievably disappeared.

In 1869 appeared Lasserre's book, *Notre Dame de Lourdes*, which had an enormous sale; it had reached its 126th edition in 1892. Henri Lasserre had been a journalist, and his paper, the *Contemporaine*, had utterly failed. He was in bad circumstances, when the bright idea struck him to puff Lourdes. He went there in August, 1867, and placed himself in the house of the *curé* Peyramale, and took in without criticism everything that he was told. He did more; he dressed up every incident fantastically, turned the story into a romance, giving details and conversations that could only have been obtained had he tracked Bernadette from day to day with a camera snap-shotting her, and with a note-book and pencil taking down everything heard in shorthand. He made no scruple to falsify facts which did not suit him, and he had his reward; the book sold with an unprecedented rapidity, and filled his pockets with gold. Now the Jesuit Cros also wrote about Lourdes; but his work, that appeared in 1901, while exposing many of Lasserre's falsehoods and exaggerations, had to be gone through and cut about by his superiors before that it was suffered to be published.

It causes some surprise, and it convinces some people that miraculous agency has worked in the grotto, in that so much water flows away from the taps supposed to discharge that which issues from the spring in the cave. This water is drawn off, evaporated, and sold in pastilles (big boxes, 2 francs; *bonbonnières*, 75 cents). But does it really come from the source pretended? The water of the cave is merely the dripping and sweating of the walls and the oozing up of infiltration of the Gave, that is little lower than the floor; but hence now issues a copious spring.

An experienced scientist of Bayonne managed to break through the wire netting at the end of the grotto that conceals the miraculous spring from the public, and to pour in sufficient fluorescine to discolour 10,000 litres of water. This would have revealed itself at the taps infallibly, had this latter supply come from the grotto. No discoloration, however, appeared. The gentleman who made this experiment wrote to the superior of the Fathers of the Grotto to inform him of the test he had applied. He received no answer. Then, in a second letter, published in the *Reveil de Bayonne*, he offered to pay the superior the sum of 40,000 francs if he would allow the matter of the water to be properly investigated, and could prove that there was no trickery. The water, he asserted, was drawn from the Gave higher up stream. The Fathers shrank from the investigation.

My authority for this is Jean de Bonnefon. But I must add that I wrote to that gentleman and also to the editor of the *Reveil de Bayonne* to learn the name of the man who offered the challenge, and also the date when made, and that neither one nor the other has had the courtesy to reply. The editor may, however, be dead, as the *Reveil* has ceased to appear.

Nevertheless, the charge of fraud has been made publicly by M. de Bonnefon, and it is incumbent on the French Government to see that no trickery is used to impose on the religious public, and obtain of it money under false pretences.

The Fathers of Garaison are no longer nominally in charge of the grotto and all its belongings, but this is nominally only. They are now called *vicaires*, under authorization of the Bishop of Tarbes. The name is altered, that is all. Monte Carlo is under the protection of the French Government. A German, Captain Weihe, has brought charges against the Company of fraudulent action, of having the balls loaded and of employing magnets. The French Government should insist before extending its patronage to the gambling hell at Monte Carlo and to the grotto of Lourdes to have the proceedings in both thoroughly and impartially investigated. But both bring vast sums of money into the country, and consequently the Government shuts its eyes upon both. When the inventories were taken in the spring of 1906 the Bishop of Tarbes gave instructions that no sort of opposition was to be offered at Lourdes to the Government authorities counting up the silver hearts, and crutches, etc., in the basilica and grotto. It mattered not to him to have the feathers of the goose counted, so long as the goose itself was not killed that laid the golden eggs. He was careful not to provoke opposition, lest an inquiry should be made that might lead to awkward disclosures.

Not that any amount of exposure of trickery—if trickery has been resorted to—would disabuse the minds of the credulous. Human stupidity is too crass for that; but it would relieve the French Government of the discredit of conniving at dishonest proceedings.

Before Lasserre's book had appeared, the Bishop of Tarbes had appointed a commission to investigate the alleged marvels at Lourdes, but there was not a name on the commission that could command confidence, only a vicar-general, canons of the cathedral, and the like, not a single man of science and of independent mind. When the bishop was satisfied—and most easy to satisfy he was—he gave his sanction to pilgrimages to the grotto, and Pius IX accorded indulgences to such as made the visit. He did more; he instituted a liturgical office for 11 February, to be inserted in the Breviary, in commemoration of the first apparition. Consequently the Church of Rome is irrevocably committed to this great delusion.

It was necessary to get rid of Bernadette; she was not indeed likely to "faire des bêtises"; but, in her own interest, it was well that she should be removed, lest her head should be turned, as people were entreating her to perform miraculous cures. And it was quite possible that she in her simplicity might let out compromising avowals—not indeed that the whole thing had been got up as a fraud, for that it was not, but might avow how greatly she had been influenced by the suggestive action of the abbés Ader, Pomian, and Peyramale, all doing their part in good faith, with no intent of deception but who, like Ader, had become, conscious *après coup* that they had brought this affair about.

Bernadette was taken off and shut up in a convent at Nevers, at such a distance from her home that there seemed no chance of relative or acquaintance ever seeing her again. There she was retained very close; hardly any one was permitted to visit her. Her health, always frail, gave way in confinement, deprived of her mountain air, and she died in 1879. When it was known that she was on her death-bed M. le Gentil very kindly undertook to pay the expenses of her brother to Nevers, so as to have a last look at his sister. Gentil accompanied him. Nevers would seem to have been chosen expressly as a place where to place Bernadette, so difficult is it to be got at from Tarbes—only by cross lines and slow trains, with long waits at every change. However difficult and tedious Gentil and Soubirous may have found it, making their way thither by train, it was nothing to the difficulties caused by wilful obstruction put in their way on reaching Nevers. Soubirous went alone to the convent, and asked for the superior. She replied to his demand for an interview with his dying sister, "It is against the rules of the convent."

Soubirous, timid as poor peasants are, returned to the hotel and told M. Gentil his want of success. Soubirous went again to the convent and was again refused. Then the two men called at the palace on the bishop. He said, "I can do nothing. The superior is mistress in her house."

Then Soubirous and his companion went again to the convent and entered the parlour, where they declared firmly that they would remain till the request was granted.

The superior in great agitation entreated them to depart and not provoke a scandal. "I am but a feeble woman," she said, "and the bishop has forbidden me to allow you to see your sister."

Throughout the day the two men remained at their post seated in the parlour. Emissaries ran to and fro between the convent and the bishop's palace. The house was like a disturbed ant-heap. Sisters passed and repassed, peeped in and withdrew. Voices were heard in discussion in the passages. But the two men would not budge.

At last night drew on. It would never do to allow them to pass it in this holy prison. At last, pale and trembling, the superior entered, and said, "Monseigneur has consented."

Soubirous was then conducted to the infirmary. The whole community of twenty nuns, and all the serving sisters, were there crowded about the bed. On it Soubirous caught a glimpse of the white face of his sister with her great burning eyes looking at him, and tears rolling down her cheeks. The dying girl in a feeble voice said, "The fathers will give you work. They have promised it." That was all. The head sank back on the pillow, and more tears flowed. Soubirous was then hustled out of the room, and he never more saw Bernadette.

To-day this man is well-to-do. He has a shop and a house, and fears God and the Fathers of the Grotto. So ended this poor martyr to the doctrine of the Immaculate Conception.[8] The annual number of pilgrims who visit the grotto amounts to something over 600,000, and the affluence increases every year. Trainloads of sick people leave Paris in the month of August, when the principal pilgrimage takes place. But all the festivals of the Blessed Virgin, and that of the Apparition, inserted in the calendar with proper Mass, give occasion to solemnities of exceptional grandeur, the most imposing feature of which is the night processions so beautifully described by Zola. Hideous and vulgar are basilica and chapel of the Rosary that have been erected over and by the cave. The situation is exceptionally beautiful, and would lend itself to a stately and well-proportioned church and pile of buildings; but it has been used as an occasion for the display of architectural ineptitude. Grotto and church are crowded with *ex votos* memorials of cures wrought there, cures that are reputed miraculous.

But who is to decide where the natural ends and the miraculous begins? In the present condition of science we cannot draw the line between the natural and the supernatural. None can plant his walking-stick at a certain point and say that he has reached "ubi defuit orbis," and no man can declare the exact point "ubi defuit scientia." We know that the Maladetta is in Spain, and that the Vingemale is in France, because the mountain chain has been surveyed, and the line of demarcation drawn between Spain and France. Such a tree, such a rock, such a hamlet, we know for certain is in one or other of these countries. But there is no such boundary in Nature. Where does the vegetable realm end and the animal kingdom begin? Psychology and physiology overlap and interpenetrate one another. The body acts on the mind, and the mind on the body. Those who come to Lourdes come in a condition of nervous exaltation, in a fever of faith and hope; not only so, but they come in crowds, and the magnetic, electric influence exercised by great masses of men and women on one another, is prodigious, when all are actuated by the same impulse.

That cures have been wrought at Lourdes I do not doubt. Similar and as many, and as genuine cures were wrought of old in pagan temples, which were also crowded with *ex votos*.

And what guarantee have we that these cures have been permanent? A man

[8] Bonnefon, *Lourdes et ses tenanciers*. Paris, 1906. The value of this book is in the second part, that contains the hitherto unpublished documents from the Paris and Departmental archives relative to the course of development of the Lourdes story.

with a rheumatic leg prays at the cave, dips in the dirty pool, feels that he can walk, and hangs up his crutches. Next day he is as much crippled as before, but he has not the courage to go back to the grotto and resume his crutch; he orders another from Paris.

But that some of the cures are permanent need not be doubted. The effect of imagination on the body is immense. Every nervous person can make himself ill by imagining himself to be ill; and a good many can get well by persuading themselves that they are convalescent. There was much truth in Mrs. Chick's saying that Mrs. Dombey died because "dear Fanny wouldn't make an effort."

# CHAPTER X

## THE LAVEDAN



A FUNICULAR railway takes a visitor to the top of the Pic de Gers, whence he can obtain a fine comprehensive panorama of the mountains. A cross surmounts the peak that is illuminated at night.

On quitting Lourdes to ascend the Valley of Argelez the mountain sides are seen to be bare, having been denuded of their trees by the ruthless axe of the peasant. Presently the train passes a mound on which stands a solitary tower called after the Black Prince, who is held to have ordered its construction to watch the upper portion of the valley. Then the basin of Argelez opens up, with villages and culture, vines, chestnuts, walnuts, running high up the sides of the mountains, mainly on the right bank of the Gave, and maize in the plain standing up as high as a man, or in the season sheets of forget-me-not-blue waving flax, alternating with crimson stretches of the *Trifolium incarnatum*. On the rubbly slopes the glistening box flourishes luxuriantly. Argelez is a delightful resort in spring and summer. It has its bathing establishment, to which the waters of Gazost are led, its casino, and a park in which the bamboos grow rank, and the acacias in spring flower and scent the air. Avenues, bordered by hotels, link the Argelez of the tourist and those who go there for what the Germans call "Sommerfrische" with the old Argelez. Among the villas is the château of Vieusac, from which that scoundrel Barrère took a title, that he dropped in the Reign of Terror, and reassumed as soon as he was safe under Louis Philippe, when he represented Argelez in the Conseil Général.

This place was formerly a Romano-Gaulish settlement; in a field near the town a considerable number of cinerary urns have been dug up. A mile below Argelez is the Balandrau, a huge block of stone balanced at the edge of a crag, held from falling by a small stone of different nature, that retains it in position, and looking as though all it needed was a touch to send it hurtling down upon the roof of a farmhouse planted beneath. A Mass is said annually in the church of Argelez to invoke Divine intervention against such a catastrophe. The Balandrau has been supposed to be a megalithic monument of the dolmen builders, but it is natural, a relic of the Ice Age in the valley when it was choked with glaciers. Farther down a stream flows into the Gave. Here, at Ouzous, is an intermittent spring that turns a mill, when it pleases it to flow. Before it bursts forth it is said to growl and grumble. Here also, in the face of the limestone cliff, is a cave that served as a church during the Reign of Terror, when priests were hunted down like wolves; and here the peasants assembled to hear Mass. Fifty years ago the rude stone altar, made like that of Gilgal, was standing; I have not been to the grotto since.

Facing Argelez, the right bank of the Gave to the crest of the mountains, from Préchac to the mouth of the Valley of Isaby constitutes one of the seven valleys of the ancient confederation of the Lavedan. It is not a valley at all, any more than is that of S. Savin, which formed another, both being mountain slopes, one on the right, the other on the left bank of the Gave. This was the Devantaïgue, which means literally, "in face of the waters," and comprised five communes. In it is the Castle of Beaucens, the former residence of the counts of Lavedan, before it passed into the hands of the King of Navarre. It is an imposing ruin, with the little village clustered about the feet of the rock on which it stands. Tradition is, as we were informed by the peasants, that up to the Revolution a terrible toll was exacted of this little commune; it was bound annually to supply a girl to become a prostitute in Paris.

The Valley of Azun, next to that of Barèges, is the largest of the seven of the confederacy. It is cut off from the basin of Argelez by a barrier of rock, through which its steel-blue Gave has sawn a way. The road to reach the valley has to mount high to surmount the barrier; and this point was strongly defended by three fortresses, the most considerable of which was Castelnau-d'Azun. The ruins are dominated by a donjon and a square tower, of the fourteenth century, which castle was held by the English till taken by assault by the peasants in 1404. Above the ravine cleft by the river is a rock from which the inhabitants hurled a collector of taxes into the abyss, a simpler proceeding than paying their dues. But they were always an independent people, self-governing, almost autonomous. Every householder, female as well as male, voted to elect their consuls and representative at the common parliament that sat at Argelez, comprising those sent from each of the seven valleys to regulate such matters as concerned all conjointly. One can understand how restive they were under the English tyranny. The kings of Navarre respected the privileges of the confederate little republics, and did not interfere with them, but sent a bailiff to administer justice in his name.

The Valley of Azun had to be watched and well guarded, as down it came one of the passages from Spain over a col. Accordingly, the castles on the barrier were but one link in the defence. Arras, farther up, had two more castles, now degraded to prosaic use. Above Arras again is Aucun. The church contains two *bénitiers*, one, richly carved, represents a wedding, with tumblers, and a musician playing the bagpipes. The other, also of white marble, has on it rudely-sculptured bears in various postures. Aucun was the capital of this miniature republic. A little below it a road descends to and crosses the Gave, and then mounting to the village of Bun leads up the narrow valley of the Gave de Lebat to the pretty bottle-green lakelet of

Estaing lying at the foot of the Soum de Monné, behind which is Cauterets.

Farther up the valley of Azun is Arreins, whence started the track leading into Spain by the Col de la Peyre S. Martin. The church served as a refuge in time of danger. It still keeps its crenellated wall of enclosure.

Hard by is the pilgrimage chapel of Puy-al-Hun, on a rock standing boldly up out of the midst of the valley. A writer in 1837 thus describes it:—

> "We went up to Notre Dame Pouey-la-Unt, beautifully set down upon a platform overlooking a world of sweet and serene aspect, and having for its rough pavement the rock on which it is built. A fissure runs through it, and when it rains, a stream through the fissure; but the walls are panelled brown and gold, the roof is azure starred with gold, the pillars of the high altar twisted like those of the baldaquin of S. Peter's at Rome, gorgeously gilt and gracefully wreathed with vine leaves and tendrils and bunches of grapes, all gold or its likeness."

The chapel is much the same now as it was when this was written, but the stream no longer flows in the channel athwart the floor. The Commissioners of the Directory visited the place to plunder the shrine and destroy the image of the Virgin, but when they entered the church they were scared by unearthly noises proceeding from above, and they ran away. These noises were produced by some young peasants who had secreted themselves between the vaulting and the roof. However, the chapel was sold, and bought by a farmer's widow in the place. Next a small garrison was quartered in it, for the protection of the frontier against the Spaniards, and the impression of their muskets on the balustrades may still be seen. One evening the women of Arreins, disguising themselves as Spanish soldiers, to the roll of drum, in the dusk made an attack on the chapel, and the garrison, thinking discretion the better part of valour, decamped, and did not halt to take breath till they reached Argelez.

The chapel was visited by Queen Hortense in 1807; she had recently lost her son, the Prince Royal of Holland, and she founded here a Mass to be said in perpetuity for the repose of his soul. The Abbé Pome, then owner and chaplain of the sanctuary, wrote to give the Queen an account of the first anniversary Mass.

> "That day, which should have been one of mourning by recalling the memory of a prince born to be the successor of the great Napoleon, has become a day of joy and thankfulness through the birth of another prince, who, generated in our mountains, and, if I may presume to say so, under the special protection of the Virgin, has dried up all our tears, has reanimated our courage, and has become the object of our most flattering hopes."

This prince just born was Louis Napoleon, who became Emperor of the French.

In 1870 Mr. Lawlor published his *Pilgrimages in the Pyrenees*, and in it says of Napoleon III:—

> "The protection of Our Lady of Poëy-la-hun would seem nev-

er to have deserted him through all his adventures and dangers."

An unhappy sentence written shortly before the disaster of Sedan in 1871.

On a beautifully wooded height on the right as ascending the Valley of Argelez are seen the tower and church and buildings of S. Savin, where was an abbey of great importance, but of which now all that remain are the church and the chapter-house. The abbot was Seigneur over the so-called Valley of S. Savin, and that of Cauterets, then desert and poor, which belonged to the confraternity. But although seigneur, the abbot was by no means a despotic lord. The little republic of S. Savin would not admit him into his monastery, let him even cross the bounds of the "valley" till he had taken oath to respect the ancient rights and liberties of the place. Its electors went by the name of *voisins*; but the abbot alone represented S. Savin in the Estates of Bigorre, and he presided over the deliberations of the assembly of *voisins* and *voisines*, for women as well as men were the representatives of the will and rights of the little republic, and a single veto would suffice to prevent the execution of any measure voted. On one occasion a *voisine*, named Galhardine de Fréchon, opposed her veto to the rest of the assembly which was otherwise unanimous, and thus paralyzed their action.

The abbot and his monks doubtless lived well: hunted, and lounged and slept in their comfortable quarters, without discharging their religious duties other than in a perfunctory manner, for the Chevalier Bestin, in his verses relative to a stay in the Pyrenees, boasted of—

> "Le long dîner, la courte messe
> Du bon abbé de Saint Savin."

The abbey occupies, it is believed, the site of the Palatium Æmilianum, which served as a retreat for Savinus, son of a Count of Barcelona, and nephew of the Count of Poitiers, in the eighth century. The abbey was erected by Charlemagne, and here, so goes the legend, Roland fought and cleft from head to waist two Saracen giants, and constrained a third to submit to baptism. In 843 the terrible Northmen destroyed the monastery. Raymond I, Count of Bigorre, rebuilt it in 945; and he it was who granted the Valley of Cauterets to the monastery. It also possessed sole rights to the interment of the inhabitants of the Val d'Azun. When, on one occasion, these people ventured to bury one of their dead near the church of Arreins, the monks forced them to dig up the body, although in an advanced state of putrefaction, and transport it to S. Savin. It is probably in reference to this that Frossard, a Protestant pastor, and one of the first writers on the Pyrenees, says that the monks enjoyed "several privileges at once destructive to individual liberty and to sound morals."

The first appearance of S. Savin is eminently striking; the massive walls, the large rude blocks of which they are constructed, the lofty apse, the fine portal, and even the clumsy fifteenth-century tower, with its ill-shaped spire, are all impressive.

The present church is of the beginning of the twelfth century, and the architecture is of the plainest and most severe Romanesque. On the tympanum of the west door is a figure of Christ between the evangelistic symbols, but so weathered as to be scarcely distinguishable.

In the interior is the marble tomb of S. Savin; far more ancient than the present church, it is a rude, early sarcophagus. But what is of special interest are the two large paintings on wood, each in nine compartments, representing the legend of the saint, the inscriptions under each group are in patois. In the sacristy are preserved the hood and comb of Savin.

A "bénétier des cagots" is a holy water vessel, near the entrance, supported by figures, supposed to represent members of the proscribed race. The organ case is of 1557, and is adorned with three faces that loll their tongues and roll their eyes, hardly to the edification of the congregation, when the bellows are worked.

The village itself of S. Savin is small, silent, and deserted, and impresses one with a sense of melancholy. But the great beauty of S. Savin is the view one enjoys from it, especially from the chapel of the Pietà, of the upper portion of the basin of the Valley of Argelez. Villages and hamlets are strewn thick over it and on the mountain side opposite. One can see up the Valley of Isaby to the ruin of Saint Orens, and the Pic de Viscos towering as a pyramid above Pierrefite, where open the gorges of the Gave from Luz and from Cauterets.

A scramble up the Valley of Isaby to S. Orens will repay the trouble.

Orens was born at Huescar, in the marches of Aragon. He sold his estate and retired as a hermit to the Valley of Lavedan. He was elected Bishop of Auch about 419, and was dispatched as ambassador from Theodoric the Ostrogoth to sue for peace from Aetius, the Roman general, and was successful. He was the author of a religious poem, the "Commonitorium," still extant, and died in 439 at his monastery in the Lavedan, to which he had retired at an advanced age from his see.

This monastery had fallen into bad ways in the eighteenth century, and the repute of the monks was so evil that the Bishop of Tarbes visited it in 1738. The prior took to his heels when he heard that an investigation into his malpractices was to be held. At the time the entire community was reduced to prior, sacristan, and a single monk, and these no longer resided in the monastery, but lodged with the *curé* of Villelongue. In the *procès* instituted against the convent we read:—

> "One of the three above-mentioned is the craftiest and most dangerous man conceivable. He is the cock of the village. He attempted to murder the prior. He stole one of the chalices. The other monk is the most imbecile and stupid creature in the place. He has lived on in the house for the last fifty years, and does not know how to read."

The ruins of the church stand boldly above the torrent that descends in a series of cascades. The stream may be followed up to the Lake of Isaby, from which it rises.

The basin of Argelez comes abruptly to an end at Pierrefite, surmounted by a ruined castle; here the Pic de Viscos divides, with the chain running from it, the valleys of Luz and of Cauterets; the Gaves from these break out of the cleft rock, for that is what Pierrefite means, on one side and on the other, and here unite. At this point terminates the railway; but hence electric trams ply to Cauterets up one ravine, and to Luz up the other.

The line to Cauterez rises rapidly up steep inclines and describing curves that command views down the chasm where the Gave boils and thunders. A tunnel is entered, passed through, and the view back of the sun-bathed, fertile Valley of Argelez, of the walnuts and chestnuts of S. Savin, is excluded. We have passed from one world into another; from golden sunlight into mountain gloom, from one vegetation to another as well. The rocks add to the effect of transition, for they are of dark schist streaked with ferruginous stains, and there are long spreading refuse slides from the lead mines of Pierrefite, too poisonous to allow any shrub, even grass, to grow on them. There are no gaps up which the eye can look to gleaming snow fields, till all at once we emerge on the basin of Cauterets, where the mountains fall back and open and show us the sunlit snow, and a river dancing down in a fine fall, and before us a bit of Paris dropped out of the clouds into this solitude.

But Cauterets and Luz must be reserved for another chapter.

I cannot quit the radiant Valley of Argelez without a kindly tribute to the simple, warm-hearted peasantry. As I have already said, we spent a summer in a château on the mountain side, high up opposite Argelez. My mother visited the poor cottagers, and where there was sickness did what every English lady would do, sent relief, and did better than that, showed tender sympathy. When we left, in the autumn, to return for the winter to Pau, our carriage was surrounded by the poor people, bringing their humble offerings of stewed pears, grapes, figs, apples, cakes, and we were laden with their gifts, more than we could consume, but were unable to refuse; and what was better still, as we whirled away, were attended by their best wishes, and not a few sincere regrets and tears.

# CHAPTER XI

## LUZ AND CAUTERETS



FROM an early period Cauterets enjoyed great repute. By a charter of 945 Raymond I, Count of Bigorre, granted the valley to the abbey of S. Savin, on condition that they built there a church in honour of S. Martin, and that they maintained at the hot springs a hospital for the patients who visited them.

Of these springs there are two groups. The upper, La Raillère, is at some distance from the town, but is reached by electric tram. It takes its name from the avalanches (raillères) that have made their pathway down the mountain side above it, and have left their white and ghastly scars on the rocks, and heaped wreckage below. This is the most abundant group of springs, but the space there is narrow, and lies in a gorge. The thermal establishment has to be maintained on huge walled terraces. There is no hotel there; but those who use the waters for baths or for gargling come and go by the tram. The platform on which the baths of La Raillère are constituted command a view of the deep valley of Lutour, down which descends a stream issuing from a chain of little lakes lying in the lap of the Pic de Mallerouge, 9740 feet, the lowest of which, the Lac d'Estom, discharges its waters by a beautiful cascade, and they further leap down into the basin of Cauterets at its extremity in a white streak. Above the Lac d'Estom in a wild chaotic cirque are the tarns that feed it; one of these retains its coat of ice almost all the year through.

The Lutour joins the Gave de Jerret above La Raillère, and it is up this latter that the way leads to the Pont d'Espagne and the Lac de Gaube, about which more presently. Another Gave, that of Cambasque, unites with the Gave of Pierrefite by the station of the electric tram at Cauterets, and below the town itself.

The Thermes des Œufs, so designated from the smell of rotten eggs, sulphuretted hydrogen, emitted by the waters, is one of the most luxuriously furnished establishments of the kind in Europe. Six springs contribute their water to the baths. Above these is the casino.

> "Cauterets," said Taine, "is a bourg at the bottom of a valley, dismal enough, paved, and furnished with an *octroi*. Innkeepers, guides, all that ravenous population surround us. We are annexed by touts, children, donkey-drivers, by the first *garçons* who can hitch on to us. We are handed cards, we receive recommendations to this hotel for its situation, to that for its cuisine. We are attended, cap in hand, by the crowd, elbowing one another out of the way, to the end of the village. 'This is my traveller,' shouts one, 'come near him and I will horsewhip you.' Every hotel has its herd of touts. Here all are hunters. In winter they hunt the chamois, in summer the tourist."

Cauterets has been considerably enlarged and improved since the above was written, but the tout is ever with you. Something like ten thousand persons visit Cauterets during the season to drink the waters or to bathe in them. But in fact it has a double *clientèle*, one of patients and the other of excursionists. The former move like clockwork to the baths and back again, like a long black revolving chain; then to their hotels or lodging-houses, to their meals, to their promenade, to their beds; and throughout the day thus mechanically passed, the tick-tack of their talk, always about their symptoms and their sufferings, their progress or their relapses, is maintained without cessation. But the second class of visitors are such as desire to climb the Vignemale, to ascend to the highest tarns above Estom; at the least to see the Lac de Gaube. These pertain to an order of beings very distinct from the patients. They have no aches and pains. They turn away their noses from the savour of the springs. They are quivering with energy, muscular, and restless. They look upon the patients with undisguised contempt, and the latter scowl at those who enjoy rude health with querulous dissatisfaction. There is yet another category of visitors — the pilgrims to Lourdes; they arrive fagged with their devotions and overstrained emotions, to relax, laugh, and perhaps entertain some incredulity as to the marvels of the Grotto of Massabielle. The market at Cauterets is gay with stalls during the season, that lasts from 1 June to the end of September; every trifle is to be found in them, from gay-coloured Merino shawls, rock-crystals, toys, rosaries, sacred images to picture cards.

The Pont d'Espagne, that can be reached by a carriage, and the Lac de Gaube, are points omitted by no excursionist who visits Cauterets. The former is a stone bridge thrown over the river formed by the junction of the Gave de Mascadou and that which issues from the Lac de Gaube. Higher up the first of these is a picturesque wooden bridge thrown across the torrent.

The path to the Lac de Gaube leaves the road just before reaching the Pont d'Espagne. The lake is a lovely mountain tarn two miles and a half in circumference. The sides are steep, in places clothed with dark masses of pines; and in the background rises the Vignemale, 10,820 feet, with its crevassed glacier, that feeds the lake by a cascade.

By the water is a white marble monument to the memory of a Mr. Pattison and his wife, who were drowned here whilst on their wedding trip, within a month of their marriage, on 20 September, 1832. Mrs. Ellis thus describes the accident. Her husband was acquainted with the relatives of both:—

> "It is said to have been a bright and beautiful morning when the English bride and bridegroom went out upon this lake, in the fisherman's rudely-constructed boat, the very same that we saw lying by the shore, than which a more unsafe or unmanageable vessel could scarcely be imagined. Little seems to be known of the awful event which followed, except what those who stood on the shore relate, that when the boat was about the middle of the lake, the figure of the man was seen stooping overboard—that the female, alarmed for his safety, rushed to the same side—and thus, the vessel being overbalanced, both were plunged into a watery grave. The bodies were both found, though one not till a month after. They were conveyed to England, and buried at Witham, in Essex."

The recklessness of the villagers in times past had threatened Cauterets with destruction. The forests had been cut down, and free course given to the avalanches to fall into the valley and cover all with stones and mud. If something had not been effected to bridle the torrent above La Raillère, the springs there would have been overwhelmed with rubble, and the thermal establishment utterly wrecked. The ravine down which the avalanches fall is that of Péquère, and it was not snow and small stuff only that was brought down, but huge masses of rock.

Great pains have been taken, by means of replanting the slopes and the erection of barriers, to protect the baths, and these efforts have been happily crowned with success. Since 1897 another avalanche path has been taken in hand, that of the Lizey, which menaced the road to Pierrefite, and had in fact cut all communication during three weeks in 1895.

Even the esplanade of Cauterets was threatened. The winter of 1903–4 tried the place severely; in the month of January the masses of fallen snow reached the town itself. In spite of themselves the inhabitants of the basin have had to yield to the resolution of the Board of Forestry and allow extensive replantation.

The journey up the ravine to Luz by electric tram presents a succession of beautiful peeps of the bottle-green river thundering through the gorge, breaking into masses of foam at every leap; waterfalls descend the mountain sides right and left—everywhere is rich and luxuriant vegetation.

The gorge opens to reveal the green meadows of Viscos, then contracts again, once more to expand into the basin of Luz. High aloft on a terrace stand the villages of Vizos and Esquièze, with their church spires. In the background is seen a superb circle of snow-clad mountains, those of the ridge of the Mont Perdu, nearer the Soum Blanc on one side and the Pic Long on the other.

The Templar Church, Luz

*From a photograph by Messrs. Levy and Sons, Paris*

The whole of the district, from the opening of the gorge at Pierrefite upwards, formed the Pays or Val de Barèges, which formerly enjoyed to a high degree the rights of self-government. It was practically an independent republic till the time of the Revolution, its liberties accorded to it in acknowledgment of services rendered in wars with Spain. Few taxes were imposed; that most severely felt elsewhere, on salt, did not trouble the Barègois. They had entire liberty to chase and to fish, rights so jealously reserved by the princes elsewhere. Even in diplomacy Barèges preserved a sort of autonomy, and treated with delegates from the Spanish valleys without reference to the counts of Bigorre or the kings of France.

What strikes the eye at once on arriving at Luz is the old Castle of Sainte Marie, now reduced to a ruin, perched on a height; and the curious parish church, built and fortified by the Templars, who had a commandery here. The crenellated walls now enclosing the small area in which stands the church were built by the Knights of Malta, who succeeded to the place that had been occupied by the Templars, after the suppression of this latter order.

On each side of the apse is a tower, one of which resembles the keep of a castle. The ramparts surrounding the old cemetery of the Knights are passed through an embattled gateway.

There are two portals into the church, that on the north being the main entrance, and it is Romanesque. The tympanum, surrounded by inscriptions of the twelfth century, contains symbols of the evangelists surrounding a figure of Christ. The bases of the columns of the doorway also bear inscriptions. The interior of the church is dark, dungeon-like, and the decorations and furniture are barbaric. On the south side of the nave is a late chapel dedicated to S. Mary Magdalen. A child's stone sarcophagus serves as a *bénitier* at the entrance to the church. Here, as at S. Savin, is a Cagot's door.

This is perhaps the best preserved Templar church in France. So far it has not undergone restoration, but it is far too small for a growing place, and a new church will have to be built elsewhere.

Above Luz, on a height, is a hermitage, formerly occupied by a Père Ambrose, who died in the odour of sanctity in 1778. He was a Capuchin friar, born in 1708, who had embraced the religious life at the age of sixteen. He wrote some godly works, one on the Joy of the Soul, one on the Peace of the Soul, and a third consisted of letters giving spiritual advice.

The chapel is dedicated to S. Peter. Napoleon III had it rebuilt, and entitled S. Pierre-de-Solférino. Near by is a cairn, under which lie the bones of Ambrose, the last hermit to occupy the place. The ruins of the Castle of S. Marie date from the fourteenth and fifteenth centuries. There are two keeps. This fortress was formerly the principal stronghold commanding the Valley of Barèges. It was built by the English originally, and held by them, terrorizing the inhabitants of the basin, till the Barègois peasants rose in a body against them in 1404, stormed the castle, and put the garrison to the sword. After that it was rebuilt and strengthened.

Saint Sauveur consists of a long street of hotels, and is occupied in the summer alone. In winter and spring every door and window is barred. It is reached from

Luz over a bridge, erected in 1860 by order of Napoleon III. The keystone of the arch is 198 feet above the torrent.

**La Brêche de Roland**

*From a photograph by Messrs. Levy and Sons, Paris*

Another bridge, farther up, is that of Scia; like the former, constructed of white marble, and thrown at an amazing height above the Gave, where huge blocks of

granite intercept its course, and it roars and tumbles savagely over the obstruction. A French guide-book asserts that at the spot an English lady, the Lady Clara,
standing on the bridge, recited the celebrated soliloquy of Hamlet, in this fashion:
"To die, to slip!" and then flung herself into the abyss. No such an incident ever
occurred there.

The Brêche de Roland, a gash in the high ridge of snow and rock above Gavarnie, now becomes visible, as Pragnères is reached, but it is invisible from Gavarnie
itself.

The story goes that Roland hacked this opening in the rock with his sword
Durandal in the hopes of breaking the blade, so that the Saracens might not get
possession of it at his death. But the tale has been transferred hither from Roncevaux. It is certainly curious to note how that legends of Roland have attached themselves to numerous places in the Pyrenees from west to east. He occupies there the
place that King Arthur does in England, Scotland, and Wales. We have seen how
that at S. Savin he was said to have fought with giants. Now it is a curious fact
that according to tradition Vizos, near Luz, was occupied by a race of giants called
Empresous, *les Preux*, and that representatives of them remained on there till the
end of the eighteenth century. The Revolution seems to have cut them down, for
we hear of no others since then. In the Archives of Luz is a record of the death of an
Empresou named Barèque, in 1771, at the age of a hundred and ten. These giants
had a cemetery of their own, and a baptistery of their own. They seem to have been
regarded with something like the repulsion with which the Cagots were considered. In the churchyard have been turned up human bones of extraordinary size.

The valley or gorge of the Gave has been much belauded and often described.
This naturally has produced a revulsion. M. Ardouin-Dumazet has led the way.
He says:—

> "The road is fine, without exactly deserving all the hyperbol-
> ical praises lavished upon it. That which is the spoiling of this
> country is the extravagance of the admiration expressed for it.
> Since the time of Ramond no one who speaks of the Pyrenees can
> describe a site without declaring it to be incomparable. If they
> have judged it incomparable, it is because they have seen nothing
> with which to compare it. The panorama from Pau, truly marvel-
> lous, I admit, is not superior to that of the Alps, the Jura, and the
> Cevennes, seen from the hills above Lyons on a clear day. It is so
> with this country. I do not venture to use the expression Gasco-
> nading with reference to these descriptions, but I cannot pitch my
> note at the diapason of the Pyrenean infatuists."

This may be true enough of the way to Gavarnie, but I do venture to believe
that the Cirque of Gavarnie—the end of this expedition up the Gave—is, *pace* Ardouin-Dumazet, incomparable.

Gèdre was a wretched hamlet some years ago, when I first knew it, but now it
has its hotels, and is a very convenient tarrying place whence to explore the valley
of the Héas, and visit the two cirques of Estaubé and Troumousse; as also the val-

ley of the Aspé, descending from the glacier of Mallerouge.

The Héas issues from a narrow fissure, foaming over cascades. Higher up in the ravine is the chapel of Notre Dame de Héas, planted on a huge block fallen from the mountain above. It is held that the Virgin once appeared to a shepherd at this spot.

This mass is but one portion of a landslip that took place in 1650, which dammed up the river and formed a lake, which in its turn was destroyed by a flood in 1788. Among the fallen rocks may be found the beautiful *Saxifraga pyramidalis* or *longifolia*, and the *Ramondia pyrenaica*. Pilgrimages are made to the chapel on 15 August and 8 September.

The Cirque de Troumousse is above Héas. It is less remarkable than that of Gavarnie, though more extensive. It lacks the series of bold escarpments capped with glacier that form the distinguishing feature of the latter.

Above Gèdre, on the route to Gavarnie is a *chaos*, an agglomeration of fallen gneiss rocks from above; it is as if half a mountain had been precipitated into the valley from the Coumélie. Farther up may be seen a cleft rock, between the jaws of which hangs a mass, arrested there on its way down. The scenery becomes grander, but at the same time more dreary; the cirque opens before one, and we reach the village of Gavarnie.

The Cirque of Gavarnie has been already briefly described in my first chapter. To see it to advantage it should be visited in spring or early summer, when, from the melting of the snows, the great fall is full of water. It resembles the Staubbach only in the long drop of the stream and its resolution into fine spray. The setting of it is immeasurably superior to that of the famous Swiss fall. The height is 1385 feet, and is the highest in Europe, except one or two in Norway. If there be plenty of water it shoots down in one single column; but in summer it descends in two leaps. This is not the only cascade in the cirque; down every part of the huge curve threads of water drop into the basin. Towards the end of a hot summer many of these fail, and the great cascade is much reduced.

The first sight of the cirque is disappointing. There is nothing by which to scale it, and the appearance is only one of size, gloom, and cold. The bottom of the great bowl is heaped with rubble brought down from above. But at Gavarnie we are four miles from the foot of the cirque, and it looks as if not more than a quarter of an hour's stroll was required to reach it. A thousand feet seems to be no more than a hundred, and the huge rocks hurled down from above are reduced in appearance to mere pebbles.

A stone dropped from the top of the Pic du Marboré, 10,600 feet, will fall 5500 feet into the cirque. In the church of Gavarnie are to be seen twelve skulls, held to have belonged to the Templars of Luz, who fled hither, and were here executed. A story is current that on the last night of the year, just before the clock strikes midnight, a Templar clothed in white, and with a red cross on his breast, enters the church at Gavarnie and cries, "Ho! who are there that will stand up and fight for the temple?" Whereupon one skull after another replies, "None; the temple is destroyed." This white-robed Templar is Du Molay, the Grand Master, burned alive at Paris, with four other great dignitaries of the Order. King Philip the Fair coveted the great possessions of the Knights, and Pope Clement V had obtained the tiara by the help of the King; the price he paid for it was the dissolution of the Order, and the sacrifice of the Knights to torture and death. In the midst of the fire Du Molay cried out, "Clement, iniquitous and cruel judge, I summon thee within forty days to meet me before the throne of God." According to some accounts he cited the King as well. Du Molay was burnt on 18 March, 1314; on 30 April, Clement was dead; and Philip the Fair on 29 November, in the same year.

The road over the pass of the Tourmalet branches off below Luz and ascends the desolate Valley of Bastan, ravaged by avalanches, to Barèges, a long street of hotels and lodging-houses closed during the winter. The baths here have been famous for long. The waters impregnated with sulphate of soda are the most powerful in the Pyrenees, and are charged with a peculiar nitrogenous substance called glairine that renders them oily to the touch. Their great use is for the healing of wounds and ulcers, and for scrofula. They have been employed for a military hospital since 1760. Barèges stands over 5000 feet above the sea, yet it is more bleak and inhospitable in appearance than many a town such as Briançon, little short of it in altitude. A covered tank for bathers was erected here in 1550; and hither, to take advantage of the waters, came Mme. de Maintenon, in 1677 with the young Duke of Maine.

The scourge of the place has been the avalanches, mainly those that shoot down by four great paths from the Labas Blancs, the mountain to the north, and which bring the town or village, call it which you will, under 100,000 cubic feet of snow. Extensive works have been undertaken to prevent the complete destruction of the houses, baths, and hospitals. Huge barriers of masonry 40 feet high and 46 feet long by 18 feet wide have been drawn across the ravine of Le Theil, and extensive replanting of the sides with pines has reduced the danger; but it will take many years of growth before the trees attain a sufficient height to be able to completely screen the place. The ravine of Le Theil may be said to have been already rendered innocuous; but that of Midaou caused disaster in July, 1897, when an avalanche carried away a portion of the baths, and choked the valley as far as to Luz. Since 1900, however, this trough of the avalanche has been blocked.

On the left bank also the work has been energetically pursued to arrest the fall of torrents of snow from the Pic d'Ayré, where the avalanche path is formed of glacial clay, hard as cement when dry, but in time of rain forming a flood of mud falling 1200 feet. Here replanting has proved efficacious, and barriers of masonry have been erected, that have served the purpose intended. This work was begun in 1862, and since 1869 no lava-like flood of mud has reached the Valley of Bastan. The inspector Dellon says:—

> "The regulation of the system of the torrents of Rieulet and Bayet, the fixing of the glacial mud which constitutes to a large extent the banks of these torrents, and the foot of the slope of the mountains facing Barèges, the attenuation of the avalanches, so dangerous to this thermal station, all prove the efficacy of the means adopted. The contrast is most striking between the districts

within the range of these torrents acquired by the State, and such others as have not, and still belong to the communes. In these latter the devastation increases every year, annually exposing the *route nationale* and the Bastan to ever magnifying dangers of obstruction."

All the valley might be saved and reclaimed, but everywhere, here as elsewhere, the Board of Forestation meets with sullen and stubborn opposition from the peasantry.

# CHAPTER XII

## TARBES

Tarbes an uninteresting place—A large village—Inglis on the view—
Jardin Massey—Cloister of S. Sever—Horses—The Haras—
Counts of Bigorre—Petronilla and her five husbands—Her will—
Numerous claimants—A long contest—Tarbes fortified—Sack by
the Huguenots—Massacre—The Leaguers—Battle of Tarbes—Re-
treat of Soult—Barrère—Macaulay on his character.

FROM Tarbes it is possible to escape in four directions, for from it radiate lines
to Paris, to Pau, to Bagnières, and to Toulouse, and another is in prospect to
Rustan and Mayonac.

No one presumably would stay in Tarbes for two days unless he were an of-
ficial tied to duties in it and enjoying a salary, or were possessed with a passion
for horses. For, indeed, in Tarbes itself there is nothing to be seen save the Haras
and the depot for remounts to the cavalry. The cathedral is the most cumbrous,
ungainly minster in all France. The public buildings lack interest. One thing Tarbes
does possess, that it shares with the meanest village in the same arrondisement—
the view of the Pyrenees.

Inglis, who trudged the Pyrenees in 1830, thus describes the prospect:—

> "I have read in some book that the most beautiful part of ev-
> ery country is where the mountains sink down into the plains,
> and of this assertion the situation of Tarbes offers an excellent
> illustration. If I had never gone further into the Pyrenees than
> Tarbes I might have said that nothing can exceed the beauty of
> its neighbourhood. The charming plain that environs it—yet not
> altogether a plain—stretches to the foot of the mountains, rich in
> every production of the southern latitude, beautifully diversified
> with wood, and watered by the meanderings of the Adour and of
> several lesser streams. The celebrated Valley of Bagnères opens to
> the left, that of Lourdes to the right; while in the south, apparent-
> ly at but a few leagues distant, the Pic du Midi towers above the
> range of mountains that extend to the right and to the left, as far
> as the eye can reach.
>
> "After the long continuation of carriage-travelling from Avi-
> gnon to Tarbes—oh, how I enjoyed this morning! It was a glori-

ous morning, and the magnificent range of the Pyrenees, rising sharply from the plain, was bathed in sunbeams, which gilded the eminences, reposed on the slopes, and gleamed in among the valleys. If this book should chance to be read by anyone who knows the scenery of Scotland, let him recollect the road from Stirling along the foot of the Ochill Hills, and he will have a better conception of the country through which I am now conveying him, than could be conveyed by a thousand minute descriptions. It is true his imagination must assist me; he must imagine the Ochills seven to eight thousand feet high in place of two thousand; he must substitute Indian corn of the most luxuriant growth, for oats and barley; and, in place of whin-blossoms covering the knolls, he must fancy them clothed with vine; he must add the charm of a southern sky, and the balminess of a southern clime."

Tarbes is a huge, straddling city, a great village giving itself the airs of a capital. On entering it from the station the town has an unattractive aspect. An avenue has been driven from the Gave to the Place Maubourguet, which is the centre of the town; but it has few houses along it, and none of consequence, and these throughout Tarbes have the appearance of villas in a suburb, surrounded with gardens. Some effort has been made to retrieve the ugliness of the town by the erection of fountains and statues, and by planting handsome promenades. But it is a lifeless place, only acquiring animation on the occasion of its fairs. The river strays in its vast bed, broken into several streams by rubble banks. It has been drawn off above the town by numerous channels of irrigation, so that when it reaches Tarbes it is out of proportion to its bed, as might be an infant in the vast fourposter of Ware.

But the Jardin Massey is the pride of Tarbes; it is a park extending over thirty acres—space is no object in Tarbes—and is really interesting. It was the gift to his native town by the man whose name it bears. Massey left Tarbes as a journeyman gardener, and visited Holland, where he obtained a situation as director of the gardens of the king. Louis Philippe summoned him to France, and made him manager of the gardens of Versailles. As he had amassed a good deal of money, he resolved on spending it for the adornment of his native town. He bought the land where now is the park, dug a lake, formed water-courses, planted rare trees, laid out flower-beds and lawns, and built a museum of natural history commanded by a lofty tower. In fifty years the trees have grown to a considerable size; and later benefactors have enriched the gardens with statues, busts, and the museum with sculptures and paintings. In the park has been erected the beautiful cloister of the fifteenth century removed from S. Sever-de-Rustan, a monastery wrecked by the Calvinists, under Lizier, who massacred all the inhabitants of the town, with the exception of seven persons. The monks would have been also put to death but that Queen Jeanne had already suppressed the abbey, and they had been dispersed. Next to the Jardin Massey the Haras should be inspected.

In ancient days the horses of the county of Bigorre, the viscounty of Béarn, and of Lower Navarre were highly esteemed; the race was called Navarrine, and it owed its merits to the fact that it was a cross between the Arab and the native

Pyrenean stock. The Saracens had crossed the mountains, overflowed Aquitaine, and threatened Northern France, they were met at Poitiers and routed by Charles Martel in 731. Three hundred thousand Saracens, say the old chroniclers, with their usual exaggeration, fell on the field; the rest fled, the main body to Narbonne, others to such passes as they knew that led to Saragossa. A battle was fought near Tarbes, in which the flying remnant was utterly routed and exterminated. A great number of their stallions and mares remained in the hands of the victors, and it was from this capture that sprang the so much coveted and esteemed race of the Navarrine horse.

By degrees the quality declined and degenerated, reverting to the type of the Basque horse. This was due partly to lack of importation of fresh Arab blood, and partly to the mountaineers neglecting the breeding of horses for that of mules, specially serviceable to them among the mountain passes where were tracks, but no roads. The evil became so great that the Estates of Bigorre voted two thousand livres annually for the maintenance of stallions. During the Revolution, when there was great demand for mounts for the cavalry, the scarcity of good horses attracted the attention of the Council of Five Hundred. Napoleon took the matter in hand with his characteristic energy. In 1806 he founded the Haras at Tarbes, and the introduction of English blood was the basis of the transformation attempted. Later, during the campaigns in Algeria, the finest stallions taken from the Arabs were sent to Tarbes; and the result has been the production of a horse admirably adapted to the use of light cavalry, that goes now by the name of the Tarbes horse. Mm. Simonoff and Mörder, of the Russian haras, thus speak of it:—

> "The three bloods of which the Tarbes horse derives—the Arab, the English, and the old Navarrin—are so near to each other, being all of Oriental origin, that the fusion took place easily and quickly; and although as yet the Tarbes horses are not of perfect homogeneity, it is quite possible to speak of them as forming a race which by its qualities, is rather full blood; than half blood."

The stallions are in the Haras at Tarbes, but the mares are dispersed within a radius of twenty kilometres around Tarbes; and the rearing of colts is the industry, and makes the fortune of the department, at all events of the plain and fertile valleys. Within the district where they are reared there is not a village, not a farm, that has not its mares for breeding. Even *curés* supplement their scanty incomes by keeping them, and rearing from them. One, the Abbé Turon, sold to the State his stallion Mousquetaire for 20,000 francs. This roused a great outcry among the Radicals, who denounced the Government for having bought from a priest. Tarbes is the old capital of Bigorre, and here resided the Count. I have already mentioned Centule I of Béarn, assassinated in 1088, who put away his wife with the approval of Pope Gregory VII, so as to marry the heiress of Bigorre. By this union Bigorre and Béarn were not united, for his son Gaston by the repudiated Gisela became Viscount of Béarn, and his son Bernard III inherited Bigorre. This Bernard left issue, a daughter only, named Beatrice, who married Peter, Viscount de Marsan, by whom she had Centule III, and he also left an heiress, Stephanie, married to Bertrand, Count of Cominges, by whom she had one child, a daughter Petronilla.

The story of the annexation of Bigorre to Foix and Béarn is complicated through the matrimonial vagaries of this same Petronilla. And this was further complicated by the action of a pious ancestor, Count Bernard II, who in a fit of maudlin devotion placed his territory and family under the protection of the black doll, Notre Dame du Puy, promising in return for this protection that the county should annually pay tribute to the church of Le Puy. Certainly Our Lady of Puy treated Bigorre scurvily in return, allowing the inheritance to slip through heiresses, five in all, and, moreover, to involve it in a lawsuit that lasted a hundred and thirty-nine years.

Petronilla married Gaston, Viscount of Béarn, and when he died without issue, in 1215, took as number two Nûnez de Cerdagne, but tired of him speedily, got the marriage annulled, on the convenient plea of consanguinity, and married in 1216 Guy, son of Simon de Montfort. This was sharp work—three husbands in a twelvemonth. By Guy she had two daughters, Alix and Perette. In 1228 she took a fourth husband, Aimart de Rançon, and on his death, in the same year, she espoused her fifth, Boso de Mastas, to whom she bore a daughter, Martha. By her will Petronilla constituted Esquirat, eldest son of her daughter Alix, heir to her estates and titles; but in default of male issue the succession was to go to Jordan, the second son of Alix. Should he fail to have a son, then the second substitution was in favour of Martha, her daughter by Boso, who was married to Gaston VII of Béarn. Esquirat did have a son, also named Esquirat, but this second Esquirat died childless, and bequeathed the county of Bigorre to his sister Lore, as his uncle Jordan had died without issue. Now Petronilla and her third husband Guy de Montfort had left a second daughter, Perette, married to Raoul de Teisson, and had by him a son William de Teisson, who conceived that he had a right to the inheritance. Martha, wife of Gaston de Béarn, had a daughter Constance, and she also put in a claim. In fact, these were the claimants: Lore, Viscountess de Turenne; Constance, Viscountess de Béarn; William de Teisson; and Mahut, daughter of Alix and Raoul de Courtenay. But that was not all. The younger Esquirat had made over his inheritance to Simon de Montfort by a first will, and then, offended at the grasping nature of Simon, had revoked his will and constituted Lore his heiress. But Simon refused to recognize the legality of this second will, sold the viscounty to Thibalt II, King of Navarre, whose son Henry gave his claim to it to Jeanne, his daughter, married to Philip the Fair, King of France, and he was but too ready to acquire this rich district of Gascony on any plea, bad or good. The church of Le Puy also put in a claim, so did the King of England as overlord. Consequently there were from eight to nine claimants.

By decree of Parliament, in 1290, the rights of the church of Le Puy to the charge on the viscounty were confirmed.

Constance, Viscountess of Béarn, occupied Bigorre with her troops, and assumed the title of Countess of Bigorre. Jeanne of France, however, expelled her, adopted the title, and Philip the Fair asserted his right to the territory, and was prepared to maintain it by force of arms. Philip had already bought off the rights of the church of Le Puy. Bigorre remained under the crown of France till Charles VIII in 1425 granted it to John, Count of Foix, in return for his services against the

English, and in consideration of his descent from Petronilla.

From 1425 to 1566 the county of Bigorre was wisely administered by the viscounts of Béarn, who had become titular Kings of Navarre.

Tarbes was fortified in the tenth century by Raymond I. It suffered destruction at the hands of the English in 1350 and 1406. But its greatest disasters took place during the Wars of Religion. Jeanne d'Albret was resolved on forcing the Reform on the Bigorriens, but they ejected the Huguenot pastors as fast as they were sent to them, and appealed to the King of France, who sent troops in 1569 to their aid. Jeanne enlisted the services of Montgomery. He swept through the country, ravaging it with fire and sword. He sent his lieutenant, Montamat, to take Tarbes, and Montamat appeared under its walls on 20 January, 1570. The besieged, finding it impossible to hold out, evacuated the city during the night. When the Huguenots entered they found no one in the place, and they pillaged the houses and set them on fire.

When he was gone the inhabitants returned and began to restore their wrecked and gutted houses and to repair the walls. Montamat reappeared, bringing cannons with him. François de Bennasse, commandant of the garrison at Lourdes, had hastened to the defence of the capital at the head of 800 men. Montamat attempted an assault, and was repulsed. But a traitor in the town opened the gates to the Calvinists, and the captain entered. Bennasse, all his soldiers, and many of the citizens were put to the sword. The number massacred was so great that it took eight days to bury them.

> "This took place," says a contemporary writer, "about the feast of Easter, in the year 1570. After that the city of Tarbes remained without inhabitants, and the grass grew in the streets as in a field, a piteous sight to behold. And three whole years elapsed without there being a garrison in it; but indeed the town was incapable of defence on account of the ruins made by the cannon."

Peace was concluded at S. Germain-en-Laye on 15 May, 1570, and it was hoped that tranquillity would ensue. But this was not to be. Passions had been wrought to frenzy, and the thirst for revenge was consuming. The death of Jeanne d'Albret in 1579 did not allay the troubles. In 1592 the town became the prey of the Leaguers of Cominges, and from it they issued to devastate the surrounding country, till expelled in 1594. Almost the whole population of Cominges had embraced the cause of the League. "There was never before seen such disorder, such pillage, from the beginning of these wars. Captains, soldiers, valets, and volunteers were so laden with furniture that they were carrying off that they complained it was a trouble to them to be encumbered with so much spoil. Moreover, in despair, the peasants of Bigorre abandoned the cultivation of the land, and many migrated into Spain."

In 1594 the people themselves rose, and, assisted by Caumont de la Force, delivered themselves from both Leaguers and Protestants, and peace was celebrated at Tarbes.

On 12 March, 1814, a combat took place between the English and Portuguese under Wellington, and the French under Soult. After the defeat of Orthez Soult had withdrawn his dispirited soldiers along both banks of the Adour, steadily pursued by Wellington.

"A light division," says Allison, "and hussars were on the right bank of the Adour; but when they approached the town, a simultaneous movement was made by Hill with the right wing, and Clinton on the left, to envelope and cut off Harispe and Villatte's divisions, which formed the French rearguard in occupation of it.

"The combat began at twelve o'clock by a violent fire from Hill's artillery on the right, which was immediately re-echoed in still louder tones by Clinton on the left; while Alton, with the light division, assailed the centre. The French fought stoutly, and, mistaking the British rifle battalions, from their dark uniforms, to be Portuguese, let them come up to the very muzzles of their guns. But the rifles were hardy veterans, inured to victory; and at length Harispe's men, unable to stand their deadly point-blank fire, broke and fled. If Clinton's men on the left had been up at this moment, the French would have been totally destroyed; for Hill had, at the same moment, driven back Villate on the right, and the plain beyond Tarbes was covered with a confused mass of fugitives, closely followed by the shouting of victorious British. But Clinton's troops, notwithstanding the utmost efforts, had not been able to get up; the numerous ditches and hedges which intersected the plain rendered all pursuit impossible; and thus the French, though utterly broken, succeeded with very little loss in reaching a ridge, three miles distant, when Clauzel, who, with four divisions, was drawn up to receive them, immediately opened fire from all his batteries upon the allies."

During the night Soult retired in two columns, and such was the rapidity of his retreat that he reached Toulouse in four days.

A native of Tarbes, of whom the town has no occasion to boast, was Bertrand Barrère, born 10 September, 1755. He was educated for the Bar at Toulouse, and became a scrivener at Toul. As his father owned a pretty estate at Vieuzac, in the Valley of Argelez, he called himself Barrère de Vieuzac, flattering himself that by this feudal addition to his name he might pass for a gentleman. He was sent as deputy for Bigorre to the States-General. Being totally devoid of principle, when the result of a parliamentary struggle could not be foreseen he took the precaution of having in his pocket two speeches, written in opposed senses, so that he could always jump in the direction taken by the cat. Barrère had affected the moderate principles of the Girondists, till he saw that the extremists were the strongest, and then he threw in his lot with the Mountain, and voted for the execution of the King. Then seeing that the current ran strong against the Girondists, he took the foremost place in procuring the condemnation to the scaffold of those with whom he had previously acted in concert. He it was who was set up in the convention to call for the blood of the Queen. On the day on which Marie Antoinette was dragged to execution Barrère regaled Robespierre and other Jacobins at a tavern.

"In the intervals between the Beaume and the Champagne, between the ragout of thrushes and the partridges with truffles, he fervently preached his new political creed. 'The vessel of the Revolution,' he said, 'can float into port only on waves of blood. We must begin with the members of the National Assembly and of the Legislative Assembly. That rubbish must be swept away.'"

The Reign of Terror began. The Jacobins had prevailed all along the line. The Convention was reduced to silence. The sovereignty had passed to the Committee of Public Safety. Six persons held the chief power in the small cabinet which domineered over France: Robespierre, Saint Just, Couthon, Collot, Billaud, and Barrère who had hastily divested himself of his territorial appendix of De Vieuzac. Of the horrors of those days it is unnecessary to speak. As guilty as Robespierre or Couthon was the bland, timorous, unscrupulous Barrère. He it was who proposed the burning of the towns and villages of the Vendéeans, the total destruction of Lyons, the violation of the royal graves at S. Denys, the deportation of all such as could not bring irrecusable proof of patriotism since 1792. He became the declared adversary of Danton when he found it safe to take that part, and proposed his arrest on the 9th Thermidor. He contributed powerfully to the fall of Robespierre; but he had made so many enemies, was so little trusted, that instead of rising higher by the fall of Robespierre, he found himself unable to maintain his balance. He was denounced before the revolutionary tribunal, along with Collot d'Herbois and Billaud-Varennes, and was sentenced to be deported to the pestilential swamps of Cayenne, but obtained the change of his destination to the Isle of Oléron. After having sacrificed his old allies, the Hébertistes, the Dantonistes, and the Robespierristes, he himself had fallen. When moved later from Oléron to Saintes, he succeeded in escaping from prison. The *coup d'état* of the eighteenth Brumaire restored him to liberty. We need not follow in detail his further adventures. When Louis XVIII gained the throne of his ancestors by the aid of foreign bayonets, Barrère fled to Brussels. The revolution of July put an end to his exile, and he returned to the south of France, and settled at Argelez, where he died 14 January, 1841.

His memoirs in four volumes were published under the editorship of Hippolyte Carnot and David d'Angers, in 1843. They are replete with disingenuousness in the representation of the part he played, as also of falsehoods, that can be proved to be such by reference to the contemporary files of the *Moniteur*.

Macaulay, at the opening of his long and brilliant essay on Barrère, says:—

"Our opinion is this: that Barrère approached nearer than any person mentioned in history or fiction, whether man or devil, to the idea of consummate and universal depravity. In him the qualities which are the proper objects of hatred, and the qualities which are the proper objects of contempt, preserve an exquisite and absolute harmony. In almost every particular sort of wickedness he has had rivals. His sensuality was immoderate; but this was a failing common to him with many great and amiable men. There have been many men as cowardly as he, some as cruel, a few as mean, a few as impudent. There may also have been as great liars, though we never met with them or read of them. But when we put everything together—sensuality, paltroonery, baseness, effrontery, mendacity, barbarity—the result is something which in a novel we would condemn as a caricature, and to which, we venture to say, no parallel can be found in history."

At the close of the article Macaulay says in reference to Hippolyte Carnot, who states that Barrère was at no time a sceptic, that he was the author of a pious treatise, entitled, *Of Christianity and its Influence*, as also of a book of meditations on the Psalms:—

"This makes the character complete. Whatsoever things are false, whatsoever things are dishonest, whatsoever things are unjust, whatsoever things are impure, whatsoever things are hateful, whatsoever things are of evil report; if there be any vice, and if there be any infamy, all these things, we knew, were blended in Barrère. But one thing was still wanting, and that M. Hippolyte Carnot has supplied. When to such an assemblage of qualities a high profession of piety is added, the effect is overpowering.

"We have no pleasure in seeing human nature thus degraded. We turn with disgust from the filthy and spiteful Yahoos of the fiction; and the filthiest and most spiteful Yahoo of the fiction was a noble creature when compared with the Barrère of history. But what is no pleasure M. Carnot has made a duty. It is no light thing that a man in high and honourable public trust should come forward to demand approbation for a life black with every sort of wickedness, and unredeemed by a single virtue. This M. Hippolyte Carnot has done. By attempting to enshrine this Jacobin carrion, he has forced us to gibbet it; and we may venture to say that, from the eminence of infamy on which we have placed it, he will not easily take it down."

Strange irony of fate. In Barrère's native town, his victim, Danton, only less detestable than himself, is glorified with a monument, a statue in bronze. After Danton, perhaps Tarbes will erect one to Barrère.

# CHAPTER XIII

## BAGNÈRES

Visitors and residents—Pic du Midi—Ramond—Springs—Captain
Lizier—Observatory—Vaussenat and Nansouty—Death of the
former—Val de Campan—Château d'Asté—The Grammont family—La belle Corisande—Philibert de Grammont—His memoirs—Larrey—Marbles—The Lac bleu—Slate quarries—The
Cagots—Caput Mortuum—Lepers—Recuperative power of Nature—Efforts of the Church to break down the barrier—Crestiaas.

Bagnères de Bigorre is a town, but it is country as well; it has the amusements
and dissipations provided by a place of public resort, but it has also lovely and
quiet resting-places in mountain solitudes.

It swarms during the season with water-drinkers, bathers, loungers, ladies
who wear elegant toilettes, and bucks turned out by the best Parisian tailors. But
it also contains marble works, linen factories, and women who are skilful at the
knitting of the so-called Barèges shawls. The wool is from Spain, the finest Merino,
and this enables them to make the shawls delicate as lace.

To the south lie the mountains rising steeply, and commanded by the Pic du
Midi. For long a rivalry existed between the Bigorriens and they of Roussillon as
to whether the Pic du Midi or the Canigou was the loftiest mountain of the Pyrenean chain; indeed, some claimed for each that it was the highest peak in Europe.
In both cases the mistake was due to the position of each mountain starting boldly
out of the plain.

It was due to Ramond that the Pic du Midi was forced to lower its pretensions. In 1787 this secretary of the Cardinal de Rohan ascended the mountain, and
on reaching the summit, and seeing before him to the south the perpetual snows
of the gleaming glaciers above the Cirque of Gavarnie, he realized what had not
before been suspected, that the Pic du Midi was but a mountain of the second
order. Then the inspiration took him to explore the whole range. He was engaged
for fifteen years on the task, and he was the first to reveal to French people what
the Pyrenees really were. Till he had explored them they knew nothing about the
chains save what they saw from the plains, and from the passes leading into Spain,
for at that time no roads had been engineered up the gorges. The visitor went no
farther than to Laruns in the Val d'Ossau, and Pierrefite in that of Argelez, unless
he committed himself to a guide, and mounted a mule, and was led over wild
heights along mere tracks.

The explorations of Ramond and his successors have been recorded with humour by H. Béraldi in his book, *Cent ans aux Pyrenees*:—

> "He accomplished," says Ardouin-Dumazet, "that which ought to have been done for the Alps; they also were undiscovered, scientifically, till the year 1787. For, be it observed, Ramond received his inspiration on the top of the Pic du Midi, in the same year in which Saussure reached the summit of Mont Blanc, along with Jacques Balmat."

The mountains rising steeply to the south of Bagnères render the place cool in summer, when some of the sun is cut off; but it is a dreary residence in the winter, for the same reason.

There are springs of various temperatures and mineral components, ferruginous, sulphurous, etc., advertised as good for nearly every complaint under the sun. It was the Roman Aquæ Convenarum, and visitors may now bathe in the marble basins in which Gallo-Roman ladies and gentlemen dipped. Bagnères was always a town, and in the Hôtel de Ville are preserved archives containing much relative to the history of the place; among these is a charter of Esquirat, Count of Bigorre, confirming the customs and liberties of Bagnères, dated 1251.

The history of the town is one of untroubled serenity till the times of the Wars of Religion. Captain Lizier, the Huguenot, on occupying Tarbes, imposed a heavy subsidy on the neighbouring towns, Bagnères included. But Bagnères demurred to raising the contribution demanded. Lizier marched to it, got hold of the governor, Beaudéan, and shot him. The people of Bagnères resolved on revenge. They drew the terrible captain into an ambuscade and killed him to the shout of "Remember Beaudéan!"

On the summit of the Pic du Midi is an observatory, erected by the energy of two men: Vaussenat and General Nansouty. Vaussenat was a native of Grenoble, born of a labouring family in 1837. He was admitted into the school of arts, and traded at Aix, and on leaving it was engaged in search for metals in Savoy. But summoned to the Pyrenees to manage some mines there, he married a niece of a general at Bagnères, and settled there. He saw, what indeed others had seen before him, that the Pic was admirably suited for a meteorological observatory, but he could not induce the Government to take any steps towards its construction. However, he managed to communicate his enthusiasm to General Nansouty, and between them the foundations were laid and the work was begun. The general took up his abode in the cabin of Sencours, just below the terminal cone, where he passed winter and summer registering his observations, whilst Vaussenat travelled through France, lecturing, exhorting, wringing money for the work out of learned societies and from generous individuals. Nansouty underwent great hardships. On one occasion, in December, 1874, a furious tempest burst over the refuge of Sencours, and twelve feet of snow was heaped on the roof, one of the windows was blown in, and the door gave way. It was absolutely necessary to quit the place. Nansouty, aided by his two companions, took seventeen hours struggling through the snow to reach the bottom, a distance that can easily be mounted in two hours and a half.

The observatory was completed in 1882, and was made over by these two energetic men to the State, whereupon Vaussenat was appointed director of the observatory. He lived till 1891, when he fell ill in it. He was being conveyed down the mountain, when one of the bearers slipped, and Vaussenat was flung down a steep descent of ice. He was taken up and carried to Bagnères, where he succumbed eight days after.

Bagnères is at the mouth of the Val de Campan. In it are the ivy-mantled ruins of the Castle of Asté. They are inconsiderable, and in themselves hardly deserve a visit. But they are of some historic interest, as this Château d'Asté was the second cradle of the dukes of Grammont. The barons d'Asté, early in the sixteenth century, became viscounts, and Menard d'Aure, Viscount Asté, had the good luck to marry the heiress of Grammont. Thenceforth his descendants assumed the title of counts of Grammont and viscounts of Asté.

Their principal residence now became Grammont, in Labourde, on the Bidouze; but for hunting the wolf and the bear, and in the heat of summer they came to Asté. Here it was that the amorous Henri Quatre was wont to visit la belle Corisande, wife of Philibert de Grammont, who died at the age of twenty-eight, in 1580. Diana, or la belle Corisande, was the only daughter of Paul, Viscount Louvigny. By her husband she had Anthony, Count of Grammont, and Guiche, also of Louvigny, Seigneur of Bidache, Viscount Asté, Viceroy of Navarre, Governor and Perpetual Hereditary Mayor of Bayonne. One of his sons, Philibert, married Elizabeth, daughter of George, Earl of Hamilton. Her picture is in the National Portrait Gallery, and one wonders, looking at it, how she could have been called "la belle Hamilton" in the French Court.

Philibert and Elizabeth had a daughter, Claude Charlotte, who married Henry Howard, Earl of Stafford. It was of Philibert, born in 1621, and who died in 1707, that the entertaining memoirs were written by Anthony Hamilton. It has been well said:—

> "The history of Grammont may be considered as unique: there is nothing like it in any language. In drollery, knowledge of the world, various satire, general utility, united with great vivacity of composition, Gil Blas is unrivalled; but as a merely agreeable book, the *Memoirs of Grammont* perhaps deserve that character more than any which was ever written; it is pleasantry throughout, and pleasantry of the best sort; unforced, graceful, and engaging. Some French critic has justly observed that if any book were to be selected as affording the truest specimen of perfect French gaiety, the *Memoirs of Grammont* would be selected in preference to all others."

In the church of Asté is a white marble statue of the Virgin that is an object of great veneration; also a painting attributed to Philippe de Champagne. The village of Beaudéan was the native place of the surgeon Larrey, born in 1766, who behaved with great self-devotion in the battle of Eylau and the retreat from Moscow. Napoleon I said that he was the most honest man he had ever known, and the most disinterested. He created him a baron, and bequeathed to him 100,000 francs. Larrey died in 1847. The house in which he was born is a humble cottage; he bequeathed it to the parish that it might be turned into a school.

Campan, that gives its name to the somewhat overpraised valley, is chiefly known for the marbles it produces. The peristyle of the Grand Trianon, the new and vulgar opera-house at Paris, have employed this splendid marble. Even Berlin has had recourse to its quarries for twenty-two columns of the royal palace.

There are several mountain tarns more or less accessible from Bagnères. That most easily reached—but taking six hours—is the Lac Bleu, a beautiful sheet of water of the most intense sapphire-blue, girded about by rocks of a golden yellow. It covers 98 acres, and is 360 feet deep. The spirit of utility has mounted to this height, and bridled the outflow, and uses it for economic purposes. A tunnel 900 feet long has been bored through the rocks on the north side of the lake, to draw off the water as needed in times when the Adour has dwindled to a thread, and cannot feed the channels of irrigation needed in the plain.

Other tarns are the Lac de Peyrelade, lying in a cirque under the Pic du Midi, also the Lac d'Isaby.

Many delightful valleys open out into the Val de Campan, The longest of these is that through which flows the Oussonet, that reaches the Adour some way below Bagnères; but a good road takes directly from Bagnères to the lateral valley of Labassere, famous for its slate quarries. The excavations are in the flanks of the mountain, and are numerous. The products are brought down by a funicular contrivance worked by electricity, taking the place of the zigzag road by which oxen formerly conveyed the slates below. The men who split the slates wear heavy sabots scooped out of billets of beech that have not been shaped externally, so as better to resist, should the sharp, cutting flakes fall on the feet. The men's legs are bound about thickly with rags to protect them from the same danger, as the slate cuts like a razor. The slate-splitters form the aristocracy of the trade, and although their labour is less considerable than that of the quarrymen, they receive double the pay of these latter. For a slate-cutter has to learn the art before he is aged fourteen, whilst the muscles are most flexible. At the age of twenty he has to undergo military service, and when he returns to his shed and tools, at the age of twenty-four, finds it very difficult to recover the skill he possessed before he donned uniform.

One of the most interesting and perplexing themes connected with the Pyrenees is the origin of the Cagots, a "race maudit," that was found throughout the chain, but not there solely. It existed as well in Brittany.

In a considerable number of churches may be seen the Cagots' door, through which alone they might pass into a portion of the church reserved for them, and cut off from the rest, and where alone they might assist at divine worship. In some of the towns are streets called Rues des Cagots, in which these outcasts herded. At one time they were not suffered to inhabit the villages, but were relegated to isolated hamlets, and they had separate burial grounds. They might not associate with the more privileged natives, and inter-marriages with them were strictly in-terdicted. They were required to wear a distinctive badge—a goose's foot in red cloth attached to one shoulder. The expression "Cagot" is still used as a term of opprobrium. But when one asks to be shown a Cagot, after some hesitation, a *cre-tin* or a poor creature afflicted with a *goître* is pointed out.

But the original Cagot was not such.

Jean Darnal, a solicitor in the Parliament of Bordeaux, thus describes the Cag-ots, whom he calls Gahets, in his *Chronique Bourdeloise*, 1555.

> "The magistrates gave orders that the Gahets should reside outside the town on the side of S. Julien, in a little faubourg apart, that they should not leave it without wearing conspicuously a bit of red cloth. These are a sort of lepers, with the disease in an un-developed condition, with whom it is ill to associate. They are car-penters by trade, and capital workmen, and gain their livelihood by this trade in the town and in the country."

One notion concerning them was that they descended from the carpenter who had made the cross of Christ; and most of them, though by no means all, actually were carpenters. Florimond de Rémond, councillor of the Parliament of Bordeaux, wrote concerning them in 1613:—

> "We see in Guyenne this race, commonly designated Cangots or Capots, one which although Christian and Catholic, holds no communication with others, and may enter into no alliance with other Christians; even to live in their towns is not allowed. They are not suffered to approach the Holy Table along with other Christians, and have a place set apart for them in the churches. The people are convinced that they are diseased, that their breath and sweat is malodorous, and that they are to some extent lepers. This is why that in many places, as at Bordeaux, they are con-strained to wear a scrap of red cloth on one shoulder."

Florimond goes on to say that he believes them to be descended from the Ari-an Goths, and that Cagot is derived from *Canis Gots*, or Dogs of Goths.

Popularly they were held to have certain distinguishing characteristics—ears furred like those of bears and destitute of the lower lobe. That they had stinking breath, and white granular spots under the skin in parts of the body, indicating undeveloped leprosy. In parish registers they were always designated in entries of baptisms and marriages and burials as Cagots or Capots.

F. Michel, in 1847, published a work upon them. He went through the Pyre-nees, and recorded how many families of Cagots remained, and where they resid-ed.

The theory of their origin as propounded by him was that they were descend-ed from the Spanish Christians who were driven over the Pyrenees by the Moors, and whom the natives received with scant hospitality, and continued to look upon as intruders. One reason for the adoption of this wild theory was that in ancient documents they are frequently called Crestiaas. Undoubtedly refugees from Spain did settle in parts of the Pyrenees, but there exists no evidence to show that they were looked down upon. Moreover, Cagots were found also in Brittany, and Michel's theory does not fit in with this fact.

Now the word *cagot* is comparatively modern. A Cagot in old documents is called *Capot* or *Crestiaa*. Capot comes from *caput mortuum*, a legal expression used of one who is outside the pale of the law; the word is still employed in Germany for what is broken and of no further use. *Es ist caput.*

The original Cagots were probably lepers, gradually recruited from the native population. A religious service was said over a man on whom were discovered the marks of the disease. It was a form of funeral. Earth was cast upon him, and he was declared to be legally and socially dead.

Precisely the same regulations were applied to the Cagots that were made for lepers. They were forbidden to spit in the roads, and to walk in them barefooted. If constrained to handle anything that had to be used by those who were sound, they must wear gloves. They might not marry out of their caste or company. They were relegated to live and be buried apart from all others.

When we consider this identity of regulation, as also that the Cagots are spoken of by all old writers as quasi-lepers, as that in popular belief they were held to have on them marks of undeveloped leprosy; when, further, we see that their old designation comes from *caput mortuum*, I think it is hard not to arrive at the conclusion that the Cagots were the descendants of sequestrated communities of lepers. But such is the recuperative power of Nature, in the healthy surroundings of the mountains, in its pure air and in wholesome diet, that the descendants of the lepers in course of time shook off the disease and became sound and robust men and women.

The Church in the eighteenth century made an effort to break down the wall of separation, the occasion for the existence of which had ceased.

We hear of an archdeacon when visiting one church had his indignation roused by seeing the Cagots huddled together in a side chapel apart from the rest of the congregation. Taking the Blessed Sacrament in his hands, he marched out of the church through the Cagots' chapel and door, and signed to the congregation to follow him. After a moment's hesitation they obeyed, and from that day the prejudice against these outcasts failed in that parish. In the Middle Ages no Cagot could become consul, mayor, juror, or be admitted to Holy Orders. But De Romagne, Bishop of Tarbes, who died in 1768, ordained to the priesthood several members of this proscribed race.

It was due to the French Revolution, that beat down all barriers, that the distinction between Cagots and other men was wholly obliterated. In the Val de Campan, between four and five miles from Campan itself, is a hamlet, situated high up on the mountain side, that is occupied by six families, all by descent Cagots. The place where they live is called "Le Quartier des Cagots." Doctor Abadie, about 1840, wrote concerning them: —

"I know the heads of these families. They are carpenters. Half a century ago these families intermarried among themselves, and were not suffered to contract unions outside their narrow circle. Now they are mingled with and are melted into the mass of the population. In physiognomy they have nothing peculiar. One remarks only that the individuals of the families Pescadère, Latoure, Lacôme, and Daléas have a white skin and grey eyes; but this is perhaps due to a lymphatic constitution, the result of living in a cold and damp locality."

M. Dufresne, who filled an important, though subsidiary, post in the administration of finances under Necker, and whose bust, under the First Consul, was placed in the hall of the Treasury, in recognition of the public services he had rendered, was by birth and ancestry a Cagot; so we see that careers were open to these members of an outcast and despised race even before the Revolution. What that great upheaval did for them was to destroy the popular prejudice entertained against them.

The derivation of the word *cagot* has been given; that of *crestiaas* is not so simple. The name is never spelt with an *h* in early documents, as if it were derived from Christians. It probably comes from these unfortunates having been originally compelled to wear a bit of red cloth on the cap as a cock's comb, or *crest*, and that later this more conspicuous mark of infamy was modified into one placed upon the shoulder. Still, however, the expression "the crested" was applied to them.

It is in vain to look for a genuine Cagot at the present time, and in the words of an old ballad sung by the people—

"Encouere qué Cagots siam
Nous noun dam;
Tous qu'em hilhs deü pay, Adam."

That may be rendered—

"Then let them say just what they will, and call us Cagots vile,
We all the sons of Adam are, on all God deigns to smile."

# CHAPTER XIV

## THE VAL D'AURE

Mauvezin—Escaldieu—Lannemezan—The Neste—The lakes uti-
lized—Lortet—Fortified caves—Marble quarries—Sarracolin—
Canal—Val d'Arros—The rival lords—Arreau—Bordères—The
Armagnacs—John IV and his sister—His ingratitude and death—
Extinction of the race—Lac de Caillaouas—Cadéac—The deadly
sins—Tramesaïgues—Lac d'Orredon—Republic.

BEFORE the train reaches the dreary moorland of Lannemezan, on its way from
Tarbes to Toulouse, a glimpse is obtained of a picturesque village grouped
about a castle on a pointed rock. This is Mauvezin, the Bad Neighbour, *par excel-
lence*. It witnessed many exploits during the English occupation of Guyenne. It
was besieged in 1374 by the Duke of Anjou, at the head of 8000 men. The strength
of the fortress was such that it would have been impregnable had it not lacked a
well within the walls. The besiegers cut off communication with the water-supply,
and as not a drop of rain fell during the six weeks of the siege, the garrison was
constrained to come to terms. The Duke of Anjou allowed them to depart, saying:
"Get you gone about your business, each one of you, to your several native lands,
without entering any fort that holds out against me; for if you do, I engage to get
hold of you, and deliver you up to Jocelin (the headsman), who will shave you
clean without a razor."

Upon the tower, which bears the arms of Béarn, may be seen the device, "J'ay
belle dame." It was a fancy of the boy Gaston, son of Gaston Phœbus, when he
was affianced to Beatrix d'Armagnac, to whom Mauvezin was given as a dower
by her father, Count John II. But Gaston was murdered by his father, as already
told, before the marriage was consummated, and Beatrix was afterwards married
to a viscount of Milan.

Near Mauvezin are the remains of the once famous Abbey of Escaldieu. The
church was destroyed by the Huguenots, and rebuilt in the seventeenth century.
It is devoid of interest, and is now converted into a coach-house. Only the chapter-house remains of the original abbey, a structure of the fourteenth century, the
vaulting sustained by marble pillars.

The great mass of Lannemezan, lying across the threshold of the Val d'Aure,
diverts the Neste from flowing north, and turns it to the east, just as the heap of
the *lande* of Pontacq acts at the mouth of the Lavedan, but there deflects the Gave
to the west. It falls into the Garonne at the confines of the department, which also

for the same reason takes an easterly course for some way, then struggles to the north-east, and only after passing Toulouse turns to take its direction so as to empty itself into the Atlantic. The Neste is a river of very great importance. It rises in two main branches under crests clothed in eternal snows, discharging glaciers into a series of upland lakes. These natural reservoirs have been artificially raised, and their waters conducted into a canal that is carried high above the bed of the river, so as to convey its fertilizing streams over the plateau of Lannemezan. The lake of Caillaouas, under the Pic de Batchinale, and the glacier cirque of the Gours Blancs has been captured at the head of Neste de Luron, and the lakes of Aumar, Aubert, Caplong, and Orredon, that feed the other Neste of Aure have also been utilized for the same purpose, at an enormous expense and by remarkably daring works of engineering. This has had a subsidiary advantage, that the superb scenery at the sources of these streams is now accessible by good roads, whereas formerly it could be reached only by difficult and dangerous mule-paths.

At La Barthe the Neste debouches from the mountains through a deep valley, the canal passing above it on the left bank; and although the river has been thus tapped, it still continues to bring down a considerable amount of water, the overflow from its reservoirs far away in the laps of the high mountain ridge.

The Val d'Aure constituted a viscounty, and of the viscounts there were several branches: one that of the Viscounts of Larbouste, another that of the viscounts of Asté, one of whom, as already mentioned, married the heiress of Grammont. The whole of Aure was under the overlordship of the counts of Armagnac.

La Barthe, commanded by a castle of the end of the eleventh century, will not long detain a visitor. But a short way above it is the village of Lortet, where are caverns in the face of the limestone cliff that have been occupied and fortified, it is thought, originally by the Saracens and the Visigoths; but the structures that remain, notably the tower, were the work of the Templars, to whom were confided the defence of most of the passes of the Pyrenees. At Hèches is a picturesque, ivy-clad tower occupying the summit by a rock. Here are quarries of marble, rose-coloured, grey, and white, spotted with black; as also of black marble veined with white. But the principal marble quarries are farther up, at Sarrancolin on the left bank, others are on the right. Those on the former are famous. The finest are red, veined with grey, or flesh tint with yellow veins; other marbles are green, blue, violet. Versailles was adorned with columns of Sarrancolin. Thence comes the marble now employed in the Louvre for most of the pedestals.

The church of Sarrancolin was originally strongly fortified, and served as the key to the valley; it is early of the twelfth century, with Romanesque windows. There are no aisles, it is a cross church. The choir grating is of the fifteenth century. In the church is the shrine of a Spanish bishop, S. Ebbo, and is the sole specimen in the district of Limoges work, and is of the thirteenth century. To the north of the church is the chapter-house in ruins. Fragments of the town walls remain, as does a gateway and tower of the fifteenth century. The houses are all built of the marble of which the hill is formed on which the place stands, and they are crowded about the church, in the constrained area within the old walls. The place recommends itself to the painter and to the archæologist.

The canal takes its waters from the Neste above the little town, and the river accordingly has in the upper portion of the valley a freer and fuller flow.

But before we have mounted so far up the Neste, a diversion may well be made to the valley of the Arros, which rises in the mountains between the Val de Campan and that of Aure. We might have supposed that it would speedily throw itself into the Adour or the Neste. But not so. It holds on its independent course far away to the north, and does not condescend to unite with the Adour till it enters the department of Gers.

In this narrow valley, high up in the mountains, stand near each other the two castles of Lomné and Espêche, concerning which the following legend is told. I will give it in the words of Mr. Inglis:—

"The lords of these two castles were enemies, and constantly disputed with one another the possession of the valley that lay between their castles; but along with the enmity each was enamoured of the wife of the other, though the ladies themselves loved their own lords, and gave no encouragement to the enemies of their husbands. At this time the Crusades were published, and both of the nobles resolved to forget private animosities for a time, and join the standard of the cross. It so happened, however, that after travelling during several days the devil entered into their hearts, and they both reasoned after this manner: 'My enemy has gone to the Holy Wars, and has left both his lands and his wife. What hinders me from returning and making the most of his absence?' And so both the Lord of Espêche and the Lord of Lomné returned and took the road not to their own castle, but to the castles of each other.

"But it so happened that on the very night upon which these nobles left their own castles their ladies had a vision. Each was warned in a dream of the intention of her husband to return and go to the castle of his enemy. Accordingly the ladies left their own castles to cross the valley, and met each other by the way; and having communicated the mutual vision, resolved upon a method of avoiding the danger. They determined to change castles, and that very day they put their resolution into effect.

"Meanwhile their lords arrived under cover of the night, each at the castle of his enemy, and were greatly surprised to find that no wonder was expressed at their return, for the ladies had forewarned their household of what was to be expected; but still greater was their surprise when, upon being ushered into the castle hall, each beheld his own spouse. The explanation that followed wrought a miraculous change. Touched with the affection of their wives, they abjured their mutual enmity, swore unutterable fidelity to their own wives, and set out in company together for the Holy Land."

Arreau stands at the junction of the two rivers called Neste, and also where the Lastie enters the stream. It has a cheerful appearance. The church of Notre Dame is of the fifteenth century, castellated, with additions a century later, built on the foundations of a church of the twelfth century, of which a good doorway remains. The chapel of S. Exuperius is of the eleventh century, and has a Romanesque portal. It stands above the Neste of Aure. The mairie is over the wooden market-hall. The entrance to the valley of the Neste de Luron is through a ravine with precipitous sides. Presently it opens out and reveals the little bourg of Bordères, commanded by the ruined castle of the Armagnacs. For now we are in Armagnac territory, and with this castle is connected the story of the last of that evil and ill-omened race. Michelet says of them:—

> "Frenchmen and princes as they were become, their diabolical nature broke out on every occasion. One of them married his brother's wife, so as to be able to retain the dower, another married his own sister, by means of a false dispensation. Bernard VII, Count of Armagnac, who was almost king, and ended so ill, had begun by despoiling his kinsman, the Viscount of Frézenzaguet, flinging him into a cistern, along with his sons, his eyes plucked out. This same Bernard, pretending to be a servant of the Duke of Orléans, made war against the English, but only worked for his own ends, for when the Duke came into Guyenne he made no attempt to assist him. But no sooner was that prince dead than he posed as his avenger, brought up all the South to ravage the North, made the young Duke of Orléans marry his daughter, and gave her as dower his bands of robbers, and the malediction of France.
>
> "What made these Armagnacs specially execrable was their impious levity allied to their innate ferocity."

The Armagnac territory extended as a strip from the Garonne to the Pyrenees. It was a fertile and well-peopled land; its principal towns were Auche, Mirande, Vic, and Lectoure.

The Armagnac family derived from a Garcias Sanchez, Duke of Gascony in the early part of the tenth century. He was nicknamed the Hunchback, and he seems to have bequeathed a moral distortion to his descendants.

John IV, Count of Armagnac, was especially associated with the castle at Bordères; and his story must now be told.

This headstrong man fell in love with his own sister, Isabella, and failing in his application to Rome for a dispensation to allow him to marry her, he forged one, and presented it to the chaplain of the castle, and demanded that he should unite them. When the priest demurred, Count John threatened to throw him headlong from the window into the river unless he obeyed. When others remonstrated, he drew his dagger on them. The cowed chaplain submitted to celebrate the incestuous nuptials.

The Pope now excommunicated the Count, and King Charles VII vainly endeavoured to recall him to a better mind; but Armagnac resisted kind instances, and defied force. Soon after he associated himself with the insurrection of the Dauphin. The Duke of Clermont was sent against him. His guilty passion had enfeebled the mind of John, and in place of resisting the invasion, he abandoned his dominions, and fled with Isabella to the protection of his relative, the King of Aragon. He was summoned by the Parliament, and having been rash enough to appear, was arrested and imprisoned. Soon after he managed to escape. The sentence of perpetual banishment was passed upon him, and his dominions were forfeited. The Valley of Aure was, however, exempted so far that it was granted as a dowry to his sister.

Then, as his last place of refuge, he retired to the Castle of Bordères, in the depths of the mountains. The once powerful and haughty Count of Armagnac was reduced to the deepest destitution, shunned by all, shrunk from even by his own subjects in the valley of the Neste, as though he were a leper or a Cagot. At last, impelled by his necessities rather than moved by remorse, he begged his way to Rome to obtain absolution for himself and for his sister. This was granted, but on hard conditions for himself, and that Isabella should retire into a convent at Barcelona.

At this time Louis XI ascended the throne of France, and by him the Count of Armagnac was restored to his former rank and possessions. He now married Jeanne, daughter of the Count of Foix, and the past was forgotten, or at least forgiven.

But this restless man, incapable of feeling gratitude for favours, allied himself with the enemies of the King, Charles the Bold, the Duke of Guyenne, and the King of England.

Louis XI took occasion of the first moment of tranquillity allowed him by the ambitious projects of the Duke of Burgundy, to chastise John of Armagnac. In 1473 he confided the task to the Cardinal of Albi, who besieged him in Lectoure. The town, which was strongly fortified, defended itself bravely. Proposals of surrender were made to the Count, but whilst negotiations were in progress, one of the gates was forced, and John's son, of the same name as his father, was killed fighting in the streets. John IV of Armagnac was stabbed in the presence of his wife, who was pregnant at the time. By order of Louis XI, who had no desire to see the line of Armagnac continued, she was thrown into prison and poisoned.

The title and claim to the county now devolved on Charles, another son of John IV; but Louis XI had him cast into prison, and retained there till he died of chagrin. There existed at the time another branch of the family, that had likewise received favours from King Louis, and had repaid them with treachery. Jacques d'Armagnac had been given by Louis XI vast estates in Meaux, Châlons, Langres, and Sens. The king had married Jacques to Louise of Anjou, and had created him Duke of Nemours. But Jacques was false to his benefactor, and joined in the League of Public Good against him. At the Treaty of Conflans he returned to his allegiance, swore fidelity on the relics in the Sainte Chapelle, and had the governorship of Paris conferred upon him. The very next year, 1469, he went over to the enemies of the King, and sided with his cousin, John IV, entering with him into negotiations with the English. But alarmed at the fate that befell John, he solicited pardon, and took an oath of fidelity, the most solemn and binding that could be devised.

Two years later, when Louis XI was in embarrassment, the Duke refused the King the succour he demanded, and prepared to lay his hands on Languedoc. No sooner was Louis delivered from his anxieties than he besieged and took Nemours, in his Castle of Carlat, and confined him in an iron cage in the Bastille. His wife, feeling confident that he would experience no mercy at the hands of the justly incensed King, died during her confinement at Carlat.

Jacques d'Armagnac's hair turned white within a few days. He was not mistaken about the gravity of his position. Louis was alarmed at these incessant conspiracies, and indignant at the ingratitude of the Duke, whom no oaths could bind. In vain did Nemours implore permission to speak with the King face to face; Louis refused to see him, and gave orders that he should be tortured. One day, hearing that the prisoner had been treated with some consideration, he wrote sharply to the gaoler, "Give him Hell (the extremity of torture); let him suffer Hell in his own chamber. Take care not to let him out of the cage except to be tortured." Jacques d'Armagnac was executed on 10 July, 1477. The assertion often made, that by the order of the King his children were placed under the scaffold so that their father's blood might fall over them, is asserted by no contemporary writers. His sons died without issue, and so ended this wicked family.

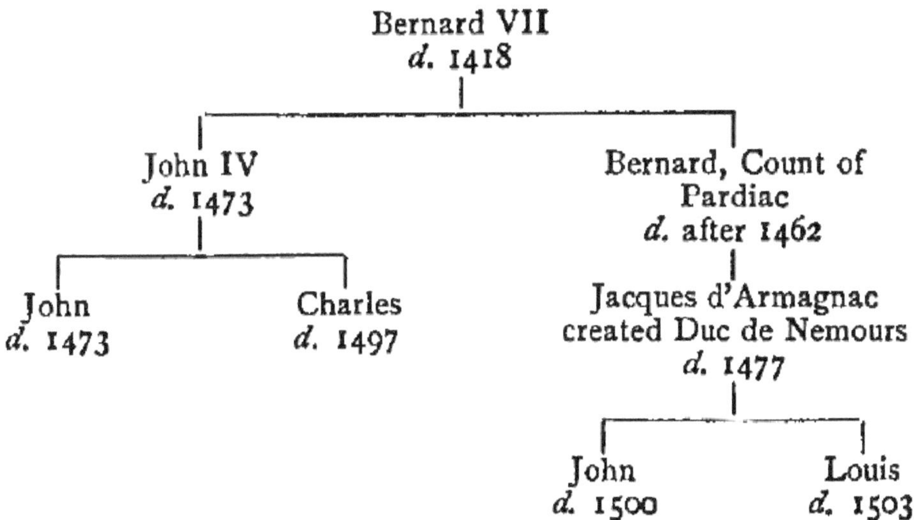


For some way above Bordères the Neste of Luron traverses a gloomy ravine; but then all at once it opens out and we come on a basin well cultivated, fringed with woods, and studded with twelve villages, about their church spires. The road ascends steeply past slate quarries that send down their avalanches of grey refuse over the base of the hill surmounted by the donjon of Gélos. It is still a long way on to the Lac de Caillaouas, that lies at the height of 3500 feet, and covers 120 acres; its blue waters are fed by some small tarns higher up under the glaciers of the Gourgs Blancs. This is one of the scenes of most savage grandeur in the Pyrenees. The lake is of great depth, and swarms with trout. A tunnel has been driven fifty-five feet below the surface through the rock that retains the lake, and through this the water can be drawn off to supply the deficiencies in the Neste and the canal that leads from it in time of drought. The work was completed in 1848.

The other Neste, that of Aure, is of even more economic importance. It rises under the Pic de Campbieil, 9550 feet; but receives a large influx of water from the Neste de Couplan that is supplied from a whole series of lakes, the largest of which is Orredon.

Above Arreau is Cadéac, one of the most ancient sites in the valley. Hither came the representatives of the various communes of the valley of the Neste to discuss their affairs, and decide their policy; for here, as in Lavedan, the people enjoyed great liberties, of which the Armagnacs did not care to deprive them. Cadéac occupies a hill surmounted by a feudal tower of the twelfth century. The church has an early north doorway, and sculptures let into the walls. The road passes up the valley under the porch of a chapel, Notre Dame de Penetaillade, that has a curious fresco representing the death of the Virgin on the façade. Vielle Aure is a village lying on both sides of the river, with a church of the twelfth century, and is an excellent centre for excursions. The road then crosses the river and reaches Bourespe, with a church of the fifteenth century, but a much earlier tower. In the porch are curious paintings of the date 1592, with representations of the deadly sins as ladies (why as ladies, and not as men?), in the costume of the period, mounted on strange beasts, and carrying behind them demons with hideous faces on their stomachs and breasts. Pride is riding on a lion, Avarice on a wolf, Gluttony on a pig, Luxury on a goat, Anger on a horse, and Idleness on an ass.

Surely Gluttony, Avarice, Anger are traits of man's intemperate passions rather than of woman's humours. *Vitium* is neuter, it will serve for either or none. But it is the old story of the sculptor and the lion. He showed the King of the Beasts a group finely carved that represented a man slaying a lion. "Ah," said the royal beast, "if a lion had been the sculptor, the figures in the group would have been in reversed positions."

It was men, not women, who wrought these representations of the cardinal vices.

Tramesaïgues (between the waters) occupies a rock, the road passes below it.

The cluster of lakes in the Néouville basin of mountains have been taken in hand as well as the Lac de Caillaouas. The undertaking was difficult, as work was possible there for only three months in the summer; all the rest of the year the basin in which they lie is buried in snow, and some of the tarns remain hard frozen. The largest of the lakes is Orredon, lying 5600 feet above the sea; it is the lowest of all, and receives the waters of the Lac d'Aubert and the Lac Aumar, lying in one valley, separated by a gravelly ridge of glacial rubbish; the Lac de Cap-de-Long reposes in another. The works were begun in 1901 and terminated in 1905.

The Four Valleys—Magonac, Neste, Aure, and La Baronne—formed another of those confederate republics of which there existed so many in the Pyrenees. Of these Magonac, with its chief town Castelnau, lay to the north of Lannemezan, and was not properly a valley at all.

After the extinction of the Armagnacs, the overlordship passed to the kings of France, and each and all from Louis XII to Louis XVI had to recognize and allow their very extended privileges. From the year 1300 no seigneur could withdraw an inhabitant of the Four Valleys from the jurisdiction of their own judges; every citizen could own land, marry, create an industry, or carry on any trade without authorization. The right to bear arms belonged to every one; and up to the eve of the Revolution the Four Valleys were exempt from all war-tax and from the obligation to have troops quartered on them.

La Fayette had no occasion to have gone to America to have seen what republican self-government was. It existed at his doors.

# CHAPTER XV

## LUCHON



A T Montréjeau the line branches off to Bagnères de Luchon from the trunk to
Toulouse. Montréjeau was Montroyal, then Montreal, and then what it has
now become through deformation by the Gascon tongue. It was a bastide, one of
those artificial towns, created first by Edward I, and then copied by great nobles,
and by the kings of France, in which every street was either parallel to another, or
cut it at right angles; and the houses were built in blocks, the whole surrounded by
walls, and the church usually serving as part of the fortification.

Montréjeau was the capital of the Marquesate of Montespan. The site is beautiful; and from the terrace, in clear weather, the giants of the Pyrenees are seen
to stand up due south, and the chain stretches away into the vaporous distance,
east and west. The church has a huge octagonal tower that served as keep to the
fortress. The town stands a little away from the station, to its disadvantage. From
it visitors usually start to see the Grotte de Gargas, the finest in the Pyrenees; it
might be visited equally well from S. Bertrand de Cominges, but that no carriage
can be obtained in that decayed city. The train, moreover, halts at Aventignan, the
station next before reaching Montréjeau, to allow of a visit to the grotto. The floor
bristles with stalagmites, and the stalactites from the roof have in several places
united with the stalagmites below. The strangest forms have been assumed by the
calcareous deposits, and the custodian points out an organ front, a cascade, a bear,

an altar, and the bed of the savage. A spring rises in the cave. Excavations made in the floor have exposed two beds of palæontological deposits of different epochs: human bones, flint tools, and bones of long extinct animals.

The discovery of this grotto is due to a series of ghastly crimes committed just ten years before the outbreak of the French Revolution.

A panic terror pervaded the neighbourhood. Among the rocks, somewhere, none knew exactly where, a monster had his lair, fell upon those who travelled along the roads, robbed them, maltreated them, carried them off, and devoured them. And this monster was a man. In 1780 the Parliament of Languedoc was called upon to try and sentence the cannibal, who was actuated by no other motive than a ravening appetite for human flesh.

Soon after the first disappearance of his victims every one had come to the conclusion as to who he was. He was Blaise Ferrage, commonly known as Seyé, a native of Ceseau, born in 1757. He was a small man, broad-shouldered, with unusually long arms, and was possessed of extraordinary strength. By trade he was a stonemason, and had worked at his trade till aged twenty-two. What induced him, in 1779, to throw up his work, quit his home and human society, in order to abandon himself in solitude to his wolfish appetite for blood, is not known; whether it was originally due to his having committed some criminal act that impelled him to fly to the rocks for refuge was never ascertained.

High up in a limestone cliff he discovered a cavern, the entrance to which was at that time so small that it had to be passed through on all fours. But within it was spacious, and provided with a running stream.

After he had spent the day in sleep Blaise would descend in the twilight and ramble over the country through fields and gardens, and appropriate to his use what he listed—fruit, fowls, sheep, pigs—and bear them away in the darkness of night to his den. Luck favoured and emboldened him, and his ferocity increased. He delayed his return till dawn. Lurking behind a wall or a bush he watched for milkmaids who were so unfortunate as to come in his way. There was no escaping him, for he carried a gun and was a sure shot. When he pounced upon his prey he tore it to pieces, or else carried it alive to his lair, and the shrieks could be heard from afar, paralyzing the timorous peasantry with fear.

His name was a terror to all the country round. In the evenings the spinners about the fire, the topers at the tavern, spoke only of the werewolf. It was thought that his tread could be heard at night among the withered leaves of autumn; that his panting breath was audible about the doors; that his gleaming eyes pierced the fog. Men pictured him lying on a ledge of rock half the day peering into the valley, motionless, watching for and selecting his prey. Imagination figured what the life must be of this man converted into a wild beast, who had renounced the society of his fellows to live among the rocks and tread the snow-fields, hearing naught save the howl of the wind, the cry of the birds of prey, and the baying of the wolves. As no single person who had disappeared ever returned, as no bodies were ever found, it was concluded that he was a man-eater.

Men he shot, strangled, or stabbed, and dragged their carcases to his lair. But he preferred to fall on women, especially such as were young; but the choicest morsels he selected were little children. On one occasion he fell short of powder and shot, and had the temerity to descend in full daylight, and in market time, to Montégu. He was recognized, and immediately the market people fled from him right and left; the dealers deserted their stalls, and the would-be purchasers hastened to take refuge within doors. He leisurely possessed himself of what he required and sauntered out of the place, not a man venturing to stay him.

At last the officers of justice seized him, and conveyed him to prison. But he broke loose the same night, and again disappeared among the mountains. The peasants were convinced that he had a talisman concealed in his hair, which enabled him to break the strongest chain and to open every lock.

He was again secured, and this time his hair was cut and searched for the supposed talisman there concealed, but, of course, ineffectually. He again, nevertheless, effected his escape.

Fear of him now passed all bounds. Girls and grown women, even the strongest men no longer ventured abroad after dark, not so much as to cross the street.

Then occurred two acts of violence which stirred the magistrates to greater activity.

Ferrage entertained a suspicion that a certain landowner in the district had instigated the police to track him. He set fire to this man's barns, stables, and cowsheds; and most of the cattle and all his grain were consumed in the flames. The other case was that of a Spanish muleteer who was driving his beasts over the mountains of Aure. Ferrage associated himself with the man on the way, volunteered to act as his guide, and the muleteer was never seen again.

High rewards were offered for the apprehension of Blaise Ferrage, but no dweller in the district dared attempt to earn it. Moreover, to track and arrest the cannibal was not a light matter. None knew precisely where he concealed himself, and it was certain that he would send a bullet into the first man whom he saw approach his place of refuge and concealment.

Finally he was taken, but only by subtlety. There was a fellow who had been guilty of more than one crime, and whom the officers of justice desired to secure. In order to make his peace with them, this man offered to assist in capturing Blaise, if he were assured of a free pardon and a reward. This was promised. Accordingly he climbed the rocks, yelling out the name of Seyé, by which Ferrage was commonly known, and crying for help. The cannibal cautiously thrust his head out of his cave, and seeing the man fleeing as for his life beckoned him to approach. The refugee breathlessly told him that he was flying from justice, that he had broken out of prison, and entreated to be sheltered. Ferrage took him in, and the fellow gained Blaise's confidence. He lived with him for awhile in his cave. However solitary a man may be, he yet craves for the society of a companion, and Blaise and this man became intimate. They went together on predatory excursions, and the betrayer finally lured Ferrage into an ambuscade laid for him, where he was taken, and firmly secured by a body of police. He was led to prison and kept there strongly guarded. The whole country breathed with relief when it was known that he was in chains and behind strong bars.

The trial was expedited and short. For three years this monster had terrorized the countryside. The number of charges of robbery and murder brought against him were innumerable.

On 12 December, 1782, the Parliament of Languedoc sentenced him to be broken on the wheel. He was then aged twenty-five. On the following 13th December Ferrage was executed. The sentence was carried out in the following manner. The culprit was fastened to a cart wheel, his limbs twined in and out among the spokes. The executioner smote with an iron bar on the limbs and broke them, one by one. Then came the *coup de grâce*, given across the chest.

It was estimated that he had murdered and eaten eighty persons, the majority of these were women and children. When he was executed crowds attended, palpitating with alarm, for they expected that at the last moment he would burst away and resume his murderous career.

He walked to death with florid countenance and with seeming indifference to his fate. Whether the prison chaplain induced him to express remorse for his guilt is not known. Only when the mangled body was cast down from the wheel, and consigned for burial to the grave-digger, did the crowd feel satisfied that they were relieved from a nightmare of horrors.

A little way above the station of Montréjeau the two great Pyrenean torrents of the Neste and the Garonne unite their waters and flow towards the east. The line to Luchon does not follow the Garonne, that issues from a gorge, but crosses it farther up at Barbazan, in a broad basin studded with villages set in luxuriant verdure.

On an isolated hill, an outlier of the Pyrenees, rises a lofty and beautiful church, with houses grouped about it; apparently a stately medieval city, actually a poor village of less than four hundred inhabitants. This is S. Bertrand de Cominges. At one time it was as splendid a town as any in Gaul, and was the capital of an important people, containing from 30,000 to 50,000 souls. These could not all be accommodated on the rock, and the town flowed down the side into the plain, where now stands Valcabrères, the Vale of Goats. S. Bertrand de Cominges is one of the few towns in France of whose foundation we know the precise date.

Sertorius was one of the most extraordinary men in the later times of the Roman Republic. He was a native of Nursia, a Sabine village, born of obscure but respectable parents, and a devoted son to his widowed mother. In B.C. 83 Sertorius went to Spain to organize a national revolt against the intolerable oppression of Rome. Availing himself of the superstitious character of the people, he tamed a fawn, so that it accompanied him in his walks, lived in his tent, and was regarded by the Iberians as a tutellary spirit that communicated to him the will of the gods.

**Choir of S. Bertrand de Cominges**

He maintained a stubborn resistance against the power of Rome for many years, defeating army after army. In B.C. 77 Pompey was appointed by the Senate to command in Spain, along with Metellus. Sertorius, at first, defeated both. Pompey was obliged to appeal to the Senate for men and arms. Unless supported efficaciously, he declared that he must infallibly be driven out of Spain. At length the tide of success turned. Disaffection broke out among the troops led by Sertorius, and a conspiracy was formed to destroy him among some of his most trusted comrades. One of these invited him to a banquet, at which they endeavoured to provoke him to anger and make an excuse for a fray by the employment of obscene language, which they were well aware that he detested; then by grotesque and undignified capers, as if they were drunk. Sertorius turned on his couch so as not to see their buffoonery, when they rushed on him with their daggers and slew him, B.C. 72. His faithful adherents fled through the defiles, and over the passes of the Pyrenees, and settled in the district afterwards known as the land of the Convenæ, and built Lugdunum Convenarum as their capital in that same year, B.C. 72.

Even after the fall of the Roman Empire this Lyons of the Convenæ remained a rich and populous city. But a terrible disaster fell on it in 584, that caused its utter and irretrievable ruin. This forms one of the most striking and detailed episodes of the history of the Franks by Gregory of Tours. In the words of Guizot:—

> "Southern Gaul, that is to say Aquitaine, Gascony, Narbonne, called Septimania, and the two banks of the Rhone near its mouths, were not comprised in the partition of the Frankish dominions. Each of the co-partners assigned to themselves, to the south of the Garonne and on the coasts of the Mediterranean, such and such a district, and such and such a town, just as heirs-at-law keep to themselves severally such and such a valuable jewel out of a rich property to which they have succeeded, and which they divide among themselves. The peculiar situation of these provinces, at their distance from the Frank settlements, contributed much to the independence of Southern Gaul, which was constantly striving and partly managed, in the tempestuous fortunes of the Frankish monarchy, to recover its independence. It is easy to comprehend how that these repeated partitions of a mighty inheritance, these domains incessantly changing hands, must have tended to increase the anarchy of the Roman and Barbaric worlds thrown pell-mell one upon another, and fallen a prey, the Roman to the disorganization of a lingering death, the Barbaric to the fermentation of a new existence, striving for development under social conditions wholly different from those of their primitive life."

An opportunity seemed to offer for Aquitaine to establish its independence.

The Merovingian dynasty was represented by an old man and by two children, and the Aquitanians thought that their chance had come to have a king of their own. They summoned from Constantinople one Gundowald, reputed to be of royal Frank blood.

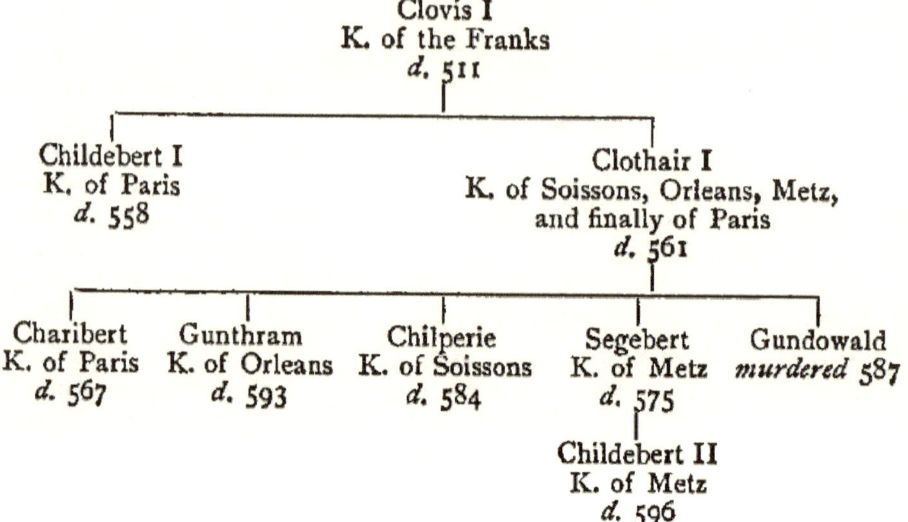



Gregory of Tours says:—

> "Gundowald, who said he was the son of Clothair I, arrived
> at Marseilles, coming from Constantinople. He had been born in
> Gaul, had been carefully educated, taught letters, and, as is the
> custom with kings of the Franks, had his hair flowing in long curls
> over his shoulders. He was presented by his mother to King Chil-
> debert (his uncle, King of Paris), and she said to him, 'Behold your
> nephew, the son of Clothair. His father ever hated him, but do
> you take him to you, for he is your own flesh and blood.' And this
> Childebert did, as he had no son of his own."

This was the prince whom the Aquitanians invited to rule over them. Clothair
I had divided the kingdom of the Franks among his sons, but three of these were
dead; Sigebert, King of Metz, however, had left a son, Childebert II. Gunthram,
King of Orleans, still lived. Gundowald visited his nephew, Childebert, at Metz,
and was favourably received by him. Childebert and Gundowald sent Duke Boso
with a deputation to Gunthram, King of Orleans, to demand the recognition of the
prince, and that he should be given Aquitaine as a kingdom. The deputation was
roughly received by Gunthram at Orleans, seated on his throne. "Pshaw!" said he,
"Gundowald's father was a miller, or, to be more exact, a carder of wool."

Then one of the deputies said boldly, "Do you pretend that Gundowald had
two fathers—one a miller, the other a wool-carder? Who ever heard of a man having two fathers?"

Another deputy broke out with—"Take care, King, the axe that cut off the
heads of your brothers has not lost its edge."

In a fury Gunthram ordered the embassy to be driven out of the palace and
pelted with horse-dung and rotten vegetables.

The Aquitanians flew to arms; Gundowald was crowned at Brives, and marched to secure Toulouse. The ecclesiastics of the south to a man favoured the pretender. Gunthram was alarmed, and at once detached his nephew Childebert from the side of Gundowald, by the bribe of an offer of the succession to the kingdom of the Franks after his death.

The reconciliation of the two kings discouraged the party of Gundowald. The fickle Aquitanians were as hasty in deserting him as they had been in acknowledging him. As a large army of the Franks was pouring south, Gundowald was constrained to throw himself into Lugdunum Convenarum, along with the grandees most compromised, as Duke Mummolus, and two bishops, Sagittarius and Waddo.

Duke Boso, who had been foremost in instigating the rising, secured all Gundowald's treasures and fled with them. Mummolus and the bishops only waited for an opportunity to betray him. The army of Gunthram surrounded the town, lying all along in the plain. Then Mummolus and the bishops advised the prince to throw himself on the mercy of his brother Gunthram. "It was at your invitation," answered he, "that I came to Gaul. I was in Constantinople with my little children, in high honour with the Emperor, when Boso sought me out and informed me of the death of all my brothers save Gunthram, without issue, and that Childebert, my nephew, was a poor creature. I allowed myself to be persuaded to return to Gaul; and now this same Boso has stolen the treasures I had brought with me, and has gone over to my brother who is warring against me." Then said Mummolus, "Do as we bid you. Divest yourself of your golden baldric and sword and go forth. We swear to you that no harm will befall you." Seeing that nothing else was open to him, that he could trust none of those who had egged him on, he issued from the gates, and at once Mummolus closed them behind him. Otto, Count of Bourges, received the prince and surrounded him with armed men. Gundowald raised his hands to heaven and said, "Judge Eternal, Avenger of the innocent! To Thee I commit my cause, and I pray Thee to avenge me on my betrayers."

As he was descending the hill, Otto dealt him a sharp blow on the back that made him fall, saying, "This dauber of the walls of churches and oratories is down at last!" Then raising his spear he attempted to transfix him, but failed, owing to the armour worn by the prince.

Gundowald sprang to his feet, and turned to reascend the hill, when Duke Boso, as base as he was treacherous, dashed a stone at his head and crushed in his skull. The prince fell, and the men at arms, after making sure that he was dead, tied his feet together, and dragged him around the camp with jeers.

The rock down which Gundowald was thrown is still pointed out. It is called Mattacan, the place where the dog was slaughtered. It is some satisfaction to learn that Mummolus gained nothing by his treachery. When the town was entered by the troops of Gunthram he was put to death. The city was delivered over to the soldiery of the King, and the inhabitants—men, women, and children—were massacred, so that, to use the expression of Gregory of Tours, there did not remain even a dog alive in it—"ita ut non remaneret mingens ad parietem." The city was levelled, and the bishops of Cominges, finding no asylum among the ruins, settled at Valcabrères, where they erected a church dedicated to S. Justus. This is an interesting structure, standing alone in the fields, built out of the ruins. The choir, very archaic in form and of rude construction, probably dates from its erection after the destruction of the Lyons of the Convenæ. The nave, less ancient, of the eleventh century, has been also built of old materials. A delicious lateral portal enriched with sculptured capitals, and fine statues of life size, and a bas-relief of Christ between the evangelistic symbols, is of the twelfth century. Within are ancient columns taken from the Roman town, and a curious stone sarcophagus or shrine of the fourteenth century, much mutilated, and reached by two stone flights of steps. It is not known whose tomb this was. Against the wall at the end of the nave is the tombstone of a priest named Patroclus, of the fourth century.

After five centuries of abandonment, one of the bishops of Cominges resolved on the re-edification of the city of Lugdunum. He built a cathedral on the height of the rock, in the midst of the ruins. This was in the eleventh century, towards its close, when religious fervour was at its height; and this new church is one of the most beautiful monuments of medieval art in the south of France. About the new cathedral canons were installed; the prelate erected for them a residence and a cloister. He built himself a palace, and in every way encouraged the people to resettle on the site of their ancient capital.

The man who did this, the second founder, was Bertrand de l'Isle-Jourdain, and he has given his name to this new foundation, or, to be more correct, the people have called the new city on the old site after his name. Bertrand's mother was daughter of William Taillefer, Count of Toulouse. He was trained in the abbey of Escaledieu, but quitted it for the profession of arms. However, before long he abandoned the life of a camp to accept a canonry at Toulouse. He was appointed Bishop of Cominges about 1073, and ruled the see for fifty years. According to popular legend, he killed a dragon that infested the neighbourhood; and the stuffed monster hangs in the church to this day. It is a crocodile from the Nile. He died in or about 1120, and his day of commemoration is on 17 October, when the decayed town is thronged with pilgrims to visit his shrine.

At the time of the Papacy at Avignon Bishop Bertrand de Got was elected Pope, and took the title of Clement V. He retained a liking for the place, revisited it several times, and contributed sums towards its completion; and to raise money without having to dip into his own purse instituted a grand Pardon or Jubilee, charged with Indulgences, for the Feast of the Invention of the Cross (3 May). This is still celebrated, and attracts pilgrims to gain the Indulgences, during three days. The vaulting of the church was begun in 1304, and completed by Hugh de Châtillon in the middle of the fourteenth century. The apse is surrounded by five chapels. The windows of the choir, very tall and narrow, are partly walled up, and partly filled with fragments of Renaissance glass. The magnificent Renaissance woodwork choir-stalls, screen, organ-case, and altar-piece are due to Bishop Jean de Mauleon, and date from 1525. In a chapel is the stately tomb of Bishop Hugh de Châtillon, who died in 1352; it is of white marble, and was executed at least a century after his death, probably at the expense of the Cardinal de Foix, to whom also is due the mausoleum of S. Bertrand behind the high altar.

Cloisters, S. Bertrand de Cominges

But bishops cannot create a town, even though they enrich a site with a superb cathedral. S. Bertrand de Cominges never thrived, and little by little the bishops tired of it, and then abandoned it for their Château of Alan, near Aurignac; they were rich men, enjoying large revenues, for the diocese of Cominges, in addition to that part which is in France, comprised also the whole of the Val d'Aran—that is to say, thirty-three parishes under the Crown of Spain.

Some of them rarely visited S. Bertrand, some not at all. One of them, Urban de S. Gelos, an ardent Leaguer, only went thither to dislodge the Huguenots, who thrice between 1569 and 1593 entered the town and committed great ravages.

At the Revolution the see was suppressed, and the small world of canons, vicars-general, and diocesan functionaries who had inhabited the capital of Cominges dispersed, and the little town sank to be a *chef-lieu de Canton*, and then lost even that dignity, which was transferred to Barbazan.

S. Bertrand would be abandoned altogether by its inhabitants, who would settle on the plain were it not much resorted to by visitors from Luchon, by artists and antiquaries, and by pilgrims.

There were counts of Cominges from a very early period, indeed from 900; but the county came to the Crown of France in 1442 through a domestic quarrel.

Margaret de Cominges was left an heiress in 1376. She married John III, Count of Armagnac Fézansac. He died in 1391, having had by her two daughters. She then married Jean d'Armagnac Pardiac, who was aged eighteen. As she treated him with contempt as a mere boy he was offended, and left her so as to reside with his father. But after awhile, finding that Margaret had installed a lieutenant in the county, and refused him those rights in it which had been assured to him by the marriage contract, he appealed to Count Bernard VII of Armagnac for assistance. This treacherous man went over to the side of Margaret, and when John hastened to Auch to urge the Count to assist him Bernard had him arrested, carried to a castle in the Rouergue, and there blinded by a red-hot basin applied to his eyes. The poor lad died in prison in great misery. Margaret being free of her boy-husband, looked out for one who was a man, and pitched on Matthew de Grailli, brother of the Count of Foix, and married him.

But Matthew proved a little too much of a man for her. He treated Margaret as roughly as she had treated Jean. He shut her up in the Castle of Saverdun, where he retained her for fifteen to sixteen years. At the end of that time she appealed to Charles VII when he was at Toulouse, and Matthew was forced to surrender her into the King's hands. Then Margaret, to vent her spite against her husband, made over the county of Cominges, in 1442, along with all her estates, to the Crown of France. Next year she died at Poitiers at the age of eighty.

The Garonne does not rise in France, but in Spain, and, by what is an apparent caprice, the frontier does not follow the crests of the highest mountains, but runs north, making a loop so as to include the Val d'Aran in Spain.

But though the valley is reached by a good carriage road from France, and can communicate with Spanish neighbours only by a mule path over a pass 8000 feet high and impassable for many months in the year, yet the valley has pertained to Spain since 1192.

Of the Val d'Aran more presently. We must first, after the antiquity and decay of S. Bertrand, refresh ourselves with the novelty and up-to-datedness of Luchon; certainly one of the most delightful centres from which to radiate in all directions, that is to be found in Europe. All the comforts, distractions, and amusements that go to make a watering-place pleasant are to be had there as elsewhere, and better than elsewhere in the Pyrenees.

A Frenchman shall describe it, lest I should do it scant justice:—

> "Forty thousand visitors come every year to Luchon, bringing with them an atmosphere of luxury not to be found to the same degree in other Pyrenean stations. Their artificial existence has for corollary an artificial existence in the population living upon them:—Coachmen and postilions in the livery of the Opéra-Comique, guides who have adopted an imaginary Pyrenean costume. The hotel-keepers are not behindhand; correctly dressed cavaliers, spruce amazons, toilettes changed frequently during the day, toilettes the product of the best Parisian dressmakers, affectation of the extreme of fashion, such is the picture of life at Luchon. Even for mountain excursions there must be a faultless costume.

> "With the exception of a few guides worthy of the name and knowing the loftiest crests, these cicerones in costume conduct walkers to spots to which they could go perfectly well without them. The mountains are very much humanized here, there are plenty of carriage-drives, walks innumerable, well kept up, to reach even great altitudes. But beyond all this Luchon is one of the principal centres of Pyrenean-Alpine climbing, it is the point of departure for bold climbers who go to the Mont Maudit, the loftiest of all the chain, but on Spanish soil" (Ardouin-Dumazet).

But even easy ascents lead to superb and savage scenery. The Lake of Seculejo is easily reached, and is accessible even in a carriage. It stands 6500 feet above the sea, and is the most visited of all the Pyrenean sheets of water. It is a mere tarn, but is singularly beautiful, lying amidst rugged mountains, with the eternal snows above it spilling their melted waters into it in a fall of 620 feet, after having paused to spread in two loftily situated tarns, one of which is frozen almost throughout the year. Inglis thus describes it, at a time when it was but occasionally visited:—

> "I dedicated a day to the Seculejo, and have seldom passed one more to my mind. I left Bagnères de Luchon about sunrise. The road to it is wild and pastoral, rapidly rising towards the south, and having constantly in view the majestic scenery that lies upon the Spanish frontier. The Lake of Seculejo is wild, solitary, and sombre. The low ripple of the water, the noise of the cataract, and the cry of a bird of prey, are the only interruptions of silence

that are in keeping with the scene; and these were the only sounds that disturbed its tranquillity as I stood upon the margin of the water. The lake is entirely surrounded by high mountains, excepting where it finds egress; and its shores are generally bold and rugged. At the upper end, a cascade falls from the top of a perpendicular rock into the lake. After lingering upon the margin of Seculejo an hour or two, I climbed up the eastern bank, by a path which has almost the appearance of a ladder, and which, indeed, bears the name of Scala. Having reached the summit of the bank, I entered a gorge, through which I passed to a hollow lying at the base of the mountain, called the Espingo; and, still proceeding to ascend the first ridges of the mountain, I reached the two lakes of Espingo. These are very elevated mountain tarns lying almost in the region of snow. All is here sombre, melancholy, rude, and dismal—great rocks, a few stunted trees, and still, deep, dark water, are the features of the scene."

We return to Luchon. Do you desire health? It is to be found there, if we may believe the advertisements of the wonders wrought by its waters, more potent than that from the lips of the Grotto of Lourdes: "Toutes les maladies de la peau, comme d'autres de toute espèce, les maladies occassionées par le lait répandu, quelques graves qu'elles soient, les rheumatismes, maladies des yeux, maladies des parties conservatrices des yeux, lésions d'oreille, maladie du système osseux, blessures; gale ventrée, rougeole, maladies des articulations; maladies des glandes salvaires; humeurs froides; maladies des voies urinaires; catarrhe pulmonaire; asthme; phthisie pulmonaire, obstructions de toutes sortes, et jaunisse." And, nevertheless, there is a cemetery at Luchon.

Luchon was well-known to the Romans, as the number of *ex voto* altars to the god Ilixion that have been found go to prove. The name of this god of healing is to be recognized in a very altered shape in the modern Luchon. In 1036 Luchon, with Upper Cominges, passed as dower to the Crown of Aragon. Later it was restored to the counts of Cominges. In 1711 the valley was ravaged, and Luchon burned by Charles of Austria, who was disputing Spain with the Duke of Anjou.

No one staying at Luchon should omit to read J. H. Michon's powerful novel, *Le Maudit*, the scene of which is mainly laid at S. Aventin on the Neste d'Oucil, a picturesquely situated village, with an interesting church of the eleventh and twelfth centuries. It has two towers—one at the west end, the other at the transept. The *grille* is specially noticeable, as it is ironwork of the twelfth century. The tomb of the patron saint is in the church. He is said to have died in the year 538.

One stormy night a bear bounced against the door of his cell. Aventin spent the night in great alarm, but on opening the door in the morning he saw the bear still there, crouched on the threshold, and it stretched forth a paw to him. Then the hermit perceived that a splinter of wood had entered it. So he said, "Poor beast, thou wast in pain, and didst seek relief, and I thought that thou wast raging for my life." Then he took the paw in his lap, drew out the splinter, bathed and bandaged the wound, and let the bear depart. It is the story of Androcles and the lion, without the termination.

Perhaps the finest excursion is up the Valley of Lys to the Cirque of Crabioules, where the glacier sends down a fine fall, the Cascade d'Enfer. Nothing can surpass the scenery in this valley.

La Cascade D'enfer, Luchon

Le Lac D'oo

The Val d'Aran should be visited on account of its magnificent scenery, running up as it does to the roots of the gloomy Maladetta. On the way to it S. Béat is reached, planted in a narrow defile, into which the sun penetrates for little more than two hours in the day in mid-winter. It owed its importance as a key to Spain, that is to say to such part of Spain as is in the Val d'Aran; and it has a key for its arms. It maintains a population of quarrymen. The marble there has been exploited since Roman times with long intermission. A votive altar has been discovered, erected by Q. J. Julianus and Publicius Crescentinus to commemorate their having been the first there to cut and dispatch columns twenty feet long. In the Middle Ages these white marble quarries were abandoned, but were worked again under Louis XIV, when hence were sent the marble basins for the gardens at Versailles. S. Béat is commanded by a castle of the fourteenth century, with a keep still more ancient. The castle is reached by steps, some hewn out of the rock. A colossal statue of the Virgin in bronze has been erected on the rock within the castle precincts.

From S. Béat it is not four miles to the frontier, at Pont-du-Roi, where some speculators have built a casino; a restaurant, and gambling tables are provided; but, of course, this fact is veiled, and it is called La Société du Vélo Club du Pont-du-Roi.

The Maladetta with its glaciers now bursts on the sight.

It is somewhat absurd that the Val d'Aran should not pertain to France, with which it has a natural connexion. Indeed the Spanish officials who come to the valley arrive by train either from Bayonne or from Perpignan, and leave it at the little station at Marignac near Luchon. The people of Aran who drink Spanish wine have the barrels brought round one way or the other by French lines, but do not pay duty, only the long carriage; whereas French wine has to pay at the Customs, coming only a few miles up from the level land.

The dialect is Catalan, but so is that of French Roussillon; and nearly every man in Aran can speak French. The position of the inhabitants is difficult, as for only two or three months in the year can they reach a Spanish town beyond the mountains, so that they must purchase French goods, and these have to be examined at the custom-house, and taxed, some heavily.

Curiously enough, at the Treaty of the Pyrenees in 1659 nothing was said about annexing Aran to France. Napoleon alone saw the necessity for it, and did annex it in 1808; but the treaty of 1815 restored it to Spain. As Aran is now situated, inevitably smuggling thrives and cannot be suppressed.

Viella is the capital of the district of Aran. Before reaching it a monolith is passed, a prehistoric monument, supposed to be dedicated to the presiding deity of the valley. Viella is planted on the banks of the Rio Negro, and possesses a church and chapels of massive construction, overcharged with gilded decorations, in accordance with Spanish taste. The houses are provided with balconies.

We are here at the roots of the Maladetta, the accursed mountain, because devoid of vegetation, and near the Cirque of Sabourede. The highest peak of the Maladetta is 10,230 feet, and in its flanks rises the western branch of the Garonne. The melted waters of the glaciers of the peak Aneto falls into a chasm, the Trou de Toro, and it was long supposed that after an underground course the same waters broke forth in the Goueil de Jouéou, which is the true source of the western Garonne. But sufficient colouring matter has been poured into the gulf to dye the water issuing from this spring, without its staining the source any more than the dye poured into the *source* in the Lourdes grotto discoloured the water a few yards distant, that issues from the taps from which the miraculous fluid is drawn. Where the stream issues that precipitates itself into the Trou de Toro has not yet been discovered. There is no doubt about the source of the eastern Garonne. That rises at the foot of the Port de Béret, in two little springs that go by the name of the Eyes of the Garonne, but which is speedily lost in the turbulent and mightier stream of the Ruda descending from the snows of Sabourede. From Luchon the passage into Spain by the Port de Venasque is to be effected, disclosing views of mountain crest and suspended glacier hardly to be surpassed in Europe. A hospice is planted half-way, where is the custom-house. "It is," says the Commandant de Oliver-Copóns, "like a great barrack in disorder, a muddle of hotel, pot-house, and workshop. There are stables that can shelter sixty beasts, but hardly a room in which a traveller can lodge comfortably." However, there is no need to stay the night there; one can push on to Venasque, and make that a centre of excursions to the lakes clustering at the heads of the wild valleys that descend from the Pic d'Eristé, the Pic des Posets and the Maladetta.

# CHAPTER XVI

## COUSERANS

Cobweb of lines—The Viscounty—S. Lizier—S. Girons—S. Lizier a
double town—Two cathedrals—Bishop Bernard—His palace—S.
Marie de la Sède—The other cathedral—Bridge and inscription—
Ramparts—The training of dancing bears—Bear hunting—Mendicity—Improvidence—Factory of La Moulasse—Job cigarette
papers—Vic—Sully tree—Oust—The Nine Springs—Aulus—The
Planturel.

THE railway lines in the central portion of the Pyrenees converge on Toulouse, and to get across country from west to east is no easy matter. In the Eastern Pyrenees they form a cobweb amidst which the traveller gets entangled and spends a day unprofitably in endeavours to extricate himself, for French railway directors ingeniously contrive to make through travelling by branch lines most difficult, or at least most tedious. To reach S. Girons it is necessary to run northwards from S. Gaudens to Boussens, then change trains and turn the face due south, following up the Salat, past the salt springs of Salies.

We now enter the old viscounty of Couserans, of which the civil capital was Massat, and the ecclesiastical was S. Lizier. It pertained for awhile to the counts of Carcassonne; Roger II gave both the district and the bishopric to his younger son, Bernard, with the title of viscount, in or about 990. But in 1257 Esquivat, Count of Bigorre, inherited the land from Roger, Count of Pallier, and thus the Couserans passed into the possession of the house of Foix-Béarn, and so to the kings of Navarre.

The capital of the whole country in early days was Lugdunum Consoranorum, now S. Lizier, and one of the nine cities of Novempopulania. The Couserans, situated between the basins of the Ariège and the Garonne, has much the shape of a vine-leaf, having the valleys of the Arac, Garbet, Salat, and Lez converging at S. Girons into the one broad stream of the Salat, as the stalk of the leaf. If S. Bertrand de Cominges has fallen from its high estate to be a miserable village, it is not alone in its fall, in that S. Lizier has shared the same fate. But Lugdunum Convenarum went out in one tragic drama of blood and flame. Lugdunum Consoranorum is dying of slow decline, its life-blood sucked out of it by the parasitic growth of S. Girons. Indeed, so low is it fallen that the railway does not afford it a station, only a *halte*. Once the fifth in order of size and splendour of the cities of Novempopulania, it now shelters within its walls not more than five hundred inhabitants. This was a double town: one portion was the city, the other the *ville*; and what is more, it possessed two cathedrals—one in the city, Notre Dame; the other, S. Lizier, in the town. As just before death a patient often brightens up, puts on an appearance of renewed life, and enjoys buoyant hopes, only to sink in relapse to death, so was it with this Lyons of the Couserans.

Bishop Bernard de Marmiesse (1653–80), not content with the medieval residence of the prelates, erected an enormous and splendid palace, commanding the whole town with its long façade flanked by semicircular towers, embracing the cathedral of S. Marie de la Sède within its walls. Where the bishops ruled and feasted in purple and fine linen lunatics are now installed. Lazarus has crept into the shell of Dives. The bishopric was suppressed at the Revolution and never restored. There had been on the cathedral staff twelve canons and twenty-four prebendaries, having under them a swarm of sacristans, *curés* to relieve them of burdensome duties, and workmen.

Ste. Marie de la Sède is a Renaissance church, but built when the spirit of Gothic architecture had not gone out of the land; but the portal is Romanesque. The interior woodwork is of the eighteenth century, and is fine for its period. To the north is the chapter-house, of the twelfth century. The materials of which cathedral and palace were built proceeded from the ruins of the Gallo-Roman city.

The other cathedral is more interesting. It consists of a nave without aisles, and an apse constructed out of fragments of Roman buildings, and over a Roman gateway. The central tower is of the fourteenth century: octagonal, lighted by windows with triangular heads, and the whole crowned by a crenellated platform. It affects the Toulouse style, and is of brick. The magnificent cloister of the twelfth and thirteenth centuries has thirty-two round-headed arches resting on alternate single and double pillars with quaintly-carved and varied capitals. Above it is an open walk or cloister, with the pantiled roof supported on beams, dating from the fifteenth century. Probably the town would expire altogether were it not kept alive by the lunatics installed in the episcopal palace, which is lighted by electricity, and such light as is not wanted in the asylum is distributed over the town.

Like S. Bertrand, this Lyons changed its name and assumes that of one of the bishops, a native of Lerida, who is said to have saved the city from destruction by the Visigoths by his intercession. The town is built on the slopes of a hill above the Salat. It communicates with the *halte* by means of a steep-pitched bridge of the twelfth or thirteenth century, consisting of three unequal arches. Into one of the piers is built a votive inscription to the goddess Belisama, who was identified by the Romans with Minerva. Another inscription to this goddess has been found at Vaison. A tower formerly stood in the midst of the bridge. Above, on the right bank of the Salat, is a square tower that defended a fortified mill. This mill has been reconstructed. The old city is enclosed in the Roman ramparts forming an ellipse, flanked by a dozen towers, of which six on the north side are square, and the rest on the south are semicircular. Against the rampart within is the episcopal keep of the twelfth century, rectangular, and only to be entered by a wooden bridge that led to the first story from the palace. The lower rests on Roman foundations.

The valleys of the Couserans do not attract many visitors; they have not the boldness of those farther west. The Pic de Crabère reaches to 7200 feet, that of Mauberme to 8650, that of Roujos to 8340. There is a little lake, the Lac d'Arrainge, out of which flows the Isar, but it is insignificant; others are above Aulus. The principal business of the people in the upper valleys was the training of dancing bears, and sometimes when a father married his daughter he would hand over to his son-in-law as the *dot* a well-trained Bruin. But the taste for seeing these beasts led about and made to stand on their hind legs and plead for coppers has died out. There is no further demand for bears, and the industry is expiring, if not dead. Perhaps the last was seen by M. Ardouin-Dumazet:—

> "No sooner had we entered the hamlet of Sérac, with its steep and muddy streets, than I asked after these strange educators. Alas! it was a lost tradition. In all the commune of Uston there was but a single little bear in training. Happily he inhabited Sérac, so I could see him.

> "A little girl conducted me to the grange in which the small animal was shut up. It was still a baby, but its mark of slavery was upon it, the ring through its nostrils, by means of which the tamer can control it. The little bear, sitting up on its hind paws, waddled and hopped incessantly, as if afflicted with S. Vitus's dance. Our visit seemed to please it; it invited caresses, and rolled about at our feet. The people said that it would be easy to tame the poor little bruin."

Bears are no longer hunted on the French side of the Pyrenees, and those who seek for them must cross over the Spanish frontier, where a good many are still to be found in the forests. But, as already said, the demand for them has ceased, not only to be led about, but to show in barber's yards as evidence that genuine bears' grease is sold on the premises.

This industry having failed, the peasants have had to fall back on cattle-rearing, and dairy-farming. But this hardly suffices for their necessities, and many of the men turn into hawkers, and almost all migrate at the time of the vintage to the Bordelais and to Languedoc. Whether it be the bear association, or the migratory habits of the fathers of the household, has given a rudeness and lack of self-respect to the children cannot be said, but nowhere in the Pyrenees does mendicity prevail with such persistency and effrontery as in the valleys of the Couserans. The legend prevails in the plain that when Christ was walking over the earth with S. Peter He found these valleys unpopulated; so He took clay and moulded it into a man, and set the figure on its feet before Him, and breathed into it the breath of life; whereupon instantly the New Adam held out its hands and cried, "Un p'tit sou, siou plaît, m'ssius!" Begging has ever since been the predominant and all-prevailing instinct of the upper region of the Couserans.

The population here as elsewhere in the mountains is dwindling owing to emigration, mainly to South America, especially to the Argentine Republic. This is largely due to the peasant seeing the comfort and comparative wealth of his brother peasant in the plain, the proprietor of vineyard and olive-yard, and of mulberry trees that feed silkworms. He returns to his Alpine pastures sulky and dissatisfied with his condition. He is unwilling to change his native, deeply-rooted customs of farming, that are unscientific and wasteful, incapable maybe of realizing that he might do better if he adopted newer methods.

"Nevertheless," says M. Ardouin-Dumazet, "he might lead a better existence if he could be brought to limit the quantity of his cattle to that number which he could rear suitably; if he would consent to make a practical use of the milk of his flocks. But everywhere in Ariège one finds every little property support three times as many beasts as the soil can well sustain; the result is lean cattle, giving poor meat and milk, giving consequently but an insufficient return of revenue.

"However, nowhere has the problem of the renovation of the pastures and the animals that overrun it been more studied and theoretically resolved. The Board of Forestry has shown by example how that the extent of meadowland and the quality of the grass might be largely extended. But everywhere it encounters invincible routine.

"Every hamlet, every farm has its stables, in which during the winter the beasts are crowded in conditions of hygiene absolutely deplorable. Air, light, litter are wanting; the fodder is measured out sparingly. If the winter be long there is dearth, for the number of beasts is out of all proportion to the resources of the forage.

"So soon as the weather becomes mild, at once the animals are despatched to the pastures or the waste lands; too numerous for the space, they ruin the turf and trample up the soil. The high pastures are squandered, and, above all, are not kept up. Juniper and rhododendrons invade them without the mountaineers concerning themselves about it. The agents of the Forestry have shown them how to get rid of these shrubs by eradication and burning, and how to make the ashes fertilize the meadows; they have shown them how by irrigation to enhance the quantity and quality of the herbage. This has been seen, understood, but not followed. Channels for irrigation have been made by the foresters and abandoned. The watering places for the cattle are choked. The paths rendering access to the mountain pastures are not kept up. The carelessness of the herdsmen surpasses all that could be imagined. It makes one despair."

And the only remedy for their poverty that they can conceive is to turn their children out into the roads to beg for sous.

A watering-place at Aulus is coming into fashion. It is reached from S. Girons by a good road, and is distant from it thirty-three kilometres; Aulus lies high up in the valley of the Garbet.

On leaving S. Girons—about which I say nothing, as concerning it nothing can be said—the factory of La Moulasse is passed, where cigarette papers are manufactured in large quantities. The man who started making them was named Jean Bardon, and he put his initials on the little books of cigarette papers, with a lozenge between, thus J.◊.B. This was read as Job, and such papers acquired the name and became famous as Job's cigarette papers. The name has been accepted on the spot, and the sources of the Moulasse that feeds the factory are now called "les sources de Job."

Vic, now a little village of 150 inhabitants, was once a Roman station, and remained of sufficient consequence in the Middle Ages to give to S. Girons the name of Bourg-sous-Vic. It has a little church with three Romanesque apses, and a ceiling of the sixteenth century with paintings in squares. Beside the church is a Sully elm. Such elms were planted throughout the country as token of rejoicing in 1593, when Henry IV abjured Calvinism and joined the Catholic Church.

Oust also speaks of the Roman occupation; the name is derived from Augusta. At Oust the road leaves the valley of the Salat to ascend its tributary vale of the Garbet; to the south snowy crests appear and the cascade of Arse comes in view. The Nine Springs is passed, supposed to have an underground course from the marshy lake of Lhers, at a distance of four miles. Usually it gives but little water; but after a storm the source bursts forth suddenly with violence and pours down in cascade over the rocks.

Aulus lies in an extremely agreeable situation, surrounded by well-wooded mountains, above which soar snowy peaks. The place was well known to the Romans, who worked there the mines of silver-lead. As a watering-place it is furnished with a casino, a park, and theatre in which every evening during the season comedies and farces are performed; and in the park a band plays twice a day. Old Aulus lay on the farther side of the river, but the new site is better exposed to the sun. Aulus lies in a cul-de-sac; no road goes farther—at least none that can be utilized by a carriage. Some little mountain tarns are objects of a visit by those who spend a few days at Aulus, ascending to them on the backs of mules. The largest of these lie in the valleys scooped out of the mass of the Pic de Bassiès, 8165 feet.

But it must be allowed that in this portion of the chain the Pyrenees go in for breadth rather than height. In fact, in Ariège they become somewhat dishevelled, unwind, and straggle into separate threads. The loftiest ridge is that along which runs the frontier; the second is that which starts from the Pic de Camporeile, and is called the Montagne de Tabe, attaining in the Pic de Campzas only to 7670 feet. The third chain is the limestone Planturel that reaches its supreme elevation in the Montagne de Roquefixade, 3010 feet. This is a curious ridge running parallel with the Pyrenees, very regular, but cut through in several places, and ending at Foix. Those who desire to visit a portion of the Pyrenees less in resort than the mountains of the Haute Garonne and the Hautes Pyrénées will not fail to find in this section many delightful sites.

# CHAPTER XVII

## FOIX

Department of Ariège—Watershed—The counts of Foix—Raymond
Roger—The Albigenses—Abuses in the Church—Manicheism—
Council of Albi—Innocent III—Murder of Peter of Castelnau—
Raymond VI of Toulouse—Crusade proclaimed—Simon de
Montfort—Subtlety of the Pope—Massacre at Béziers—And at
Cascassonne—Battle of Muret—Council of the Lateran—A second
Crusade—Simon de Montfort killed—Count Roger Bernard—
Béarn annexed—The town of Foix—The Castle—S. Volusinian—
Nailmakers—Hermitage—Grotto de l'Herme—Mas d'Azil—
The River Ariège—Tarascon—Richelieu—Ste. Quiterie—Iron
mines—Sabarthès—Vicdessos—Iron industry—Cavern of Lom-
brive—Slaughter and smothering of heretics—Les Cabannes—
Lordat—Talc—Ax-les-Thermes—Self-created    nobles—Hôtel
Dieu—Andorra—The Republic—The capital—Urgel—The Count
of Spain—His death.

THE county of Foix, now constituting the major portion of the department of
Ariège, is and always was in Languedoc. The Couserans was, however, ever
regarded as forming a part of Gascony. The ridge between the Volp and the Salat
separates two hydrographic basins and two provinces. Geographically the department of Ariège belongs nevertheless to the basin of the Garonne; all its streams,
with the exception of a few at the extreme east, flow into that great artery, and
finally discharge into the Atlantic. Linguistically only the Couserans is Gascon; yet
Foix from an early date was united to Béarn and Bigorre.

Of the earliest history of the counts of Foix we know very little. Roger Bernard,
who died in 1188, was an excellent prince. His son, Raymond Roger, lived in difficult times, and was involved in the troubles arising out of the attempt of Pope
Innocent III to stamp out the heresy of the Albigenses.

To understand the spread of this heresy and the Crusade which devastated
these fair lands in the South, a few words must be said.

There can be little doubt that Christianity had not struck deep roots in Languedoc. The clergy had acquired but a smattering of Latin, and a meagre knowledge
of doctrine in the monastic schools. They entered on their cures not much raised
above their parishioners in culture, and in morals not infrequently sank below
their level. Enforced clerical celibacy was evaded, but this evasion left a scar on the

conscience. Bishoprics and abbacies were the provision of cadets of noble houses, whether religiously or morally qualified was of no account.

In what is now the department of Ariège, no bigger than an ordinarily sized English county, there were three episcopal sees—S. Lizier, Pamiers, and Mirepoix—and many abbeys.

A persecution of the Manichees in the Byzantine Empire sent a stream of refugees into Lombardy, Provence, and Languedoc, and these heretics speedily acquired a strong hold on the popular imagination. The Church had done so little to awaken the spiritual life in the souls of men, that instinctively, but blindly, they turned to welcome such as promised something better.

The Cathari, i.e. Puritans, as they called themselves, offered a very simple creed and easy conditions of salvation. The fundamental principle of this religion was a Dualism of Good and Evil principles, equally matched; the Evil Principle, the author of the visible Creation; the Good Principle, the author of the invisible, the Spiritual world. The opposition of matter and spirit formed the basis of their moral system. All that pertained to the body, all its functions, its needs, its passions, were of the Evil One; all the aspirations of the soul emanated from the Good Principle. To the people of Provence and Languedoc and Gascony the Cathari seemed to be inoffensive, self-denying enthusiasts. These had their high-priests—the "Perfect" or "Very Elect"—and it was the function of these men to "console" the believers; but the sacrament of Consolation was never administered till it was supposed that a believer was on his death-bed, for this reason, that after it had been administered the recipient might not touch food under pain of committing the unpardonable sin. If there should appear signs of convalescence after the performance of the rite, the person consoled was bled to death, or given pounded glass to swallow.

This new Manichæism offered to the people of the South just what they wanted. They had set before them a class of enthusiasts, the Very Elect, who led austere lives; but they themselves were not required to adopt a life of abstinence, even of self-restraint, for at death free justification was offered them by a simple formula. Moreover, the theological system of the Cathari was simplicity itself.

The whole of the South was infected. A council, held at Albi in 1176, condemned the heresy, and thenceforth the heretics were called Albigenses.

The princes, notably the counts of Toulouse and of Foix, did not interfere. The Albigenses were inoffensive people. If they held odd opinions, that was their own affair, with which their feudal lords were not concerned to meddle.

But the Court of Rome thought otherwise. The flow of contributions into its treasury from the rich South dwindled to nothing. What to the Pope was even more serious was that his authority was openly flouted.

Pope Innocent—is there not bitter satire in the name—in 1203 sent a legate into the southern provinces, Peter of Castelnau by name. This man visited Toulouse, but his efforts there to confute the heresy failed completely. Hopeless of success and mortified in his vanity Peter appealed to Pope Innocent to adopt drastic measures, and Innocent bade him require Raymond, Count of Toulouse, to suppress

Albigensianism throughout his dominions by fire and sword. He was ordered, on pain of excommunication, to become the inquisitor and executioner of his subjects. At the same time he deposed Raymond, Bishop of Toulouse, an amiable, liberal-minded man, and put in his place the firebrand Foulques, who had been a troubadour, and notorious for his licentious verses.

Raymond VI of Toulouse promptly refused to do what was required of him, whereupon Innocent, in 1207, pronounced his excommunication.

Possibly the Count may have let slip some expression of disgust at the conduct of the papal legate, and a wish to be well rid of him, as did Henry II with reference to Becket. The result was the same; a knight killed Peter of Castelnau in 1208 as he was crossing the Rhone. This filled up the measure of Innocent's wrath. He hurled the most dreadful imprecations against the Count, and loudly summoned all Christendom to a war of extermination against the Albigenses. "Anathema to the Count of Toulouse! Remission of all sins to such as arm against these pestilential Provincials. Go forward, soldiers of Christ! May the heretics perish out of the land, and let colonies of Christians be established in their room!"

Dukes and bishops, counts and viscounts, flew to the standard of the Cross, eager to glut themselves on the spoil of the South, so rich with merchandise, and at the same time to gain eternal salvation by violation and murder. Three armies invaded the South under the supreme command of a needy northern knight, Simon de Montfort.

The Pope was as subtle as he was remorseless. In order to weaken the opposition in the South he had entered into negociation with Raymond of Toulouse, and had deluded him into expectations of pardon, till the Crusaders were on him. They began with Béziers, although the viscount was known to be a Catholic. The city was taken and the inhabitants massacred. The Abbot of Citeaux, the legate, wrote regretfully to Innocent that he could only answer for having cut the throats of twenty thousand.

Then the papal host marched to Cascassonne, where they hung fifty prisoners, and burned four hundred Albigenses alive.

Raymond was now offered pardon if he would dismiss his soldiers, level his castles and the walls of his towns, give the Inquisition a free hand in his domains, and make every householder pay a tax of four deniers to the papal treasury. The Count indignantly refused, and the legate again sounded the attack. Raymond was defeated at Castelnaudary, and compelled to fly to Aragon. The conquerors seized on his territory, which the needy knights of the north parcelled out among themselves; and they diverted themselves in hunting out the heretics and burning them.

Urged on by his kinsman, the Count of Toulouse, Peter II, King of Aragon, passed the Pyrenees with an army, and was at once joined by the Count of Foix and many other nobles. A battle was fought at Muret in 1213, in which the King was killed, the army routed, and the nobles of Languedoc dispersed. This sealed the fate of the country. The Council of the Lateran, held two years later, ratified the deposition of Raymond, who, along with the counts of Foix and Cominges, had appeared before the Council, with bitter complaints in their mouths of the way in which their subjects had been slaughtered wholesale and the country laid waste. At once up sprang Foulques, Bishop of Toulouse. "Foix," said he, "swarms with heretics. The sister of the Count intercepted and cut to pieces six thousand Germans, Crusaders, on their way to join the legate."

"Soldiers of the Cross!" retorted the Count of Foix fearlessly. "They were mere robbers, committing every possible outrage in the country."

Then the Baron de Vilamour rose, and in a cold voice gave a detailed account of the horrors, the rapes, the murders, the ravages committed by the Soldiers of the Cross, those sent forth by the Holy See with assurance of gaining Heaven thereby. As he spoke Innocent's head sank on his breast, and he heaved a sigh; some sense of shame stole into his heart. He went to meet his account in 1216, and was succeeded by Honorius III.

Toulouse, the whole South, writhed under the despotism of Simon de Montfort, and called back its exiled count. A new Crusade was preached. Remission of sins was offered to all who would glean what the first locust swarm had left, and massacre such as had been spared. Excommunication was again launched against the Count of Toulouse and the Count of Foix. In an attack on Toulouse Simon de Montfort was killed, and the command was taken by Prince Louis of France. Before this vast army the cities of Languedoc opened their gates. Count Raymond and he of Foix bowed to the storm. Louis died of exhaustion on his return, after having secured the submission of almost the whole land.

Count Roger Bernard of Foix was excommunicated in 1228, and was forced to subscribe to the most degrading terms. The truce lasted eight years. In 1237 he was summoned to appear and answer for his orthodoxy before the papal Inquisitors quartered in his own domains, and holding their court in his own castle. Because he refused he was again excommunicated. He was compelled to submit in 1240, and died in the ensuing year.

The horrors of the extirpation of heresy continued till 1244, when the last of the strongholds of the Albigenses was taken, and two hundred of them were burnt alive without a trial.

After that all trace of them gradually disappears.

Bernard Roger III (1265) married Margaret de Moncada, second daughter of Gaston de Béarn, and as she was heiress, he annexed her territories, and thenceforth the history of Foix is merged in that of Béarn.

Foix, in local patois *Fouch,* is situated at the junction of the Arget with the Ariège, and where, most conveniently for military purposes, a rock shoots up, abrupt and bold, inviting the mediæval noble to plant his castle on the summit. The castle never was a palace like that of Pau; it never was anything but a stronghold. When the counts became lords of Béarn they abandoned their ancient nest, which if secure was inconvenient, and betook themselves to their own creations at Mazères, Orthez, and Pau. The town occupies a triangle where the two rivers already mentioned unite. It is a dull place, its sole feature being the castle, like a very plain man with a very prominent nose. That it should be capital of the department is due to association, not to size, for Pamiers, where was a cathedral, exceeds it in population. It has a theatre, in which but rarely a performance is given; a public library, open for a few hours one day in the week, into which an occasional reader saunters; baths, better known externally than within; an abattoir, where oxen past work are slaughtered, for consumption by those of the inhabitants who have digestions that could dissolve leather; a promenade which lacks promenaders; a vast prefecture, in which the prefect is dying daily of ennui. The Hotel des Gouverneurs has become Palais de Justice—"un édifice banal, malgré ce nom grandiloquent."

The rock of Foix is 178 feet above the river, and is surmounted by three noble towers that served successively as keeps. In the donjons the Inquisition had their court, their trials, and sentences, and the Count had to resign his castle to them in pledge of submission to the judgment of the Holy See. The loftiest of the towers is cylindrical, and is attributed to Gaston Phœbus, but apparently it dates from the fifteenth century. Between the noble towers appear the mean buildings of a prison, in which those who are confined yawn their time away. Below the rock, near the river, at the apex of the triangle, is the church of S. Volusinian, of the fourteenth century, and, like most of the great churches in this portion of the south of France, consists of a nave without aisles. The choir is surrounded by radiating chapels.

Volusinian was Bishop of Tours, a native of Auvergne. When Alaric, King of the Goths, invaded Gaul he carried Volusinian away with him south, and as he proved to be uncompromising in his adherence to the Creed of Nicæa, had him executed at Foix. His festival is on 11 February, and he suffered in 491. Foix has no manufactures, no trade—hardly an expectant *commis voyageur* visits it; but I am in error. It has perpetrated a joke, a miserable pun—Foix produces *patés de foie gras*.

Were there but coal-mines near at hand Foix would revive, for the whole county is full of iron ore. Foix bleeds iron from its veins, but the ferruginous springs run away into the river. The stars in their courses fight against Foix; the valley of the Arget was full of nailmakers at one time—in 1835 there were forty-seven forges. Now their fires are put out: machine-made nails have killed the hand-made nails. Those made in the Barguillère, the valley of the Arget, were for horseshoes, and the makers dubbed themselves *chevaliers*. The extinction of the little forges has led to depopulation; between 1891 and 1901 there was a loss of 27,092 inhabitants in that district.

To the north of the town rises a steep hill, on the summit of which is the hermitage of S. Sauveur, but the last hermit has departed this life; his occupation also is gone, and he has no successor. The Administration has put an end to the hermits.

In the neighbourhood of Foix is the Grotto de l'Herme, that has yielded notable finds of prehistoric man. But the main curiosity is the Mas d'Azil, where the river Arize has bored its way through the limestone barrier of the Planturel. This long chain opposed a passage northwards to the river descending from the mountains to the south. The Arize discovered a fault in the barrier and pierced it, forming a noble arch 250 feet high. Beside it is an artificial gallery bored for the passage of the road. The length of the tunnel is 1250 feet. The road follows the right bank of the Arize, separated from it by a wall of rock. The river descends into the gallery, the average width of which is ninety-five feet, breaking over masses of rock that have fallen from the roof. Above the left bank, under the huge vault, rises a natural column, called the Monk. Farther on in the gallery, a pillar thirty feet in diameter sustaining the roof. There are lateral galleries, at a higher elevation, that have yielded evidence of human occupation. The guano produced by the innumerable bats that inhabit the cave actually forms an article of commerce.

The opening to the north, through which the river effects its escape, is less striking in appearance than that where it makes its plunge underground.

The road from Foix to Ax leads up the river that gives its name to the department, and penetrates deep into the recesses of the mountains.

The first town reached is Tarascon, prettily situated at the junction of the Vicdessos with the Ariège, about a conical hill surmounted by a round tower, which is all that remains of a castle that was blown up by order of Richelieu. The great cardinal thought that the best means of maiming the independence of the nobles, petty barons, and seigneurs, was to destroy their nests. It was he, not the Revolutionists, who made the worst havoc among the stately châteaux of France. He went so far even as to insist on the pepper-castor roofed round towers at the angles of every small squire's mansion being lowered a story to the level of the eaves of the main roof. Tarascon on Ariège is a busier place than sleepy Tarascon on Rhone, that was drawn out of its obscurity by the mythical Tastarin. It is the great centre of activity to the country, "a land whose stones are iron." Formerly it was more prosperous than it is to-day. But the population remains stationary, which in the midst of a universal shrinkage may be reckoned as good. The town is divided into two parts. Old Tarascon clusters about the decayed castle. New Tarascon forms the faubourg Sainte Quitterie, where there is a ferruginous spring bearing the name of the saint, and supposed miraculously to cure insanity. The wonder in this part of the mountains is to find any springs that do not run red. Quiteria, who has given virtue to this spring, is a person of problematical existence. Once upon a time — the Bollandists even know not when — there lived a King Katillas and his wife Calsia, who inhabited doubtlessly a Château en Espagne. Queen Calsia gave birth to nine daughters at once, and being afraid what the King would say, gave them to the nurse with orders to drown them like puppies. But the nurse took them to her home, and reared all in the Christian faith. In time of persecution the nine damsels dispersed, but were caught and offered the alternative of marriage or death. They accepted the latter. One of them, named Wilgefortis, when pestered by a princely suitor, prayed, and lo! out sprouted a thick beard and moustache. She was crucified. Quiteria's head was struck off with a sword. But unwilling to be less of an oddity than her sister, after death she developed into three entire bodies. One became the perquisite of the Portuguese, another of the Spaniards, and the Gascons got hold of the third, and buried it at Aire. I have little doubt that, when a man reputed insane was brought to Quiteria's well and made to drink eight tumblers full of the red water, he remonstrated, and vowed that he was well; whereupon his relations cried out, "A miracle! He has spoken sensibly. Thanks be to Quiteria."

To Tarascon comes the iron ore from the mines in the Vicdessos valley in carts and tumbrils, and is there smelted. There are here also quarries of gypsum for the manufacture of plaster of Paris.

To the south of the town is the church of Notre Dame de Sabart, so-called from Sabarthès, the name of the little region formed by the Valley of Vicdessos and of the Ariège as far as Les Cabannes. The church is Romanesque, and there are remains of an abbey founded for an order of military knights, founded, it is said, by Charlemagne, as a protection of the population and the valuable iron-mines. This is a resort of pilgrims on 8 May and 15 September, when fairs are held at Tarascon, and business, pleasure, and devotion can be harmoniously combined. The Valley of Vicdessos is, and has been from time immemorial, the great seat of iron-mining in the Pyrenees. The ore is nearly pure, and lies in veins and pockets in the limestone of the mountains of Rance, and the deposits form bands alternating with the calcareous rock through a height of over 1800 feet.

The working of the mines is the privilege of the inhabitants of Sem, Goulier, and Olbier, and natives of Vicdessos and other villages about can only be admitted to this privilege by marrying a girl of one of the three named. Otherwise they can be employed only as wagoners drawing the ore to Tarascon.

The earliest mention of these mines is in a charter of the Count of Foix in 1293. For centuries the counts found the utmost difficulty in levying a toll on the iron carried out of the valley; the miners exercised their ingenuity in evading it, and overriding all the restrictions hampering their industry. Unhappily, for many hundred years the mining was not carried on by companies, but by individuals who grubbed where they would and carried on the works in the most wasteful manner. Now the veins of ore are giving out; but the men who have exclusive rights to the mines refuse obstinately and ignorantly to admit of new methods in the extraction of the ore, and disapprove of co-operation. The ancient medieval corporations have survived at Sem, with their traditional rites and formulas. The law on mines of 1893 has somewhat modified some of the restrictions and extended the rights of mining. But the men are stolidly opposed to improvement; they retain the prejudices of their fathers. They have cut down the trees, and the mountain torrents now devastate their little fields and carry away the roads. The State has vainly endeavoured to replant, and by so doing diminish the range of the ravages caused by goats and sheep. The output of the mines dwindles and the impoverishment of the villagers increases. From Usat may be visited the cavern of Lombrive, only an hour's walk from the baths of Usat. The last stronghold of the unfortunate Albigenses was the Castle of Montségur, in the valley of the Lasset, that flows into the Hers. Buried among the mountains, hidden from most eyes, in an apparently inaccessible position, they hoped to be forgotten and to remain in security. But they were scented and tracked by the bloodhounds of the Papacy, and the army of the Crusaders, reluctantly led by Raymond VII of Toulouse, constrained by Innocent VI, who carried on the remorseless policy of Innocent III, and as the sole means of obtaining forgiveness for himself, surrounded it in 1244. The castle stands on and amidst tremendous precipices, and is commanded by the Pic S. Barthélemy. The Albigensian chiefs held out for long, and repulsed several assaults. Then, seeing that their provisions were failing, and that they could not much longer maintain their position, they dispatched four of their number to carry away their treasures to some place of security. These four men crossed the mountain spurs, and hid the treasure in one of the many caverns that open in the cliffs above Usat, but where has not yet been discovered.

On 14 March Montségur was taken, and over two hundred heretics found in it were thrown alive into a huge bonfire that had been erected, and burnt alive to satisfy the implacable vengeance of the Papacy. After that the horde of Crusaders went to Tarascon to search the valleys for more on whom to glut their rage. All the Albigenses of the country round had fled to the caves; they were hunted out and massacred. Nevertheless, all had not been exterminated. In 1325, when John XXII was reigning in Avignon, a fresh pursuit of the heretics was instituted. It was reported that the Albigenses employed the cave of Lombrive as their cathedral. The armies of the Papacy assembled anew and filled the valley. From five to six hundred of the unfortunate heretics—men, women, and children—took refuge in the cavern that runs deep into the heart of the mountain. It has been explored for a distance of three miles. To save themselves the trouble and risk of pursuing the Albigenses in darkness through the winding recesses of the cave, the entrance was walled up, and the miserable wretches were all left to perish there of starvation in abysmal night. Their bones still lie scattered about the pit. The treasures of the Albigenses, supposed to have been hidden there, have never been recovered; but the true treasure, for which they fought and for which they died, the emancipation of the human soul from the fetters of slavery in which it had been bound by Rome, has been won by nearly all Europe.

Les Cabannes lies in a beautiful basin formed by the junction of the Aston with the Ariège. From hence the lateral valley branches off that formed the seigneuries of the Lordadais. In it is planted one of the mightiest fortresses of the counts of Foix, perched on a rock, and commanding a most picturesque site. It was blown up in 1632, by order of Louis XIII, but still retains portions of four concentric oval-en-closing walls, and a square keep. From the castle can be viewed the entire mass of the Tabe; its culminating point, the Pic S. Barthélemy, shoots up superbly to the height of 7060 feet. At Vernaux is a Romanesque church. This place has given its name to the talc that is found in quarries near by, situated at a great elevation, some 6600 feet above the sea, and where the workmen can be employed only from 1 May to 15 November. The bed of talc is about 120 feet thick, and extends for a length of 1500 feet, and is sent down to the station of Luzenac by a wire rope.

Ax-les-Thermes is planted at the junction of the Oriège and the Ariège. About it rise many bold crags; on the summit of one is Castel Maü, supposed to have been a Moorish fortress. Another supports a huge statue of the Virgin. The whole valley has been studded with castles, of which now only the ruins remain. In troubled times, when warfare was incessant between the counts of Foix and the counts of Urgel, or between them and the Crusaders, every country gentleman was obliged to pitch his house on the top of a rock, and give it the character of a stronghold. Some of these are so small that they could not have accommodated more than a little garrison; and the seigneurs must have lived cramped and uneasy in them.

Probably they had their houses in the valley, and only retreated to these castles when the clash of arms sounded. It is a pity that some of these picturesque ruins should not be restored. On the Dordogne, the Lot, and the Vezère, some rich wine merchant of Bordeaux buys up a castle, and makes it habitable in the midst of a park. When in residence there M. Blom of Bordeaux blossoms out into le Comte de Montréal, and M. Dois into le Marquis de Beausejour. In England we have to pay heavy fees when we acquire a title; it is not so in France. There a man dubs himself baron, or count, or marquis. As to the armorial bearings that they assume—"Ma foi!" exclaimed a painter, looking at the heraldic shield over one of these châteaux, "what imaginations these *nouveaux riches* possess!"

Ax (Aquæ) was probably a Roman thermal station. The place was frequented in the Middle Ages, when the Hôtel Dieu was founded (in 1260) for the reception of patients. Even before that, in 1200, a bath for lepers was constructed here. The Hôtel Dieu owes its origin to King Louis IX, who had it constructed for the use of Crusaders who had contracted leprosy in Palestine and Egypt. But it was not till the beginning of the eighteenth century that Ax was much frequented. Now it receives about ten thousand visitors in the year, seeking healing in its water. The springs are so numerous, and so thickly strewn, that the town seems as though erected over the rose of a fountain of thermal waters.

From Ax Andorra may be reached by the Port de Saldeu. Andorra is the sole remaining independent republic in the Pyrenees. It has a legendary origin. In 805 Louis "le Débonnaire" was on his way to besiege Urgel, and the Andorrans took up arms and materially aided him. In recognition of their services Louis conferred on them a charter that accorded to them the rights of self-government. Later, when Emperor, he conceded to the Bishop of Urgel half the tithe of the six parishes in the valley, as well as half his right of suzerainty over the diminutive republic. Actually Andorra formed a lordship in the county of Urgel, and it was the counts of that place who granted rights over it to the bishops of the see of Urgel. Later on the seigneural rights passed to the counts of Foix. Counts and bishops wrangled over their respective claims, till in 1278 the feud was settled by a convention that accorded to the republic the privileges that it still enjoys—local autonomy under the double suzerainty of the bishops of Urgel and the counts of Foix, to whom has succeeded the French Government. The Andorrans pay a tribute to France annually of 950 francs, and to the Bishop of Urgel 450 francs.

This duodecimo republic has an area of 175 square miles, and a population of six thousand. It is governed by a council of twenty-four, elected by the householders, and two provosts—one nominated by the French Government, the other by the Bishop of Urgel, exercising in common judicial powers. These provosts are theoretically the captains of the Andorran militia, which is composed of all the heads of houses. Of the twenty-four councillors, elected every four years, one half are renewable every two years. The republic consists of three valleys, surrounded by mountains on every side save where in the south the River Embaline issues and flows down to Urgel. The land is fertile for the altitude at which the basin lies, but its principal products are timber and iron, and its chief industry is smuggling. Some years ago a proposal was made to the little republic to convert it into a monster gambling hell. This was after the closing of the house at Homburg; but although the sum offered was tempting, the Andorrans had the good sense to refuse the offer, which accordingly was then made to the Prince of Monaco, and by him seized.

The capital is a dirty, ill-built village; the principal buildings in it are a Romanesque church and the palace, a fortified structure of the fifteenth century, which serves as the seat of government, school, Palais de Justice, and prison. On the ground-floor are stables for the horses of the councillors.

In the council hall is a great oak chest containing the archives, and fastened by six locks, the key to each being retained by each of the six parishes. The town or village has a dismal look, the houses being constructed of slate and schist rock.

The original capital was at S. Julien de Loria, where a cross marks the site.

On the heights are the remains of an old Moorish castle, called Carol, a name derived from Charles the Great, who is supposed to have expelled the infidel. The name of Andorra is supposed to be taken from the Arabic *aldarra*, "a place thick with trees." Mr. Ford says:—

> "The hills around the rich alluvial basin of Andorra abound in pine forests, which afford fuel; nothing can be prettier than the distant views of the villages, embosomed in woods; at Mont Melous are three lakes enclosed by lofty and fantastic walls of rock."

A rough road leads from Andorra to Seo de Urgel, a distance of sixteen miles. This is a quaint old Spanish town with an interesting cathedral of the eleventh century, and a cloister of considerable beauty. The town is commanded by the citadel on the height Las Horcas, "The Gallows," where the Bishop of Urgel, who was a sovereign prince, hung miscreants.

Urgel was the headquarters of a Carlist insurrection in 1827. This was put down by an adventurer of French origin; none knew his real name, and what had been his position in life, before he turned up and offered his services to Ferdinand VII and dubbed himself the Count of Spain. He served the King well, was absolutely without scruples, and remorselessly cruel. He was made by Ferdinand Governor of Catalonia. But, on the death of his patron in 1833, he passed over to Don Carlos, and fought under him for the very cause which a few years previously he had put down. But his former cruelties were not forgotten. He made his headquarters at Urgel. The Junta of the Carlists was summoned to meet at Aira on 26 October, 1839, and the Count went to attend it. He was received with expressions of pleasure and devotion by his aide-de-camp, Mariano Orteu, who engaged him in conversation, whilst the *curé*, Ferres, levelled a pistol at him, fired, and wounded him.

The Count fell, and pleaded for a drink of water. This was refused. He was then mounted on a mule, his feet bound together under the belly, and he was conducted from place to place, exposed to the insults and derision of the people, till 1 November, when he found himself at Ceselles; there, with cruel irony his former friend Orteu informed the unfortunate man that he was to be speedily "sent to his own place." Then he deliberately shot him, and the rest of the company fell on him and hacked him to pieces with their long knives.

# CHAPTER XVIII

## LA CERDAGNE

Col de Puy Morens—Etang de Lanous—Many lakes—Dreary country—River of Carol—Dam of Quès—County of Cerdagne—Divided at the Peace of the Pyrenees—Llivia—Ceretani—Bourg-Madame—Paradise of botanists—Relics of the Flood—Mont
Louis—General Dagobert—Church of Planès—Font-Romeu—
Image, object of Pilgrimage—Story of Othman and Lampagia.

FROM Ax-les-Thermes a good carriage road crosses the Col de Puy Morens to the
Cerdagne and to Puygcerda in Spanish territory. It passes through most bald
and weariful uplands, under the Pic de Carlitte, which is the highest point of the
watershed between the Atlantic and the Mediterranean. The height of this peak is
9580 feet, and its flanks are starred with lakes, many of which are frozen through
a great part of the year, more than are found in any other part of the Pyrenees.
The Etang de Lanous is three kilometres long and from 500 to 600 yards across,
pinched in the middle so as to form two basins. It is covered with ice for about nine
months. It swarms with red-fleshed *Salmo alpinus*, which is excellent eating.

> "A frame of lofty mountains, reaching above 7500 feet sur-
> rounds this lake. Behind this barrier are other sheets of water; the
> most extensive lie on the north side, in the department of Ariège.
> Among these is the Etang d'En-Beys, whence issues the Oriège;
> the Etangs of Peyrisse from which the water descends in a series
> of cascades to form the large and beautiful Lake of Naguilles, a
> reservoir to be utilized some day for the irrigation of the plain of
> Pamiers, and any number of others lying asleep at the bottom of
> valleys, in which, with the exception of a few shepherds, no other
> face is seen."

All this portion of the chain is almost barren and sad. The road leads through
a dreary country, where the snow lies long, and the scanty grass is burnt with
the frozen streams, and heaped with granitic blocks thrown up by moraines of
glaciers that no longer exist. A few miserable villages are passed till the ruins are
reached of the Castle of Carol, of which two towers remain. This was at one time
the chief place of the valley, and it maintained independence in the midst of the
county of Cerdagne.

At Quès the river of Carol, flowing south, is arrested by a barrier of rocks,
formed to serve for irrigation by means of a canal, as far as Puygcerda. It is, per-

haps, the earliest recorded instance, at least in medieval times, of such an economic undertaking. This canal was constructed in 1318, by virtue of a charter of Sanchez, King of Majorca. It was so well constructed that it serves its purpose admirably to the present day, fertilizing the fields below it, whereas above the life-giving stream the mountain side is barren. When the Treaty of the Pyrenees was drawn in 1659 it was stipulated that this barrier and the canal from it, though on territory ceded to France, should be maintained in good order.

The Cerdagne became an independent state soon after the Moorish invasion of 731. It was governed by a Berber chief, Munuza by name, who threw in his lot with the Franks against the Yemenite Arabs of the South, and even married a daughter of Eudes, Duke of Aquitaine. But he was killed near Puygcerda; his head was salted, and sent to the Caliph of Damascus.

About 928 Miro, Count of Barcelona, gave Cerdagne to his son Oliba Cabréta, and it was ruled by its own counts till 1117, when the last died childless, and then it was reannexed to the county of Barcelona, and later went to Aragon. Finally, by the peace of 1659, it was divided, much to the indignation of the inhabitants, who protested ineffectually—half went to France, and half remained to Spain. France thrust her frontier down the Spanish slope of the mountains, taking in the rivers that flow south to feed the Ebro, just as Spain carried her frontier beyond the highest crests of the range to include the Val d'Aran and the head waters of the Garonne. But this acquisition on the part of France was not as unreasonable as it would seem, for the object was to secure communication between Foix and the Conflant and Valespir valleys that opened unto the plain of Roussillon, which had also become incorporated into the kingdom of France.

There is, however, a curious little *enclave* of twelve square kilometres, about the town of Llivia, completely surrounded by French territory, that remains Spanish. The explanation of this anomaly is as follows: At the Peace of the Pyrenees Spain agreed to surrender to France thirty-three villages in Cerdagne. But Llivia haughtily protested that she was not a village, but a town, once a city with a bishop of her own, consequently did not come within the terms of the agreement. This was admitted, and Llivia remains Spanish, much to the inconvenience of the custom-house officers, who have to maintain a cordon of douaniers about the petty territory. Now Llivia, that possesses 330 inhabitants, regrets the past. Spain exacts of her taxes to the amount of 30,000 francs, and gives her nothing in return—neither a post office, nor telegraph, nor roads. The post office has to be kept up by the citizens, so also the roads till they reach the frontier. Llivia was a Roman town founded in honour of the wife of Augustus, and some remains of the Roman walls exist. It is a poor, decayed place. A castle in ruins occupies the highest point of the hill on which it is built; the large church is planted on a terrace above the cold, slated roofs of the sordid houses and narrow streets of the town.

Cerdagne is the country of the Ceretani of Pliny, and the same people occupied the Valespir, and have left their name in the town of Ceret. The race was not Iberic, but purely Celtic, and their name is the same as that given to Ceretica, or Ceredigion, Cardigan in Wales.

Whilst Llivia decays malodorously under Spanish neglect, a little hamlet on French soil, Bourg-Madame, is growing into vigorous and fresh life. Not many years ago it was nothing but a cluster of a couple of taverns and a station of the customs, and it was called Guinguettes d'Hix. But the situation favoured it, standing on the frontier at the point where the high road from Barcelona is linked on to a network of French main roads. Moreover, Barcelona derives much of its butter and cheese from the French Cerdagne, and the trade consequently passes through the place. In 1815 the Duke of Angoulême entered France by this door on the frontier, and the inhabitants obtained from him leave to alter the name of the growing town to Bourg-Madame.

The Pyrenees of this part of the chain is one of the most barren mountain systems in Europe. The passes into Spain are mere notches cut to a depth of 600 to 900 feet in the ridge, that rises to a height of about 8000 feet above the sea. Even the mountain peaks have little individual character, and from the high land whence seen do not show their true elevation.

Nevertheless this portion of the range is a paradise for botanists; plants are found here that are discoverable in no other part of the Pyrenees. The granitic elevated plateau is strewn with lakes, already alluded to, which are the sources of the Ariège, the Aude, the Segre, and the Têt. The peasants believe that these are relics of Noah's flood, patches of water that loitered and were left behind when the Deluge was past and the flood was engulfed. And they are further convinced that the ark rested on the Puyg Péne. North and east of the plateau the ground falls away in a series of terraces cleft by ravines; the finest and best known of these latter is that of the Aude, visited from the baths of Cascanières.

In this upland region is a fortress created by Vauban, Mont Louis, in which a couple of companies are quartered, and spend a joyless time, where the winter lasts ten months out of the twelve. The fortifications enclose but a handful of houses. It stands at the height of 5280 feet above the sea, and is commanded by mountains that rise to 6685 feet, as the Pic de la Tausse, but they do not impress one with sense of height. Mont Louis stands at the point of suture of the three little provinces out of which Louis XIII formed that of Roussillon—the Conflent, the Capcir, and Cerdagne.

In Mont Louis there is nothing to be seen of particular interest. The church was built from designs of Vauban. On the terrace is the monument of General Dagobert, who died in 1794. It consists of a pile of granite surmounted by a bomb. Dagobert was, however, not a native of this place, but of Saint Lô, in Manche. He had been sub-lieutenant in the regiment of Touraine in the Seven Years' War, and when the Revolution broke out he was sent as General of Division with the army of Italy, and met with some success. He was less fortunate when commanding an army in the Pyrénées Orientales; he met with defeat at Trouillas, and was relieved of his charge and arrested. But he succeeded in justifying himself, before the Committee of Public Safety, by showing that his failure was due to the jealousy and disobedience of the generals placed under his orders. He was re-established in his position and allowed to carry on the campaign according to a plan proposed by himself to the Convention. He reached Perpignan in March, 1794, but could not obtain from Dugommier more than a few battalions in place of the 12,000 infantry and 600 cavalry that had been ordered to be placed at his disposal. At the head of a small body of men he went to Puygcerda and invaded Catalonia, took the strong position of Monteska, and surrounded Urgel. On 10 April he entered that city, which redeemed itself from sack by paying a contribution of 10,000 francs. Then he attempted to besiege the citadel, but found it to be too strong to be taken, and he retreated on the morrow. He was conveyed ill to Puygcerda on 17 April, where he died.

To the south-east of Mont Louis is Planès, where there is a curious church, some suppose of Moorish constructure, by others attributed to the tenth century, by others again set as late as the twelfth. It consists of an equilateral triangle, surmounted by a cupola, and each angle rounded off. That this curious monument should be of Moorish origin is most improbable. The Arabs in France destroyed much, but built nothing.

The hermitage of Font-Romeu is a pilgrimage resort with a Calvary, situated at the height of 5330 feet, and commanding a wide panorama.

The way to it is through a pine wood, the old trees bearded with grey lichen. A hermit takes charge of the shrine—a real hermit, one of the rare survivals; they are now almost as extinct as the dodo and the great auk. The sanctuary is the very Mecca of Cerdagne and Capcir. On 8 September as many as three thousand pilgrims assemble here; the place is like a disturbed ant-heap. The visitors do not restrain themselves to devotional exercises; they also dine, drink, sing. Then may be seen the white caps, laced, of Conflent and Roussillon; the kerchief of glaring colours—red, yellow, and blue—of the women of Cerdagne; men wearing the red *barretina* and the cord-soled *spadrillos*, Catalonians these who have not abandoned their old costume. The miraculous image is a seated Madonna, with head and hands out of all proportion to the body. It spends the winter in the church of Odeillo, but revisits Font-Romeu as soon as the rhododendrons begin to flush the mountain sides.

In winter Mont Louis is a cold and wretched prison. Clouds envelop the mountain-tops, cold rain and heavy falls of snow alternate with furious and icy gales. In summer the vapours often fill the valley, and from the ramparts of Mont Louis is seen the spectacle of a vast plain of snow, recalling the scenes of winter; but the snow now is the surface of cloud lying low, silvered by the light from above.

This wild country saw the end of Othman abu Nessu, the Moorish Governor of Narbonne.

In 725 Ambessa, Moslem Governor of Spain, crossed the Pyrenees. Cascassonne and Nîmes vainly endeavoured to resist him. In the midst of his successes, however, death surprised him. But he left the Arabs masters of Septimania, where they established themselves in force and made Narbonne their capital. The struggle between Moslem and Christian for the possession of the soil of France now became a struggle desperate in its earnestness.

Eudes, Duke of Aquitania, was at the time hampered by an attack from the North by Charles Martel, Duke of the Franks. In his extremity he made overtures to Othman, Governor of Narbonne, who was not a Saracen, but a Moor. The Moors were Berbers from Northern Africa, of the same blood as the Iberians of Spain; they had been conquered by the Arabs and forced to become Mahomedans. Eudes gave his beautiful daughter Lampagia to Othman, who became deeply attached to his Christian wife, and promised his assistance against the new Emir, Abderahman. This latter came over the Col de Perche and threatened Narbonne. Othman was deserted by his men, and fled to Llivia with his wife and a few attendants. He soon perceived that it was not possible to defend the little town, and he escaped and attempted to cross the Col de Morens. In his flight he was entreated to halt by Lampagia, to slake her thirst at a spring and rest on the turf by it. Othman and she were surrendering themselves to the pleasing hope that they were safe, when they saw a detachment of Saracens in full pursuit.

The servants took to flight, but Lampagia was too weary to join them, and Othman would not abandon his wife. In a moment they were surrounded, and Othman, rather than fall into the hands of his enemies, flung himself down the precipice and perished. His head was cut off and sent to Abderahman along with Lampagia. She was so lovely in the eyes of the Emir that he sent her to Damascus to the Commander of the Faithful.

Abderahman pursued his successes, but met with discomfiture on the fields of Poitiers in October, 732, and he himself was among the slain.

# CHAPTER XIX

## THE CANIGOU

The Canigou a supreme effort of the Pyrenees before dying down—
The Corbières—Ballad—*Goigs*—Catalonian dances—Prades—
Priory of Serrabonna—S. Michel de Cuxa—Villefranche—
Castle—Imprisonment there of two assistants of Mme. de
Brinvilliars—Conspiracy—Betrayed by Mez de Llar—Castle tak-
en by Gilly—Corneilla—Vernet—Ascent of the Canigou—Funic-
ular railway—S. Martin de Canigou—Founded—Restored—Le
Boulon—Main highway to Spain—Ceret—Legend of its bridge—
Hazel-nuts—Gathering the crop—Hermitage of S. Ferreolus—
Pallada—Amelie les Bains—Arles-sur-Tech—Church—Tomb of
SS. Abdo and Senen—Miraculous flow of water—Cloister—Prats
de Mollo—Spadrillos.

THE Pyrenees, before expiring in the cliffs of Cerbère, that drop abruptly into the
Mediterranean, make a supreme effort and rise in the Canigou, which, though
not one of the first-class heights, is certainly one of the finest. A certain bashfulness
prevails among the giants. The Vignemale, the Mont Perdu, the Maladetta retreat
behind screens of less elevation and conceal their majesty. But the Canigou makes
the most of herself. The height is but 9135 feet, yet it is a stately mountain, grey
with eternal snows, as its name implies, and yielding to none in dignity.

Comeliness in a woman is enhanced threefold when she is well set up. Canigou is admirably set up. The fringe of subsidiary hills that hitherto has intervened
between the high ranges and the plain here becomes detached and drifts away
to the north-east, as the Corbières, leaving the Canigou to reap the advantage of
showing from head to foot. It is not even the highest mountain of the Pyrénées
Orientales; it is surpassed by the Carlitte, which is 9780 feet, and the Puig Mal,
which is 9730 feet; but as these two summits are confounded among a number of
other heights rising out of the elevated plateau, it seems impossible, at first sight,
to suppose them to be as lofty as the Canigou. This latter mountain is the termination of a chain that breaks away from the main range in a north-easterly direction,
built up of granite and mica schist, and is composed of the junction of two ridges,
which give to the Canigou the appearance of having two heads. It dominates the
whole plain of Roussillon, and has inspired a song known to every peasant there,
who, if he does not sing all the words, warbles the air. This song may be rendered
into English thus:—

"Of mountains that are wondrous fair
Give me the Canigou!
Where, in the glowing summer air,
Bloom flowers red and blue.
Give me thy love, sweet maid, give me thy love!

"In autumn and in spring as well
The flowers here unfold,
Blush roses, many a purple bell,
Red pinks, and broom all gold.
Give me thy love, etc.

"Her chestnut-brown and laughing eye
Has ravishèd my heart,
So neat and trim is she, but I
Feel but my cruel smart.
Give me thy love, etc.

"White is she as the Canigou,
Her face as cotton grass,
That's bathèd in the morning dew,
Her eyes are clear as glass.
Give me thy love, etc.

"Her teeth are pearls, her lips are red,
And archèd are her brows.
She wounds my heart, she turns my head;
Maid! hearken to my vows.
Give me thy love, etc."

The *Goigs* are the "Joys," sacred songs or carols in honour of the Virgin and the Saints. The best known is that in praise of Our Lady of Font-Romeu. The "Goigs dels Ous" "Carol of the Eggs," sung everywhere, an Easter song, is trolled in the streets and throughout the night on the eve of that great festival. One of the chanters carries a basket, to receive eggs and any other contributions accorded to the carolers.

On the Place at Vernet, on Sundays and on the local fête, may be seen Catalan dances about the great elm tree. Unfortunately these dances have lost much of their primitive character since the *cornet-à-piston* has displaced the old bagpipe. The ancient *bals*, *sardanas*, and *seguedillas* are danced less frequently every year. The *bal* is a musical pastoral representing the love-making of a youth and his lass; but this is changing its features, and degenerating into a gallop. The *sardana* and the *seguedilla* were ballads, the tunes of which were taken by the *joglars*, or minstrels, for country dances, but to which formerly the performers sang.

Notwithstanding the degeneration of the dances, the tourist will see in them some traits of the light-hearted character of the people, will be interested in the traditional music, and be pleased with the quaintness of the scene, like a bit out of an opera.

Vernet les Bains

The peaks of Canigou may be reached by train either on the north or on the south. The northern line from Perpignan leads to Prades and Villefranche de Conflent for Vernet, whence the visitor will be able to ascend the Canigou by a funicular railway in course of construction. The other way is by the Valespir to Amelie les Bains and Arles-sur-Tech.

We will begin with the first, and not halt till we reach Prades, though there is much on the way of interest. The plain of Prades is two and a half miles wide by two long, not very extensive, but enjoying so sweet a climate, and having such a fertile soil, and so well watered, that fruit and vegetables grow there in marvellous abundance. Prades is a pleasant little town, but without much of interest in its public buildings. The church was completed in 1686 in the unattractive style affected at that period. But if Prades itself lacks antiquities, it is not so with the neighbourhood.

If the visitor likes to run back to the third station on the line by which he has arrived, i.e. to Boule-Ternère, and ascend the lateral valley for five miles, or else take a carriage from Vinca, he can see one of the most interesting monuments of medieval architecture in Roussillon. This is an Augustinian priory of Serrabonna, founded in 1082; Artal II, Bishop of Elne, consecrated the church in 1151. The church consists of a nave and two side aisles, which are cut off from the nave; that on the south, standing on the edge of a precipice, was formerly open to sun and air, supported on columns of white marble, the capitals sculptured with all the richness and quaintness affected in the early twelfth century. The sun has mellowed the marble to a rich golden hue. This aisle is now converted into a stable. The north aisle communicated with the galilee or pro-naos, and with the choir. Between the doorway into the cemetery and that into the nave is the galilee, opening outwards, through a large portal covered with magnificent sculptures. The galilee is composed of a hall supported by round-headed arches resting on pillars, single and double, with richly sculptured capitals all in white marble.

The priory is situated in a wild and desolate region, thinly populated.

Nearer to Prades, within an easy walk, is another ruined religious house, S. Michel de Cuxa, founded in the ninth century. The abbot wore the mitre and exercised quasi-episcopal jurisdiction over fifteen parishes. The abbey obtained a high repute on account of the sanctity of several of its members, as S. Romuald and Peter Orseolo, the latter of whom had been Doge of Venice.

The situation is delightful. The monastery is planted on the summit of a hill above the waters of the Riberetta. About it is an amphitheatre of mountains, opening out to the south to afford a full view of the Canigou. Springs of pure cold water gush forth in many places. The great abbey is now in such complete ruin that it is difficult to distinguish the parts of the monastic building. The splendid cloister has been destroyed, and portions have been transferred to adorn the baths at Prades. The church is Romanesque, with a pointed choir. The nave is now roofless, and is used for a storehouse. The church formerly possessed two towers: one fell in 1839, the other leans. The story goes that the architect who built it, finding that his erection was out of the perpendicular, ran away, and was never heard of again.

The fine Renaissance doorway of the abbot's house is intact. It is richly carved in white marble, yellowed by the sun, and is surmounted by a sundial, on which is represented a Benedictine monk looking up at the sun, and bearing the inscription, *Sub uno solis radio omnem mundum collectum conspexit.*

Five miles above Prades is Villefranche, the terminus of the railway. It is a dreary little place built of grey marble that discolours and stains black. Moreover, it consists of two streets only, usually empty; and the houses are too many for the small population, numbering less than five hundred. The town was built by William Raymond, Count of Cerdagne, in 1095. He surrounded the town with a wall flanked by towers. The castle was erected by Vauban, on a spur of the limestone mountain of Belloch, 450 feet above the river Tet, and reached by a subterranean staircase of 999 steps. In this castle were confined for the rest of their lives two of the assistants of the infamous Marquise de Brinvilliers. These were La Chappelain and Guesdon. A very brief notice of the Marchioness and her crimes must suffice. She was a young and beautiful woman, connected both by birth and marriage with some of the noblest families of France, and was married to the Marquis de Brinvilliers, a man of depraved conduct. She formed a guilty attachment for Sainte Croix, a gay, handsome man, who had learned in Italy the manufacture of slow poisons, especially the Succession Powder. The Marquis and Marchioness separated, but were not divorced. Sainte Croix, who had no fortune of his own, depended on what was given him by his mistress, and as this did not suffice, he proposed to her to poison her old father and brothers and sister, so as to gather into her own hands all their succession. She agreed without hesitation, and herself administered the fatal draught to her father. The brothers were next got rid of, and the sister would have been similarly destroyed had not her suspicions been roused, and she hastily quitted Paris. Others who were inconvenient in one way or another were similarly got rid of, but all was done with such caution that no charge could be made against either. But the day of retribution was at hand, and a terrible mischance brought the murders to light. The nature of the poisons was so deadly that when Sainte Croix worked in his laboratory, he was obliged to wear a mask, to preserve himself from suffocation. One day the mask slipped off, and the miserable wretch perished in his crimes. His corpse was found on the following morning in the obscure lodging where he had fitted up his laboratory, and with it papers which disclosed the whole series of murders perpetrated by the pair. The Marchioness fled to England, where she remained for three years, but went early in 1676 to Liège. There she was caught, brought to Paris, executed, and her body burnt.

La Guesdon, along with her husband, had been in the service of Sainte Croix, and before her marriage had been in that of the Marchioness. She had been implicated in the poisonings. La Chappelain had acted in Paris the part of a fortune-teller. By means of her supposed prevision of the future she was able to presage the death of those marked down by Mme. de Brinvilliers and Sainte Croix for destruction. La Guesdon died in the prison at Villefranche in 1717, La Chappelain in 1724.

In the place itself is the opening into an extensive cavern. In 1674 a conspiracy was raised to capture the citadel and deliver it over to the Spaniards. It was widely ramified through the Cerdagne and Roussillon, neither content at having been made over to France by the Treaty of the Pyrenees. Some of the leading spirits in the plot were the men of the family of Llar, in Villefranche, whose dilapidated and dingy *hôtel* may be seen in the Rue des Juifs. The cavern mentioned served as a place of meeting and a storehouse for arms. The conspiracy was betrayed by Inez de Llar, daughter of the chief man in the plot, Charles de Llar. He and her brother and relatives involved in it were executed. The unfortunate Inez, broken-hearted at having brought ruin on her family, ended her days in a convent.

In 1793 the Spanish general Crespo succeeded in making himself master of Villefranche, on 4 August; but on 19 September, Gilly, at the head of the second battalion of the Grenadiers of Gard, composed of 450 men, retook the place by an act of audacity. He disposed his men on the heights as though the vanguard of an army, and then rode up to the outposts with sixty grenadiers behind him, and haughtily summoned the Spanish commandant to surrender to General Dagobert, whose army, he said, was at hand, and who would give no quarter if the place were not immediately given up.

The frightened Crespo consented, and an hour later Gilly entered Villefranche at the head of the little army.

From Villefranche the distance is hardly five miles to Vernet, up the valley of the Riu Major. The road passes Corneilla, where there is a curious Romanesque church with a square tower and a fine marble, sculptured doorway, as also, what is a rare feature, a retable of carved marble of 1345, by an artist named Carcall de Berga. It represents incidents in the life of our Lord. At the Revolution it was pulled down, but was re-erected by an unintelligent mason, who put it together badly, as may be seen by the disorder into which the inscriptions have been thrown. The counts of Cerdagne were much attached to Corneilla, and erected here a palace, which was abandoned later and given up to the Augustinian canons.

Vernet is built in an amphitheatre of verdure, commanded by the buttresses of the Canigou. It is composed of two distinct parts, of very different aspect. The upper town is a tangle of little streets between mean, black houses with broken windows and rickety doors, above whose red tiled or slated roofs rise the church and the castle. New Vernet lies along the road lower down, and there are found the baths, the hotels, and the casino. The watering-places of Bagnères de Luchon, Cauterez, S. Sauveur, etc., are frequented only in the months of June, July, August, and rarely September; but at Vernet the season begins in April, and bathers linger on to November. For the use of winter residents a *jardin d'hiver* has been formed. The cold here is never great; and the salubrity of the spot has induced the erection of an open-air cure sanatorium at the height of 2250 feet, in an isolated position, for the use of consumptives.

From Vernet the ascent of the Canigou can be made on foot or by the newly-constructed cog-railway. There is a station at S. Martin de Canigou, an abbey founded at the edge of a precipice in 1007 by Count Waifre of Cerdagne, and his wife Gisella. Tradition will have it that he was engaged in warfare with the Moors, and had planned to surround them. He committed one detachment of troops to his son, with strict injunctions to delay attack till he himself should appear. But the young man, in his impetuosity, fell on the unbelievers before the arrival of the Count, and was defeated. Waifre in a rage killed him, and then repenting of what he had done, went to Rome, where the Pope required him to build and endow a monastery in expiation of his crime. This is, however, mere fable. As a matter of fact, the foundation was wholly voluntary, and Count Waifre, after having built it retired from the world within its walls, and occupied his leisure in scooping out a sarcophagus that was to contain himself eventually, which sarcophagus, now empty, is still shown. He died in 1049. The abbey, having been dismantled at the Revolution, fell into complete ruin, but has been purchased, and the church restored by Bishop du Pont of Perpignan. He has also revived the pilgrimage to it, which takes place on S. Martin's Day (11 November), when a procession winds up the mountain from Vernet. Whether procession and pilgrims will henceforth go up in trucks by the cog-railway remains to be seen. The church is a very interesting example of earliest Romanesque, the aisles are separated from the nave by granite columns very massive, with Byzantine ornament on the capitals. Beneath the church is the crypt.

The second way to reach the roots of the Canigou, and, if it be desired, to ascend it, is to take the branch line from Elne to Arles-sur-Tech. At Le Boulou (lo Volo) the line crosses the Great Eastern highway into Spain, the main pass from Narbonne to Barcelona in Roman and medieval times, and used by Celts and Iberians before ever Narbonne and Barcelona were thought of. Le Boulou did well as a place through which travellers and merchandise streamed this way and that. But then came the days of steam; the iron road was carried along the coast from Perpignan to Barcelona, and Le Boulou's occupation and prosperity were gone never to return.

Beyond Le Boulou we reach Ceret, famous for its bridge, a daring medieval structure, and for its nuts and cherry orchards. The architect employed on the bridge, unable to throw the bold arch over the Tech, put himself in communication with the Devil, who promised to complete it for the usual consideration. As the fatal day approached the architect became uneasy, and in the night went to the river with a sack on his back, and waited till half-past eleven. Then he let loose a cat with a kettle tied to its tail, and the Evil One, frightened at the noise, let drop the last stone needed to complete the bridge and fled. Thus the bridge never was finished; it lacks one stone to the present day. The bridge spans the river with a single arch, and the height from the key of the arch to the level of the water is 70 feet. The opening of the arch between the piers is 128 feet. It remains the boldest achievement in bridge-building accomplished in ancient France, the only other approaching it was that of Brioude, which no longer exists. This bridge was constructed in 1321. It marked the limit of the Valespir, or upper basin of the Tech.

Ceret really flourishes on hazel-nuts. The plantations extend over other communes, but Ceret is the centre of the industry. Three kinds of nuts are grown; the best is thought to be indigenous; it has a russet shell, pointed, and is contained in a cup divided into four lobes delicately striated. The taste is superior to that of the other kinds, and it is in greater request for the making of nougat. Inferior in taste, but larger, is the second variety, usually sold to be served up at dessert. The third kind is exotic, and is little cultivated.

The gathering of the nuts is done by women in the middle of August. After that the nuts have been freed from their cases, they are dried, and the sale begins in October. For the production of nougat the shells are cracked and the kernel released, and this latter is alone sent to the factories of that dainty. A hazel-nut tree will bear the third year after it has been planted, but is not calculated to render a good crop till the fifth. A hectare (2 acres, 1 r., 35 p.) is reckoned to render a crop that will bring in 130 francs.

A little over two miles above the bridge of Ceret is the Hermitage of S. Ferreolus, on the left bank of the Tech. Ferreolus was, so the story goes, a robber chieftain who committed many murders. Seized with compunction, he resolved on expiating his crimes by being rolled downhill from where now stands the chapel, in a barrel, studded internally with nails, a process the same as that which extinguished Regulus. His festival is on 18 September, on which day the chapel is visited, and there is much eating and drinking and dancing. On the following Sunday is bull-baiting.

The line passes within sight of Pallada, most picturesquely situated, at some distance from the iron road; but Pallada is best visited from Amalie des Bains.

The baths were known to and used by the Romans, but were a dependency of Arles-sur-Tech, and so remained till that needy little town in a weak moment disposed of them in 1813, and has regretted the sale ever since.

Amelie, which takes its name from Queen Amelie, occupies a specially favoured site. Mountains fold about it, it faces the sun, and is screened from every wind. The terrible Tramontane, which has bowed the olives and plane trees in Roussillon and Languedoc, is powerless to reach this blessed valley. The north-east wind indeed can steal up the ravine of the Tech, but not till it has been despoiled of its humidity, which renders it so objectionable to the inhabitants of the plain. Frost and snow rarely visit Amelie; the mean number of days when rain falls in the winter is eleven, in spring thirty-two, sixteen in the summer, and twelve in the autumn. There is a military establishment of baths at Amelie, and the place is much frequented by officers during the winter, so that it is never utterly deserted and dead, as is the generality of watering-places.

Amelie has been formed as a commune out of scraps taken from others, but mainly from Arles-sur-Tech, to which the springs originally belonged. Arles is a very curious town, vastly ancient, and is the terminus of the line. Its principal manufacture is chocolate. The little town stands on a height, and is surrounded by mountains. Arles owes its medieval revival to a Benedictine abbey of which a considerable portion remains to this day. The abbot exercised almost episcopal jurisdiction over several parishes, of which he was also temporal lord. In the sixteenth century it was in full decay, and was so poor that its finances had to be helped out by annexing to it the funds of another abbey. The reason was that it was held *in commendam*, the revenue eaten by a titular abbot who resided in Paris, and discharged none of his duties.

The church of the monastery was finished in 1040, and is very archaic. It underwent, however, additions in 1157, when the curious vaulting was added. As a doubt was entertained whether the piers would sustain it, they were strengthened, and smaller arches added beneath those first erected. The church reminds one of the monolithic church of S. Emillon on the Garonne. The same square, massive piers rising to a great height, quite unadorned, support the round-headed unmoulded arches. Above each arch is a small, round-headed clerestory window. The church consists of five bays, and the nave has side aisles, out of which open chapels of much later construction. There was in the church at one time a richly carved altar-piece of the fifteenth century. But when the present detestable roccoco retable was erected, this was destroyed. Some of the panels were happily preserved and affixed to the pillars in the nave.

Outside the church the western portal is early, with a triangular lintel, on which is cut a shield with A.ω between A and A. The meaning of these double A's is not understood. In the diminutive yard without, behind is a grating, of an early sarcophagus that contained the bodies of saints Abdo and Senen. It possesses the curious property of filling with water, which can be drawn off by a tap at the side to supply bottles brought by pilgrims, who consider the water as efficacious in many maladies. How it is that the sarcophagus thus fills with water is not known; probably the clergy of the church do not themselves know, as the heavy lid has not been removed for centuries, nor the stone coffin shifted from the spot where it now stands.

But the greatest beauty of the church consists in the large cloister on the north side, of the thirteenth century. The arches are pointed, and rest on graceful pillars with dainty foliaged capitals, all of marble, and coupled. The cloister is not vaulted. This cloister was begun in 1261, but was not completed till the beginning of the fourteenth century.

The patrons of the church are SS. Abdo and Senen, Persian saints who suffered under Decius in 252. In the reign of Constantine the Great their relics were enshrined in Rome, and the marble sarcophagus that contained them still exists there, and their remains are in the church of S. Mark, Rome; but also here. Their day, 30 July, is a high festival at Arles, when the sleepy town is full of animation, and dances take place in the public square; then can be seen the red *barretina* and the gaily-coloured kerchiefs of the women.

Farther up the valley is a watering-place, Prats de Mollo. The name Prats, as Prades, which occurs in so many parts of the south, derives from the Latin *prates*, and signifies pleasant meadows by the water-side. The industry of Prats is the making of the red caps worn by the Catalans, and the rope-woven soles of *spadrillos*. The place enjoyed great privileges under the kings of Aragon, among these was freedom from duty on salt. Louis XIV sought to introduce it, but the people rose and slaughtered the tax-collectors. Louis sent troops to subdue them, and erected a fortress to intimidate them. On a mountain above Prats le Coral is a pilgrimage chapel containing a miraculous image of the Virgin. Crowds visit it—pilgrims from the country round, and bathers from Amelie—to see the combined devotion and jollification on 8 September.

# CHAPTER XX

## PERPIGNAN



THE old county of Roussillon, between Languedoc and Catalonia, formerly pertained to Spain; it was pledged to Louis XI of France by King John of Aragon
along with the Cerdagne. The stipulation was that these counties should remain
to France should John fail to redeem them in nine years with the sum of three
hundred gold crowns, which the crafty Louis knew was a sum John could not
raise. John, finding his inability to pay, stirred up the people of Roussillon to revolt against French domination, whereupon Louis poured thirty thousand men
into the country, and during fifteen years it underwent all the miseries of war.
Perpignan capitulated in 1475, and Roussillon remained in the hands of the French
till 1493, when the feeble Charles VIII restored it, along with the Cerdagne, to the
King of Aragon. At this time Aragon and Castille, united by the marriage of Ferdinand the Catholic with Isabella, formed from 1479 the kingdom of Spain.

In 1493 Ferdinand made his solemn entry into Perpignan, and brought the
Inquisition in his train. The already severely tried county was further tortured by
the Inquisitors, and the inhabitants were driven to desperation. They appealed to
Francis I for relief, and he was induced to attempt the recovery of Roussillon, but
was unsuccessful.

Under the fanatical Philip II the county was a prey to plague as well as persecution, so that hatred against Spain became intense. Philip III, sensible of this,
endeavoured to cajole the citizens of Perpignan by transferring to it the seat of the
bishopric from Elne, and by ennobling several of the leading citizens, but succeed-

ed in doing no more than in forming a small Spanish faction in the town.

Château de Roussillon

In 1610 all Catalonia was in revolt against Philip IV, and the county of Roussillon followed the example of Barcelona. The King of Spain sent troops to Perpignan and massacred the citizens. Those who survived the carnage appealed to Louis XIII, who sent an army into the county, and in 1642 the French, entering Perpignan, were hailed as deliverers. In 1659 the Treaty of the Pyrenees finally assured to France the possession of Roussillon and half of Cerdagne, and since then these have formed an integral portion of France.

But before all this for a while Perpignan was the capital of the short-lived kingdom of Majorca. James I, King of Aragon, in 1229 had expelled the Moors from that island, and in 1238 from Valencia; and to the title King of Aragon he added those of King of Majorca and Valencia, Count of Barcelona and of Roussillon and Urgel, and Seigneur of Montpellier. To his eldest son Peter he left Aragon, and to the younger, James, he gave the rest.

James I of Majorca was succeeded by his son Sanchez, who died without issue in 1324, and the next and last king was James II, son of Ferdinand, the brother of Sanchez. James married his cousin Constance, sister of Peter IV of Aragon.

Peter was an ambitious man and insatiate in his greed. He resolved on the destruction of his cousin and brother-in-law, and the annexation of his dominions. James had made himself unpopular by his tyranny, and the islanders complained to the Aragonese king. This was precisely what Peter wanted; he summoned James to meet him in conference at Barcelona, arrested his sister Constance, and would have done the same by his brother-in-law had not James found means to escape. In the impotence of his resentment he declared war against Aragon, and thereby sealed his own fate. In 1343 Peter landed in Majorca, and was at once joined by the islanders. Then he turned his attention to Roussillon and overran it.

The unfortunate James now solicited a safe conduct, and throwing himself at the feet of the victor, implored forgiveness in consideration of kinship. He might as well have appealed to a rock. He was informed that if he would surrender Perpignan, that still held out for him, he would experience his brother-in-law's clemency. He consented; but no sooner was Peter in possession that he declared Roussillon annexed in perpetuity to Aragon. The estates met, and offered James a miserable indemnity of 10,000 French crowns. He indignantly refused the offer. The Pope so far interfered as to obtain the release from prison of his wife Constance, and of James his eldest son. Unable to bear adversity with patience, in 1349 he sold to the French king his lordship of Montpellier, and with the money received raised 3000 foot soldiers and 300 horsemen, in the wild hope of reconquering his kingdom. With this small force he embarked, and made a descent on Majorca, but was deserted by the mercenaries when his funds gave out, and in a battle against great odds was killed, and his son James was wounded and taken prisoner. This prince had been married to Joanna I, Queen of Naples, who had murdered her first husband. Fearing to meet with the same fate, and disgusted with her levity, he had left Naples and had thrown in his lot with his father. For twelve years he languished in prison, effected his escape in 1362, and died of chagrin in 1375.

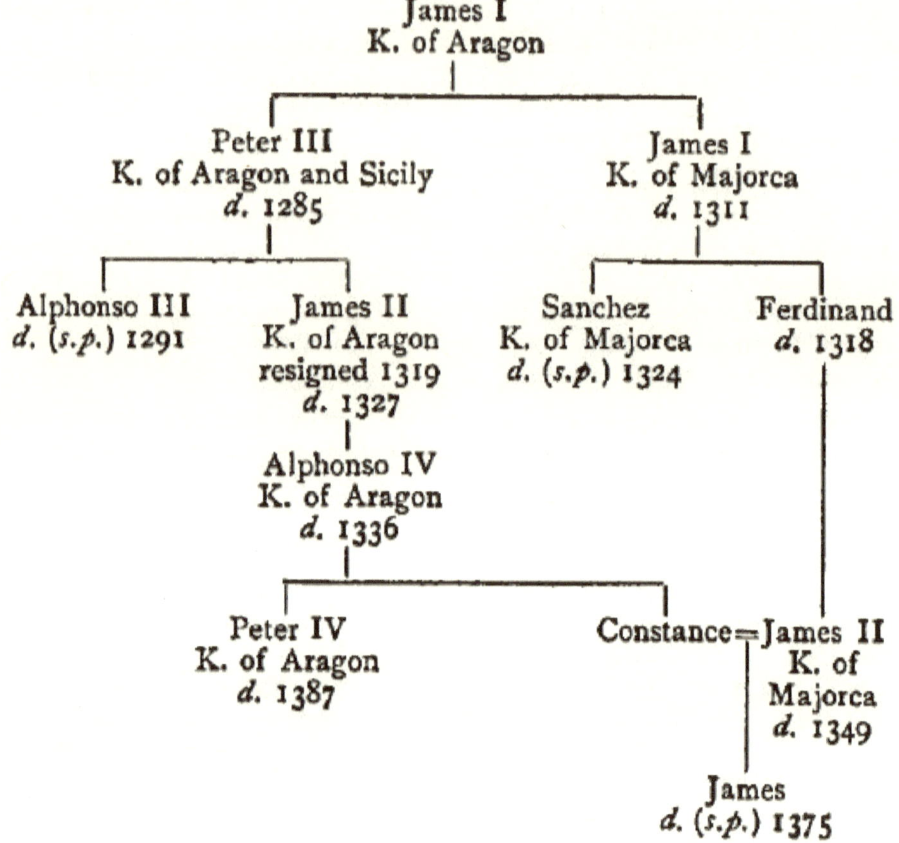


Roussillon takes its name from Ruscino, the ancient capital, which was destroyed by the Northmen in 859. The site is now occupied by a tower and a Romanesque chapel, a couple of miles from Perpignan. The name of Ruscino appears for the first time B.C. 218, when Hannibal crossed the Pyrenees on his march into Italy. The Roman Senate sent ambassadors to the people of Ruscino to urge them to oppose the progress of the great Carthaginian. They met where is now this castle, but were listened to with impatient murmurs. The tower, that dates from the twelfth century, is all that remains of the castle of the counts of Roussillon. No one has as yet undertaken serious exploration of the site, which infallibly would surrender very important relics of the ancient capital of the Rusceni, one of the Nine Peoples, and where in all probability the Phœnicians had a mercantile station; the plough, or mattock, has repeatedly turned up Iberian, Greek, Punic, Roman, and Arabic coins.

One cannot quit Castell-Rossello, as the tower is now called, without mention of William de Cabestang, who was châtelain of the neighbouring village of Cabestang. Taken with the charms of Sirmonde, the wife of Raimond, Count of Roussillon, he celebrated her in song. The husband, transported with jealousy, had him waylaid and murdered, then tore out his heart, had it roasted, and served at table. After Sirmonde had partaken of the dish he revealed to her what she had eaten. Then said she, "This meat has been to me so good and savoury that no other shall pass my lips." The Count at this drew his sword, and Sirmonde threw herself from the window and perished by the fall. Alphonso II of Aragon went to the place, ordered the arrest of the Count, and the burial of the troubadour and the Countess before the western entrance of the church of S. Jean at Perpignan.

Gateway of the Citadel, Perpignan

A few lines from one of his *sirventes* in her honour may be quoted:—

> "Before my mind's eye, lady fair,
> I see thy form, thy flowing hair,
> Thy face, thy iv'ry brow.
> My path to Paradise were sure
> Were love to God in me as pure
> As mine to thee, I trow.

> "Perchance thou wilt not bend an ear,
> Perchance not shed for me a tear,
> For me, who in my prayer
> To Mary Mother ever plead,
> To stead thee in thy hour of need,
> Sweet lady, passing fair.

> "Together from first childish days,
> As playfellows, I knew thy ways;
> I served thee when a child.
> Permit me but thy glove to kiss,
> That, that will be supremest bliss.
> Will still my pulses wild."

Perpignan, with its vast and huge citadel, cramped within fortifications planned by Vauban, was formerly a fortress of the first order. To-day, under changed systems of defence and attack, citadel and bastions have lost their value, and the walls and earthworks that gird the town about are now being levelled, and the moat filled to form a boulevard. When that red belt of bricks is completely demolished, Perpignan will expand in all directions.

The little river Basse divides the town into two unequal parts: the New Town, which is the ancient faubourg of the Tanneries, was included within the circuit of the fortifications by Vauban; and the Old Town, on the right bank of the river, comprises the hills of S. Jacques and de la Réal; and in this the streets are narrow and tortuous. In 1859 the medieval wall of defence along the river front was demolished and the Place Arago was made; a Palais de Justice and a Prefecture were erected on its site. The citadel is on high ground above the town, and contains the palace of the kings of Majorca. It is well to ascend the belvedere that surmounts the palace chapel to obtain a good view of the plain of Roussillon to the bald limestone range of the Corbières, to the soaring mass of Canigou, and the Pyrenean range— here called les Albères—and to the Mediterranean, blue as a peacock's neck, and the lagoons that lie along the coast. For what Perpignan sorely lacks is a high terrace that would give a view of the surrounding country and of the mountains.

Alphonso II, King of Aragon, to whom the last Count of Roussillon bequeathed his county in 1172, did much for the place. As a considerable part of the town lay low in marshy and unhealthy ground, he desired to move it up the height, at the foot of which was a leper hospital, and which for this reason is called the Puig des Lépreux. But he met with opposition from the inhabitants, and abandoned his intention. Nevertheless the Puig became peopled by artisans, and this portion was soldered on to the Old Town, and included later within the ramparts.

The Place de la Loge is the centre of animation to the town, the forum of the capital of Roussillon. It derives its name from the Loge de la Mer, a court for naval and mercantile affairs. This dates from 1397, but was reconstructed in 1540; it is richly carved, but is somewhat weak in design, and however elaborate is the ornamentation is not effective. From the upper story is suspended a diminutive ship with all its appointments. The lower story is given up to be a café. Before this all the rollicking and fun of the carnival takes place, not, as elsewhere, on Shrove Tuesday, but on Ash Wednesday. Before this pass the fantastic cars bearing maskers representing various trades or else allegorical groups. Here goes on the battle of the *dragées*, when every one not masked, down to the baby in arms, wears a wire vizor over his face, such as is employed by fencers, as a protection against the *dragées*, which are as large as beans and as hard as pebbles.

It is somewhat startling to note the contrast presented on Ash Wednesday between the scene in the cathedral, when the whole congregation goes to the altar rails to have a cross of ashes marked on each brow, with the words: "Remember, O man, that dust thou art, and unto dust thou shalt return!" and that in the Place de la Loge in the afternoon, when fun runs fast and furious, and every one is playing the fool.

The cathedral was begun in 1324, and terminated in the beginning of the sixteenth century. Externally it promises little, but the interior is overwhelmingly beautiful. The church is built of tiles rather than bricks, each 17 inches long by 1½ inches thick and 8 inches wide; with bands of these tiles alternate belts of cobble-stones arranged in herring-bone fashion.

The interior consists of one vast nave 56 feet wide, in seven bays and with transepts. The whole ends in a magnificent apse. Between the buttresses are chapels, 17 feet deep, in each of which is a three-light window most of these blocked by retables, and this renders the church unnecessarily dark. The high altar-piece of white marble, of the seventeenth century, is an admirable composition, purely Renaissance in character, executed by Bartholomew Soler, of Barcelona. In the niches are statues of the Virgin, S. John, and SS. Julia and Eulalia, patronesses of Elne. Particularly noticeable is a superb carved oak and gilded reredos in the north transept, of the fifteenth century, representing scenes of the Passion in eight compartments. Another, enclosing fine paintings in place of sculpture, is in the south transept. The huge organ-case is a splendid bit of work of the sixteenth century.

In the south of Languedoc a taste prevailed for churches comprising huge naves without side aisles—in fact, immense halls. At Carcassonne such is the type; but there, in the two churches in the New Town, the effect is unsatisfactory, as the chancels, or apses, bud out of the flat east wall in an ungainly manner. Here in Perpignan we have the hall interior, but leading up to and ending in an apse of the full width of the nave.

On the south side of the church is a chapel with a highly favoured crucifix in it, and Pope Leo XIII accorded plenary indulgence with remission of all sins to such as should worship before it and pray for the extermination of heresies, i.e. heretics on the Feast of the Exaltation of the Cross.

The other churches of S. Mathieu and La Réal deserve a visit. Built on the same lines as the cathedral, they have been sadly spoiled by tasteless additions in the Barroque period. Over the high altar at La Réal, as in a side chapel at S. Mathieu, are groups of coloured statuary, on which light is also made to fall from above; and as the churches are profoundly dark, this is in its way effective.

Cathedral Interior, Perpignan

The ancient Palais de Justice, much purer in style than the Loge, adjoins it, separated from it only by the old house of the consuls, now the Hôtel de Ville. The old Palais has beautiful windows, with trefoil heads cut in the block, unmoulded, supported by dainty columns. But the most strikingly picturesque edifice of Perpignan is the Castelet, erected between 1367 and 1369, with the town gate of Notre Dame (1481) at one side of it, all constructed of tiles like the cathedral. The bold projecting machicolations, and the octagonal turret surmounted by a small cupola, have a pronounced Spanish character.

When one passes out of the Porte Notre Dame the Promenade des Platanes is reached, a boulevard shaded by magnificent plane trees, but all inclined from the north, from the terrible Tramontane wind, which is the scourge of the plain of Roussillon. Here on Shrove Tuesday evening hundreds of maskers dance under the leafless branches, and sometimes in spite of the cutting wind and dropping rain. The promenade is then railed in, and soldiers are stationed to act as sentinels to prevent the crowd entering and interfering with the dancers. But the waltz music is too exhilarating to allow these sentinels to soberly pace their distances, and I have seen them holding their rifles and pirouetting up and down their beats with them as if their firearms were lovely partners.

Beyond the Basse, where it flows into the Tet, is the faubourg Notre Dame, very animated and peopled in part with gipsies, or *gitanos*. They speak a language of their own, a mixture of Arabic, Castillian, and Catalan. They are first mentioned in Roussillon in an ordinance of 1512, that required them to be cudgelled out of the country. It does not seem that this order produced the effect desired, for they have been found, and still are found, throughout the department, mainly engaged in selling mules.

The first station out of Perpignan on the line to Barcelona is Elne, long the seat of a bishop. It was the ancient Illiberis. The name tells its origin. It derives from the Iberian, and signifies the New City; and shows that it was a town founded by these people before they were expelled or subjugated by the Celts, who invaded the country in the fourth century before Christ. When Hannibal crossed the Pyrenees he planted his headquarters here, and hither came the heads of the Gaulish tribe to make terms with him against Rome. At the same time they made complaint of the conduct of some of his Carthaginian soldiery. Hannibal listened to their grievances, and decided that in any further cases of misconduct by his soldiers these should be tried by a court composed of the wives of the Gauls.

The Romans, when they occupied the land, neglected Illiberis, and planted a colony at Ruscino. The town dwindled to insignificance till Constantine refounded it and called it after the name of his mother, Helena; and this is the name it now bears, transformed into Elne. It was the scene of the assassination of Constans, the son of the great Constantine. He was an indolent, weak, and debauched prince, monarch of the West. Whilst hunting in Gaul he received tidings of the revolt of Magnentius, that the soldiers had mutinied, and that emissaries had been dispatched to kill him. He fled to Illiberis, but was overtaken here and put to death in 350, in the thirtieth year of his reign.

Devastated by the Arabs, we do not hear of a bishop of Elne till 783. After that the lordship of Elne was shared between the bishop and the chapter. The seat of the bishop was removed to Perpignan in 1602.

Elne occupies a sandstone rock, about which this town is built, and is divided into the upper and the lower town. It is a dull and sleepy place, that wakens into life only on the festival of SS. Eulalia and Julia, when there is much merry-making with processions, music, and dancing. Portions of the walls and some of the gates remain; but the great object of interest is the cathedral, with its superb cloisters of white marble. The exact date of the rebuilding is not known, but the church was complete in 1069. Externally it is constructed of rubble stone in herring-bone, set in mortar. The west front has a crenellated gable between two towers of unequal size and height. The loftiest is a bold structure that has had buttresses added to it much later, in 1415. The western doorway is unornamented. The plan of the church is a nave with side aisles and no transepts. It is very plain within as without, with huge piers supporting round-headed arches and vault. The high altar was of silver, and dated from 1069, but was sent to the mint at Perpignan to be coined into money in 1721. The new altar-piece is as Prosper Mérimée described it—"a masterpiece of meanness and bad taste."

The original choir stalls were fine. A writer in 1787 says of the woodwork: "It is grand, and remarkable for the beauty of the stall-work covered with sculpture of the end of the thirteenth century, as is known by an inscription on one of the stalls." All this has disappeared.

In the sacristy is preserved a little bell with the date on it, 1554, ornamented with a figure of Apollo playing on the *rebec*, a monkey doing the same, and dancing bears, an eagle, a rabbit, and a boar.

But the great glory of Elne is its cloister raised on a terrace of the ancient acropolis of Illiberis, on the north side of the cathedral. Entrance to it is obtained by a doorway, which for the purity of its style and the sobriety of its ornamentation deserves notice. The arch is pointed, and of marble, alternatively white and red, and dates from the fourteenth century. The ironwork of the door is simple but graceful. Alart, the historian and antiquary says: "Without dispute, from the point of view of art, and from the historic reminiscences attached to it, the cloister is the most remarkable and precious relic that remains of Roussellonnaise architecture." It was begun in the twelfth century, but was continued and retouched in the fourteenth, so that whereas some of the capitals and columns are of Byzantine or Romanesque design, others have Gothic ornament. All is in white marble, and the sculpture is of exquisite delicacy: foliage, figures of every description are there in lavish profusion. The pillars are coupled, some twisted, some plain. The very bases are enriched with ornament.

> "In the morning, in summer, when the sun lights up the galleries to north and west, all the details come out with extraordinary brilliancy. In the afternoon the eastern gallery is burnt by the solar rays that have turned the marble yellow."—P. Vidal.

In the lateral wall on the north side open two doorways, one of which must be entered with precaution, or one may fall below, for the stair that led from it has disappeared. Underneath are two large vaulted chambers paved with bricks, communicating one with another by a small opening. Traces of fresco painting may be noticed. The popular opinion is that these were the dungeons of the Inquisition, but actually they were an old chapel dedicated to S. Laurence. The other door gives access to a spiral staircase leading to a terrace, from which a magnificent view is obtained of the plain, the Albères, and Canigou.

The Cloisters of Elne

Arles-sur-Mer is a watering-place by the sea. Near it is the more interesting port of Collioure, an Iberian name signifying the port of the New Town; and Iberian coins have been found there. The fortress of S. Elne was built by Charles V. The streets are narrow, the houses dilapidated, and occupied mainly by fishermen and their families.

> "On the sea-coast these men enter into very hot discussions, use expressions somewhat rough and coarse, but rarely come to blows. Few scandals occur here, and they marry young. It is worthy of remark that among these good folk so free of tongue and freer still in opinion, these solid republicans, the religious sentiment is very developed. They pray to God and go to Mass; but they also go to the ball. The three last days of carnival are given up by the whole population to a wild frenzy. They cling to this poor carnival as though it would never return. Every café has its ball at night; if weather permit there is a general ball in the public square."

A few yards from the beach on a rock stands a chapel dedicated to S. Vincent, who is traditionally held to have been born at Collioure. He was martyred at Valencia in Spain, 304. But Huesca also claims the honour of his birth. His name is included in the English Church calendar on 22 January. From the rock of S. Vincent on 16 August, annually, at nine o'clock in the evening, starts a procession of boats that brings the relics of the saint to the town. The sailing-boats and fishing-vessels richly decked and illuminated with coloured lamps are reflected in the still sea. An immense crowd is gathered about the harbour, that is lighted by a bonfire made of vine twigs and barrels of tar.

As soon as the vessel bearing the relics arrives at the quay, the harbour-master calls out, "What boat is that?" To which the captain replies, "A boat of Saint Vincent." "Whence come you?" "From Saint Vincent-de-l'Ile." "With what are you laden?" "With the relics of the Saint Vincent, of Saint Marinus, and of Saint Liberada." "Are there passengers, and are they according to rule?" "There are passengers, and they are all according to rule." "What do you require?" "To be allowed to disembark." "In the name of God, do so."

Then the whole crowd shouts, "Sant Vincens béneit!" Whereupon the boat is hauled ashore and dragged through the town. The crowd that separated to allow of the passage then unites and follows in a dense mass, elbowing one another. The boat halts before the "Vierge des quatres coins," the relics are removed from it, and carried processionally to the church. The bonfire and the coloured lamps go out, and the scene of movement is transferred from the harbour to the Place, where the *joglars*, installed on an improvized platform, sound their instruments to lively melodies, and all, young and old, in two minutes are in full swing of a dance, that lasts from ten o'clock to midnight. "Si réellement," says a French writer, "la danse est un amusement, nulle part au monde ou ne s'amuse autant qu' ici."

The train, as it traverses the flats and athwart arms of the lagoons that lie along the coast, skirts a place called Salses, and if the traveller be looking out of the window on the right hand, he catches a glimpse of a rusty mass of building with towers, and wonders what it is. This is the fortress of Salses, erected in 1497 by a Spanish engineer named Ramirez, and it is sufficiently curious to merit a study, for it was built at a time when the use of cannon was materially altering the conditions of warfare, especially of sieges. The château, though often menaced with destruction, indeed repeatedly ordered to be levelled, has remained almost intact to the present day. It forms a rectangle with a tower at each angle. These towers give evidence of the hesitation of the engineer. He was hampered by tradition, and had to introduce them without knowing exactly that they had a purpose any longer. But, on the other hand, he adopted an innovation, destined to revolutionize the defence of fortresses, by creating bastions isolated and in advance of the walls, like the demi-lunes of modern citadels. As far as we know, this was the first instance of their being employed. The castle was of some strategic importance, as commanding the passage between the vast Lagoon of Leucate and the barren ridge of the Corbières.

The last governor of the fortress was a nephew of Voltaire, named La Houlière, who grew vines and made wine on his wife's estate; he sent a cask of the latter to his illustrious uncle, and entreated him to obtain a market for his wines in Russia. To which Voltaire replied, "I am sorry not to be able to be of use to you in this matter, but the Empress at this moment is too much occupied with the Turks who drink no wine, and with the Germans who drink too much, to be able to turn her attention to your generous liquor."

When La Houlière, who commanded at Perpignan in April, 1793, learned the defeat of the French troops by the Spaniards, he was so depressed that he blew out his brains.

Throughout the plain of Roussillon vines grow, and the wine they produce is excellent. The canals of irrigation bordered by trees traverse the plain; and, thanks to this semi-aquatic condition, the vineyards do not present the monotony of those of Narbonne and Beziers.

The dread of the cold winds over the snows of the Alps and the Cevennes is everywhere apparent. Reeds grow in the dykes to a great height, from twelve to fourteen feet, and even more, and these are cut and formed into mats to barricade the fields and gardens, and give some shelter to them from the piercing blast that has bent every tree from the direction whence it blows. Round Perpignan every patch of flower or vegetable garden is thus hedged about.

At Perpignan the Count de Grammont met the Abbé Poussatin, when he was retreating with the Prince of Condé after the unsuccessful campaign in Catalonia, in 1647. Grammont says:—

> "At last we arrived at Perpignan on a holiday; a company of Catalans, who were dancing in the street, out of respect to the prince, came forward to dance under his windows. Monsieur Poussatin, in a little black jacket, danced in the middle of this company, as if he were really mad. I immediately recognized him as my countryman, from his manner of skipping and frisking about.

The prince was charmed with his humour and activity. After the dance I sent for him, and inquired who he was. 'A poor priest, at your service, my lord,' said he; 'my name is Poussatin, and Béarn is my native country. I was going into Catalonia to serve in the infantry, for, God be praised, I can march very well on foot; but since the war is happily concluded, if your lordship pleases to take me into your service, I would follow you everywhere, and serve you faithfully.' 'Monsieur Poussatin,' said I, 'my lordship has no great occasion for a chaplain; but since you are so well disposed towards me, I will take you into my service.'

"The Prince of Condé, who was present at this conversation, was overjoyed at my having a chaplain. Poor Poussatin was in a very tattered condition, and I had no time to provide him with a proper habit at Perpignan; but giving him a spare livery of one of the Marshal de Grammont's servants, I made him get up behind the prince's coach, who was like to die with laughing every time he looked at poor Poussatin's uncanonical mien in a yellow livery.

"As soon as we arrived in Paris the story was told to the queen, who at first expressed some surprise at it; this, however, did not prevent her from wishing to see my chaplain dance; for in Spain it is not altogether so strange to see ecclesiastics dance, as to see them in livery.

"Poussatin performed wonders before the queen; but as he danced with great sprightliness, she could not bear the savour which his violent motions diffused through the room; the ladies likewise began to pray for relief."

The Eastern Pyrenees have, to my mind, been unduly neglected, and yet they present scenes of great beauty, and are very easily reached. To botanists they should be especially attractive. The Val d'Eyne, near Mont Louis, is known to possess flowers found nowhere else in the range. The ravine of the Aude is as fine as any in the Hautes Pyrénées. There are peaks that run up to 10,000 feet, and are covered with snow all the year, and if the glaciers be insignificant, glaciers are not essential to beauty. There are more mountain tarns here than elsewhere, and some of these the largest in the Pyrenees. In ecclesiastical architecture this is by far the richest portion of the chain, as the churches have not been wrecked by the Huguenots as in Béarn and Bigorre. And what is more, there is less rain, there are clearer and bluer skies. Some of the watering-places are sweet and sheltered nooks where one can be in summer sunlight early in April, even at the end of March, sheltered from every wind, and with excursions possible all about them, and what is more, are not so fashionable, not so savouring of Paris as Bagnères and Luchon, Cauterez, and Eauxbonnes. In the heats of summer no more cool and invigorating climate can be found than in some of those towns and villages on lofty plateaux, like Mont Louis. As to the Pyrenees in general, many best able to judge and with widest experience of mountain scenery, prefer them to the Alps of Switzerland and of Tyrol, so overrun with the tripper and the herds conducted by Cook. The colouring is richer and more varied, the foliage, the flowers more abundant; and the peasantry have not lost their simplicity, as have the Swiss.

I will conclude with the words of a Pyrenean poet, written in his Gascon dialect, but rendered into French: "Puisse-je remonter sur ces trônes flamboyants de porphyre et de glace, ou tout est froid, même l'éclair; j'irai révoir du haut de ces nues, ces horizons grands comme l'éternité, mais que je ne trouverais jamais assez illimités. Et quand aura sonné l'heure fatale et cruelle du repos, j'irais m'assoir au bord de l'Océan ou de la Méditerranée, mais toujours en vue des Pyrénées."

# INDEX

Lector House believes that a society develops through a two-fold approach of continuous learning and adaptation, which is derived from the study of classic literary works spread across the historic timeline of literature records. Therefore, we aim at reviving, repairing and redeveloping all those inaccessible or damaged but historically as well as culturally important literature across subjects so that the future generations may have an opportunity to study and learn from past works to embark upon a journey of creating a better future.

This book is a result of an effort made by Lector House towards making a contribution to the preservation and repair of original ancient works which might hold historical significance to the approach of continuous learning across subjects.

HAPPY READING & LEARNING!

LECTOR HOUSE
LECTOR HOUSE LLP
E-MAIL: lectorpublishing@gmail.com